TEMPLE

#1 *NEW YORK TIMES* BESTSELLING AUTHOR

MIKE EVANS

The TEMPLE

THE CENTER *of* GRAVITY

TimeWorthy BOOKS

P.O. BOX 30000, PHOENIX, AZ 85046

The Temple: The Center of Gravity

Copyright © 2015
All rights reserved
Printed in the United States of America

Published by TimeWorthy Books
Phoenix, AZ 85046

Design: Peter Gloege | LOOK Design Studio

Hardcover: 978-1-62961-081-8
Paperback: 978-1-62961-080-1
   Canada: 978-1-62961-082-5

This book is dedicated
to my lovely and selfless daughter-in-love
Jessica Renee Evans.
She is a wonderful wife to my son,
Michael David II and mother to their
three beautiful children—
Michael David III, Brooke, and Colton.

FOREWORD

t's early on a sunny autumn morning as I leave the Friends of Zion Museum and walk east, toward Jerusalem's Old City. Horns blare as traffic rushes through the streets of the city. Fumes from the vehicles are overcome by the fragrance of freshly baked bread as I walk the route that will take me from earthly Jerusalem to heavenly Jerusalem—from the modern city to the Temple Mount in the Old City. Ultra-Orthodox Jews dressed in dark suits and wearing wide-brimmed black hats rush past me with children in tow on their way to pray at the Western Wall.

As I ascend one hill in earthly Jerusalem, I can see that at the bottom lies the beautiful new Mamilla Pedestrian Mall. Built on the site of the former no-man's-land between Israel and Jordan, it is now a thriving commercial center filled with tourists and local shoppers. Leaving behind the mall's elegant shops and restaurants, I stroll straight toward the Old City's Jaffa Gate, where I enter the Arab market on my way to the Temple Mount.

This is a special day, as it comes in the midst of the Jewish Festival of Sukkot, when thousands of Jewish worshipers gather at the Western Wall to receive the Priestly Blessing. It is also the day of celebration of the Feast of Tabernacles, when 10,000 Christians from 100 countries will gather in Jerusalem. The Old City will be packed with the faithful of both religions, all converging at the same holy place, the Temple Mount.

As I exit the Mamilla mall and climb the stairs to Jaffa Gate, I pause and look to my right across the Sultan's Pool and see the King David Hotel atop the next hill. It is a symbol of resistance to British rule during Israel's struggle for independence. As does every part of Jerusalem, the Sultan's Pool also carries an echo of biblical history; it slopes down to the Valley of Hinoam, where ancient worshipers of the god Moloch would sacrifice their children on burning altars—until Moses brought the law of God to ancient Israelites.

My mind returns to the present, to the walls surrounding the Old City. Dominated by David's Citadel, the walls stand as if on guard above Jaffa Gate, one of the city's eight gates. It points toward the port of Jaffa, the destination of Jewish and Christian pilgrims in previous centuries. Although the walls were built by Sultan Suleiman the Magnificent in the sixteenth century, Jaffa Gate was widened to accommodate the carriage of Kaiser Wilhelm of Germany during his visit to Jerusalem in 1898. His pompous demand was contrasted some twenty years later at the end of World War I, when conquering British general Edmund Allenby dismounted his horse outside the widened gate and declared he would enter the holy city on foot as a Christian pilgrim. I feel Allenby's presence as this pilgrim follows in his footsteps through the Jaffa Gate.

Walking down narrow David Street through the Arab market, I pass colorful shops selling every kind of merchandise, including a wide variety of souvenirs and religious objects for every faith. The winding streets of the *souk*, the Arab market, are divided into sections much like an open-air department store: dry goods on one street, grocery stalls on another, and on yet another, shops selling exotic oriental spices that perfume the air.

Walking past the Church of the Holy Sepulchre on the Via Dolorosa with its Stations of the Cross, I enter a street devoted to patisseries, among which one can buy a chunk of *halva,* the Middle Eastern sesame-and-honey confection in assorted flavors—pistachio is recommended.

The Arab merchants eagerly call out to passersby to inspect their wares—and bargain for them—and I am no exception. The shop owners expect to do a good business with all the tourists. Today, the Old City is packed with foreign visitors adding to the crush of religious Jews on their way to receive the Priestly Blessing.

This benediction is, in Hebrew, *nesiat kapayim,* or "raising of hands." In Yiddish, it is known as *dukhanen,* from the word *dukhan,* or platform, the place from which the blessing is traditionally offered by the *Kohanim,* or priests, descendants of Aaron. The Torah decrees that the priests are to raise their hands and bless those gathered in order to transfer Jehovah's blessings upon the people. Although the temple was destroyed in AD 70, this practice is carried on today in synagogues during prayer services. The verbatim text in the Torah is:

> May the LORD bless you and guard you—
>
> יְבָרֶכְשִׁיְוֶ ,הוהי וְכִרְבִי
>
> (*Yevhārēkh-khā Adhōnāy veyishmerēkhā . . .*)

> May the LORD make His face shed light upon
> you and be gracious unto you—
>
> :הְנֶחִיו ,רִיְלֶא וִיְנְגְפ הוהי רֵאָי
>
> ("*Yā'ēr Adhōnāy pānāw ēlekhā viḥunnékkā . . .*")

> May the LORD lift up His face unto you and give you peace—
>
> סוֹלָשׁ רֶל סֵשְׁיְו ,רִיְלֶא וִיְנְגְפ הוהי אֹשִׁי
>
> ("*Yissā Adhōnāy pānāw ēlekhā viyāsēm lekhā shālōm.*")

It can be found in the Bible in Numbers 6:24–26.

The crowd jostling through the streets is in a jovial holiday mood. One marvelous thing about Jerusalem's Old City is that it is always open: On the Jewish Sabbath, the Christian and Muslim shops are open; on Sunday, shops of Jews and Muslims are open; and on Friday, Jews and Christians conduct business. Turning aside from the Muslim Quarter, I enter the Jewish Quarter at the Cardo— the ancient Roman market and the country's first shopping mall. It was Jerusalem's main street fifteen hundred years ago. Today the Cardo is a combination of upscale shopping and archeological sites dating back to Roman Emperor Hadrian, including original paving stones upon which Jesus might have walked.

Since entering the Old City at Jaffa Gate, my stroll through the Arab market and the Cardo has been shaded from the harsh Middle Eastern sun. Now, as I climb the stairs and exit into the Jewish Quarter, I emerge into bright sunlight that makes the stone buildings of the quarter glow with a golden light. The first building on my left is the nineteenth-century Hurva Synagogue, rebuilt after having been destroyed by the Jordanian army during the War of Independence. Restored to its former glory, including its magnificent dome, it is the center of the Jewish Quarter, itself lovingly rebuilt after 1967. The plaza at the center is filled, not only with visitors but also with many children at play from the quarter.

I pause in the midst of the usual array of shops and restaurants to note an exceptional site: the ruins of the Burnt House. This magnificent building, uncovered by archeologists, was burned down at the time of the conquest of Jerusalem by the Romans in AD 70 in the same fire that destroyed the temple.

As I slowly descend the stairs from the Jewish Quarter toward the Western Wall plaza, I turn a corner and am struck by a study in contrasts. Part of the silver gray dome of Al-Aqsa Mosque appears framed against the background of the Mount of Olives in the distance. I gaze upon the thousands of graves of the oldest Jewish cemetery in the world; the mountain that Jesus is meant to cross on His next visit to Jerusalem. It is also the place overlooking the Valley of the Dry Bones that the prophet Ezekiel prophesied would come to life (Ezekiel 37:1–28) and restore the nation of Israel.

Farther in the distance to the east, the sky is clear enough for me to just make out the Dead Sea some thirty miles away. Just visible in Jordan beyond the Dead Sea are the Mountains of Moab, which conceal the burial place of Moses, who was not allowed to cross into the Promised Land. As I turn the corner, suddenly the entire majesty of the Temple Mount is before me: the plaza leading up to the Western Wall, the Kotel; above it on the left is the sparkling golden Dome of the Rock shrine, and to the right Al-Aqsa Mosque. I am humbled by the incredible holiness of this place that is most sacred to the Jews.

The Dome of the Rock is built over the Foundation Stone, which Jewish tradition teaches is the center of the universe. Centuries before the Dome of the Rock was completed in AD 691, the stone was covered by the Holy of Holies in the temples. Centuries before that, Jewish tradition ascribes the site to Mount Moriah, where God tested Abraham's faith in his willingness to sacrifice Isaac.

Before the second temple was destroyed, a social activist rabbi from the Galilee expelled the money changers from its holy premises, as related by all four gospels of the New Testament. For the Believers who have flocked to the city for the Feast of Tabernacles, not only is Jerusalem the City of David, it is the City of God. It is the location of the garden of Gethsemane, Golgotha, and nearby, the Garden Tomb. It is the home of numerous churches that have been erected over the centuries, including the ancient Church of the Holy Sepulchre and the colorful Church of All Nations. The city is also home to the Cenacle, believed to be the place where the Last Supper was celebrated by Jesus and His disciples.

I stand reverently before the history that resonates from this place, from the presence of Jesus to the ingathering of the exiles foretold by the prophets. I have walked across the modern, earthly Jerusalem to the one place Jews, Christians, and Muslims believe is the gateway to heaven. These very stones speak to me as I cross the plaza and ascend the ramp to the Mughrabi Gate of the Temple Mount that welcomes me and all who come in peace. Jerusalem. It all began here, and will all end here.

JERUSALEM:
CITY *of* GOLD

Atop the Mount of Olives outside the ancient city of Jerusalem and looking toward the east, the sun rises over the Judean desert. I can see the buildings in the distance as the sunlight tints the ancient stones with the rosy glow of red and ocher. The sun races across the sky until it reaches apogee and then begins the descent toward the Mediterranean Sea. As the waning sunlight bounces off the royal stone—the crystalline limestone covering the cream-colored façade of one ageless edifice and then another—it produces a golden tinge. It is from this reflection that Jerusalem has become known as the "city of gold." This sunset is as brilliant as the sunrise—an oft-captured picture-postcard moment in time.

The sweeping panorama of Jerusalem is overwhelming. The multi-towered landscape is a splendid drama written in stone, one that has received rave reviews from countless pilgrims to the Holy Land. Seen from atop the mount are landmarks such as the ancient ruins of the City of David, the gilded cupola on the *Haram esh-Sharif,* the Dome of the Rock, and the Kidron Valley, where tombstones dot the hillside beneath the crenellated walls of the ancient city. These

massive stone walls, with their battlements intact, have proudly wit-
nessed countless sieges of invading armies. The parapets of these
walls once sheltered archers; today soldiers patrol those same bul-
warks, not with bows and arrows, but with automatic rifles.

The Olivet view entices pilgrims to descend into Jerusalem,
a city of magnificent hewn stones, and visit the Old City with its
Jewish Quarter. Stones, stones, stones. As the traveler wanders
through the tangled labyrinth of narrow alleyways, one can almost
touch those stone walls on either side. There are stone arches above
and paving stones beneath. From the ancient ruins to the medieval
ramparts, these streets and walls that have baked in the warmth of
innumerable sunrises each have a story to tell.

Those most beloved by the people of Israel are the stones that
rise to form the Western Wall, the holiest shrine of the Jewish faith.
The fifty-feet-high wall is all that remains of Herod's temple as it
existed in the first century. The stones stacked one upon another to
build this wall are so massive it's hard to imagine how they were
chiseled out of the quarries outside Jerusalem and then transported
up the hills into the city.

To grasp the perspective, it is helpful to look backward across
the centuries and to follow the course of events that has led to
today's impasse in the City of David. Consider the view from the
temple when the stones were newly hewn and the city of Jerusalem
shone like alabaster in the morning sun; Herod the Great began
rebuilding Solomon's temple in 20 BC; the project occupied the rest
of his administration. While the fifteen-story-high temple was constructed during Herod's reign, the outer courts and walls were not
fully completed until AD 64, some sixty-eight years after his death.

One day, after Jesus had been teaching in the temple precincts,
He called His disciples' attention to the buildings:

"Do you see all these things?" he asked. "Truly I
tell you, not one stone here will be left on another;
every one will be thrown down." (Matthew 24:2)

The words of Jesus were precisely fulfilled in AD 70 when Roman armies swept through Jerusalem and reduced Herod's magnificent temple to a pile of blackened rubble. The stones of the temple have been buried in antiquity, somewhere deep beneath the Old City.

The remaining stones of the Western Wall have become a symbol of the enduring hope of the Jewish people. Even nonreligious Jews venerate the Wall as a national monument. The plaza in front of the Western Wall can accommodate 100,000 congregants. It is the gathering place of the people of Israel, the scene of both joyous celebration and solemn memorial. For a city that has been completely destroyed twice, occupied by enemies twenty-three times, surrounded fifty-two times, and liberated forty-four times, the Wall remains a testimony of God's all-encompassing providence.

The walls of Jerusalem summon pilgrims to return again and again to that eternal city. They speak to the soul and hum with the sound of ancient songs in a minor key—songs of anguish and suffering—songs of, "Rachel weeping for her children and refusing to be comforted, because they are no more" (Jeremiah 31:15).

The Western Wall is also known by some as the Wailing Wall. Worshipers who have gone there to pray over the centuries have washed those stones with rivers of tears—tears of mourning, tears of joy, tears of intercession. Visible in the cracks and crevices between the huge stones are tiny pieces of paper, crinkled and wedged in the nooks and crannies of the Wall. It's a tradition to write a prayer on a slip of paper and place it among the stones. It has become a place of prayer for peoples of all nations. Once each month, caretakers of the

Western Wall carefully remove the scraps of paper and bury them ceremonially.

Stand in front of those hulking stones and a spiritual connection is made with the other worshipers offering their prayers and praises to God. Reach out and touch the ancient weathered boulders. Listen to the eerie sounds of the *muezzin*, the Muslim crier who heralds the Islamic call to prayer from atop Mount Moriah; it is also a reminder of the many Jews killed for daring to stand beside the wall to pray to *Yahweh*. It has long been a silent witness to the sufferings of God's Chosen People. If only those ancient weathered rocks could speak.

The very fact that the Jewish people and the nation of Israel exist today is a miracle. No other group of people has been so systematically targeted for destruction. Most Jews were exiled from their homeland after having been conquered by one kingdom or another, and even then were hunted and humiliated, menaced and massacred by the millions. The Jews as a people would not have survived were it not that the sovereign Lord of the universe ordained their preservation.

The nations that ransacked, burned, and leveled Jerusalem while trying to annihilate the Jewish people are rife with devastation. We have only to examine history to ascertain that the remnants of those once-great empires are now dust and ashes. Many nations have come against Israel from the beginning of her existence. Yet, like the proverbial Phoenix, she has risen from the ashes each time. Nebuchadnezzar conquered Jerusalem in 586 BC and was doomed to live as a beast of the field for seven, agonizing years. He was restored to sanity when he recognized the God of the Israelites. (See Daniel 4.) His kingdom of Babylon was conquered by Cyrus the Great.

In 332 BC, Alexander the Great captured Jerusalem. His empire fragmented after his death, and the followers of Ptolemy in Egypt and then the Seleucids of Syria ruled over Jerusalem. The Jews, horrified by the desecration of the temple under the Seleucid ruler, Antiochus IV, staged a revolt and regained independence under the Hasmonean dynasty. It lasted for one hundred years, until Pompey established Roman rule in the city. The Holy Roman Empire collapsed after destroying the temple and leveling Jerusalem.

The British, who ruled over Palestine and Jerusalem following World War I, boasted that the sun never set on the British Empire. Indeed, one-fifth of the world's population was under its rule. However, after turning away Jews seeking asylum in both Britain and Palestine as they fled Hitler's gas chambers, and after arming Arabs to fight against them in the Holy Land, the empire quickly began to disintegrate. Great Britain today is comprised of just fourteen territories, consisting of a number of islands. Gone are the days when the empire stretched from India to Canada and from Australia to Africa.

Jerusalem, however, continues to stand as a testimony to the determination and courage of the Jewish people. That God has ordained the preservation of His chosen people is written throughout the pages of the Scriptures.

It was first noted in His covenant with Abraham:

> The LORD had said to Abram, "Go from your country, your people and your father's household to the land I will show you. I will make you into a great nation, and I will bless you; I will make your name great, and you will be a blessing. I will bless those who bless you, and whoever curses you I will curse; and all peoples on earth will be blessed through you."
> (Genesis 12:1–3)

In addition to the covenant, the Lord gave Abraham and his descendants, Isaac and Jacob, the title deed to the land of Israel. He declared that it would be in their possession perpetually. In Genesis God again spoke:

> On that day the LORD made a covenant with Abram and said, "To your descendants I give this land, from the Wadi of Egypt to the great river, the Euphrates— the land of the Kenites, Kenizzites, Kadmonites, Hittites, Perizzites, Rephaites, Amorites, Canaanites, Girgashites and Jebusites." (Genesis 15:18–21)

In secular terms, this would be called a royal land grant. This type of grant, common in antiquity, was perpetual and unconditional. The king, or sovereign, possessed all the land and granted parcels of it to loyal subjects as reward for faithful service. In biblical terms, God is sovereign over all the earth—He created it, and there are no greater rights of ownership than that—so the land is certainly His to bequeath as He wishes.

Years after He made His original covenant with Abraham, God confirmed it. The patriarch accepted the terms of the covenant by the right of circumcision:

> "As for Me, behold, My covenant is with you, and you shall be a father of many nations. No longer shall your name be called Abram, but your name shall be Abraham; for I have made you a father of many nations. I will make you exceedingly fruitful; and I will make nations of you, and kings shall come from you. And I will establish My covenant between Me and you and your descendants after you in their

generations, for an everlasting covenant, to be God to you and your descendants after you. Also I give to you and your descendants after you the land in which you are a stranger, all the land of Canaan, as an everlasting possession; and I will be their God." And God said to Abraham: "As for you, you shall keep My covenant, you and your descendants after you throughout their generations. This is My covenant which you shall keep, between Me and you and your descendants after you: Every male child among you shall be circumcised . . . " (Genesis 17:4–10 NKJV)

This covenant with Abraham is an eternal one with no preconditions or expiration date. It was given as an everlasting possession to Abraham and his descendants. Only mankind is capable of impeding the fulfillment of the contract through disobedience, but the pact can never be rescinded. Moses declared:

God is not human, that he should lie, not a human being, that he should change his mind. Does he speak and then not act? Does he promise and not fulfill? (Numbers 23:19)

To avoid any confusion or equivocation, God reconfirmed the covenant with Abraham's son, Isaac. Moses related God's promise:

"For to you and your descendants I will give all these lands and will confirm the oath I swore to your father Abraham. I will make your descendants as numerous as the stars in the sky and will give them all these lands, and through your offspring all nations on earth will be blessed . . ." (Genesis 26:3–4)

Neither did God leave out Abraham's grandson Jacob, or the generations that followed. He declared:

> "I am the LORD, the God of your father Abraham and the God of Isaac. I will give you and your descendants the land on which you are lying. Your descendants will be like the dust of the earth, and you will spread out to the west and to the east, to the north and to the south. All peoples on earth will be blessed through you and your offspring. I am with you and will watch over you wherever you go, and I will bring you back to this land. I will not leave you until I have done what I have promised you." (Genesis 28:13–15)

Of what value is this ancient covenant between God and Abraham today? God remains sovereign over the land He bestowed upon Abraham and his offspring. He has never vacated the title deed, nor, as some believe, has He rescinded His covenant declaration. The land still belongs to Abraham, Isaac, Jacob, and their descendants—as numerous as the sands of the sea.

Today, the place where God made and confirmed this covenant lies in an area north of Jerusalem between Bethel and Ai. It is in the heart of the West Bank (actually Judea and Samaria) on land the United Nations has decreed that Israel occupies illegally. World leaders demand that Israel forego the area for the sake of an ever-elusive peace.

2

JERUSALEM:
CITY *of* GOD

The Jewish people have a God-given, inalienable right to possess the land of Israel. Many have the mistaken idea that an inalienable right is one that cannot be taken from you. In reality, it means just the opposite: It is one that cannot be given away, sold, surrendered, or legally transferred to another.

The all-time best-selling book—the Bible—confirms it. Since it is an inalienable right, it means Israel does not have the authority to give away her land or convey the property to another party. The children of Israel were forbidden to sell the land permanently, even to another Jew. God instructed:

> "The land must not be sold permanently, because
> the land is mine and you reside in my land as foreign-
> ers and strangers" (Leviticus 25:23).

Giving away any of the land violates the covenant God made with Abraham, Isaac, and Jacob and places the nation of Israel outside God's covenant blessings. Likewise, the nations that are coercing Israel into giving up the land come under the curse of God.

God's sovereignty over the land of Israel extends in a special way to the city of Jerusalem. It is the only city He has ever claimed as His own. In the Scriptures it is called the "City of God" and the "Holy City." For that reason alone, Christians should be concerned about the fate of Jerusalem. If Jerusalem is dear to God's heart, it should be dear to the hearts of every Bible believer.

In order to look forward, we must first walk back through the pages of Jerusalem's history, the history of the temple and its influence on the children of Israel. The city seems always to have been exceptional—almost an oddity. Back in Joshua's time, when the Israelites were fighting to take the land of Canaan from its previous inhabitants and conquered Jerusalem, its name was omitted from the review of Joshua's conquests. We see later in Joshua 15:63 that the tribe of Judah was unable to rid the village of the Jebusites who controlled it. It remained that way until roughly four hundred years later.

When David became king something important happened. After King Saul's death on Mount Gilboa, David ceased to be a fugitive running for his life. God told him to establish his headquarters in Hebron in the midst of his own tribe. This is where the people of Judah anointed David king. Abner, King Saul's cousin and commander-in-chief of his armies, ruled over the northern tribes after the king died, but after Abner's murder, the elders of Israel made a pact with David and anointed him their king. The prophet Samuel's words had come to pass, and the nation of Israel was reunited.

Now David needed a city from which to rule a united Israel. Jerusalem was ideally located. It stood on the border between the northern tribes and Judah, and, more importantly, it had never been associated with any specific tribe. It would be the capital of all the tribes and a center for the worship of Yahweh, to whom David was deeply devoted.

Determining it would be his seat of government, David and his men marched to Jerusalem. The Jebusites refused to take David's challenge seriously. They had successfully held the Israelites at bay from their high perch before; why should things be different this time? David, however, succeeded where others had failed. He used a water channel to get inside the Jebusite fortifications surrounding Jerusalem. In short order, David took the city and began to consolidate his people from the new capital.

Hiram, King of Tyre, sent men and material to assist in building a palace. David saw it all as God's favor and understood that his rule as king was blessed for the sake of His people Israel. But David's success would not go unchallenged. Enter the Philistines. They viewed David as merely a renegade shepherd, who had been lucky in killing the giant Goliath, and set out to punish this upstart! David soundly defeated them in two separate battles and sent them back to their fortresses along the south coast.

Afterward, David mustered his troops to escort the ark of the covenant to the new capital. This was of vital importance to him. It was Yahweh, the God of Abraham, Isaac, and Jacob, who had brought him through his years of shepherding, Samuel's anointing and prophecy, battling Goliath, Saul's attempts to kill him, and David's years of exile. Never had God forsaken him.

The false gods of Astarte and Baal held no allure for King David. Yahweh was his one true God. He was so devoted that he was unashamed to let everyone know of his dedication. His wife Michal, Saul's daughter, ridiculed and scorned her husband for being foolish as he danced before the ark of the covenant as it was being returned to Jerusalem. David was unperturbed and informed Michal that he would gladly do that and much more. No display of heartfelt exuberance was inappropriate to the worship of this great and wonderful God who had blessed David so abundantly.

Once David had settled in Jerusalem, it became the center for worship of the God of the Hebrews. King David wanted to build a temple for the Lord he loved, but the prophet Nathan told him his warlike ways had made it inappropriate for him to carry out such a task.

During David's reign, although the ark of the covenant continued to dwell in a tent, it in no way hampered David's enthusiasm in promoting the worship of Yahweh. Animals were sacrificed morning and evening, and the Sabbath was rigorously observed. Even today, David's intimate relationship with his God and the worship that relationship evoked is preserved in the book of Psalms. Both Christian and Jew are deeply affected by the beauty and sense of awe of Almighty God that flows through its pages.

King David, who conquered Jerusalem and made it his capital city, is described in Scripture as a man "after God's own heart." The desire of David's heart was to build a temple in Jerusalem as the dwelling place of God. Because David's kingdom was so associated with warfare and bloodshed in the conquest of Israel's enemies, the Lord would not allow David to move forward with his plans. He did, however, promise David that his son and successor, Solomon, would fulfill the dream.

God made an unconditional promise, another "everlasting covenant" with David. This covenant promised that his line would endure forever, and that the Messiah would come from the Davidic lineage:

> The LORD became angry with Solomon because
> his heart had turned away from the LORD, the God of

Israel, who had appeared to him twice. Although he had forbidden Solomon to follow other gods, Solomon did not keep the LORD's command. So the LORD said to Solomon, "Since this is your attitude and you have not kept my covenant and my decrees, which I commanded you, I will most certainly tear the kingdom away from you and give it to one of your subordinates. Nevertheless, for the sake of David your father, I will not do it during your lifetime. I will tear it out of the hand of your son. Yet I will not tear the whole kingdom from him, but will give him one tribe for the sake of David my servant and for the sake of Jerusalem, which I have chosen." (1 Kings 11:9–13)

Solomon's disobedience precluded his participation in the covenant blessing, but because God had made an unconditional promise, and for the sake of Jerusalem, Solomon was not totally cut off. God is faithful to always keep His promises. Not only did He choose Jerusalem as His city and the symbol of His intent to dwell among His people, He continued to exercise control over it. His sovereignty over Jerusalem is demonstrated in that He decreed both its destruction and rebuilding.

Jerusalem is what it is—a center of worship. No river flows through it; it sits beside no harbor. No other reason can be offered for its importance. It is a mystery to be pondered at length. It sits astride a range of unremarkable hills at a narrow neck of land that joins the two largest continents on Earth: Asia and Africa. From ancient times great and prosperous societies flourished both north of Jerusalem in Mesopotamia, that fertile region around the Tigris and Euphrates, and south of Jerusalem around the Nile River valley. Alternatively those great societies sought to impose their rule over each other. To do so, they had to pass through Israel—everyone's doormat.

For one shining moment, all that changed when God found in David a man after His own heart. During David's reign the great tides of history that generally governed events around Jerusalem were interrupted. Neither Mesopotamia nor Egypt was active; both great centers of civilization were stagnant. During this temporary lull, David's star rose to heights unimaginable in the little backwater province he ruled. To this day, it is difficult to imagine a kingdom centered in Jerusalem that would extend almost from the Nile to the Euphrates. But that is the land David and his son Solomon ruled in peace and prosperity.

It was a golden age unforgotten by the Jews. In the dark days during Solomon's reign, his heart began to follow the false gods of some of his many wives and concubines. The prophets of Israel comforted those who remained faithful to Yahweh. They announced that God would one day bring another like David, an anointed one, a Messiah who would reestablish Zion (Jerusalem). He would exalt it in the eyes of all men so that the nations, the *goyim*, would come from the four corners of the earth to acknowledge the God of Israel as the one true God of all creation—the King of Glory, *Yahweh Sabaoth*. It was to this promise alone that God's people clung over succeeding centuries.

3

GENESIS:
SIN *and* SACRIFICE

The long history of sacrifices by the children of Israel to Yahweh began within the confines of the garden of Eden. The beautiful and luxurious garden was the first tabernacle on earth, the first meeting place where God took up residence among His creation and communed with man face-to-face. It was truly a heavenly tabernacle on earth before sin polluted its inhabitants.

It is in Genesis that God first exhibited grace to His creation. Adam and Eve were formed in the likeness of God. He created them with the ability to reason, with emotions, and with free will. It was the Creator's desire that man would serve Him with mind and heart and would choose to obey Him. The truth is that Adam and Eve were completely free to love God, or to reject Him. It was a wonderful design: Man was meant to willingly and fearlessly love and serve Yahweh. Unfortunately, Adam and Eve heeded the wrong voice.

In Genesis 3:1–6 (NKJV), we read the story of a willful decision:

> Now the serpent was more cunning than any beast
> of the field which the LORD God had made. And he

said to the woman, "Has God indeed said, 'You shall not eat of every tree of the garden'?" And the woman said to the serpent, "We may eat the fruit of the trees of the garden; but of the fruit of the tree which is in the midst of the garden, God has said, 'You shall not eat it, nor shall you touch it, lest you die.'" Then the serpent said to the woman, "You will not surely die. For God knows that in the day you eat of it your eyes will be opened, and you will be like God, knowing good and evil." So when the woman saw that the tree was good for food, that it was pleasant to the eyes, and a tree desirable to make one wise, she took of its fruit and ate. She also gave to her husband with her, and he ate.

With the decision to pluck the fruit from the tree, sin entered the world. In Genesis 2:25 (NKJV), we read, "And they were both naked, the man and his wife, and were not ashamed." Adam and Eve were untouched by evil—either in thought or deed. Seven short verses later and after partaking of the forbidden fruit, the entire universe changed, for "the eyes of both of them were opened, and they knew that they were naked; and they sewed fig leaves together and made themselves coverings" (Genesis 3:7 NKJV).

In his book *The Genesis Record*, Dr. Henry M. Morris wrote of their nakedness:

It may be noted incidentally that the shame of nudity is no artificial inhibition introduced by the conventions of civilization, as certain anthropologists and self-service sophisticates have urged. It has its source in this primeval awareness of sin, and is only discarded when the moral conscience has been so hardened as to lose all sensitivity to sin.[1]

What horror the man and woman in the garden must have experienced when they immediately realized that something had changed. What do you think Eve might have given for a do-over? She and Adam had gone from being God-centered to being Self-centered. Before sin entered in, they conversed freely with God. Is it possible that their clothing was the same light that shrouded Moses' face after he talked with God on Mount Sinai? If so, the light had been snuffed out and Adam realized that their holy covering had vanished; now they were naked. The reaction was to cover their nudity with the leaves of the fig tree. The sanctity of the tabernacle in the garden had been breached by sin. In his article "Fig Leaves and Pharisees," minister and author Doug Batchelor made this observation:

> When we sin, one of two things will happen. We either start looking for fig leaves to make our own flimsy coverup, or we look to Jesus for His robe of righteousness.[2]

Having hurriedly fashioned aprons of fig leaves, Adam and Eve waited fearfully for their daily time of communion with God. Yet when that time approached, they hid among the lush greenery of the garden. The setting had not changed, but the two in the garden had been changed forever:

> Then the LORD God called to Adam and said to him, "Where are you?" So he [Adam] said, "I heard Your voice in the garden, and I was afraid because I was naked; and I hid myself." And He said, "Who told you that you were naked? Have you eaten from the

tree of which I commanded you that you should not eat?" (Genesis 3:9–11 NKJV)

Excuses poured forth from the two who had been so privileged to sit at the feet of Yahweh. Adam blamed Eve, and perhaps even God, when he replied:

> "The woman whom You gave to be with me, she gave me of the tree, and I ate." And the LORD God said to the woman, "What is this you have done?" The woman said, "The serpent deceived me, and I ate." (Genesis 3:12–13 NKJV)

Little has changed since that long-ago evening in the garden of Eden. Mankind continues to make excuses, shift blame, and refuse to accept responsibility for his/her actions. How often do we read or hear an apology such as this offered: "If you find my remarks/actions/lifestyle offensive, I apologize that you were upset." No personal responsibility, only a guilt trip laid on the one who was insulted. Apologists admit little if any wrongdoing, following the tradition set by Adam and Eve.

The two inhabitants of the garden were about to discover that God's admonition was true when He said, "For in the day that you eat of it you shall surely die" (Genesis 2:17b NKJV). They would soon know firsthand that sin required a blood sacrifice. Beyond that, they had no idea of the door that had been opened and how one bite—just one bite—would affect mankind from that moment forward. Adam and Eve tried to hide their sin with the leaves of a smelly, itchy fig tree, which was totally incapable of providing atonement. Was God forced, then, to turn His back on His creation? He cannot look upon sin; therefore, God had to provide a way to impute righteousness to those who were separated from Him. No longer could Adam and Eve sit at the feet of Yahweh and commune with Him.

Animals would have to die in order for garments to be fashioned to cover their nakedness, and eventually a practice for postponing sin would be given to Moses in the wilderness. But there in the garden, God initiated the first sacrifice. Some two thousand years later, He would give the ultimate sacrifice, the Lamb that would not simply cover sin, but remove sin for all eternity. Only when we accept Christ and put on His righteousness are we ever fully clothed to stand in the presence of Jehovah. The apostle Paul wrote to the Romans in chapter 13, verse 14, "But put on the Lord Jesus Christ, and make no provision for the flesh, to fulfill its lusts" (NKJV).

There in Eden, Jehovah laid the foundation for grace. Nothing Adam and Eve could do would cover their sinful state. God selected an animal, probably a lamb, slew it, skinned it, and fashioned skins to cover His children. It was God's gracious gift; Adam and Eve could only stand by in horror as the animal bleated and then bled out to provide a substitutionary covering. The leaves the two had so painstakingly sewn together covered only their hindquarters. Jehovah provided a garment to hide their shame. The Hebrew word for "garment" is *kuttoneth*, from the root meaning to cover as with a coat or tunic.[3]

God's provision was sufficient; man could add nothing. That is grace, and the actuality that the pair did feel guilt and shame gave hope for salvation and reconciliation with the Creator. As the old hymn reminds us:

> Grace, grace, God's grace,
> grace that will pardon and cleanse within;

grace, grace, God's grace,

grace that is greater than all our sin![4]

Wayne Stiles, executive vice president at Insight for Living, wrote in his blog:

> In the Garden of Eden, Adam's choice to commit sin had the potential of bringing condemnation to everyone. In the Garden of Gethsemane, Christ's decision to die for sins provided potential justification to everyone (Romans 5:18).
>
> Adam *never* would have eaten the fruit had he known the consequences to himself and to his race. But he couldn't see the results.
>
> All he had was God's Word and its warning. That's all we have as well . . . . Every day, we walk in the gardens of decision. The two choices in two gardens give us pause to consider our own decisions today:
>
> ✧ Like Adam in the Garden of Eden, we can compromise God's Word in favor of what we think or feel—and live with overwhelming regret. We don't have to wonder if this will be our outcome. Adam has shown us it is so.
>
> ✧ Like Jesus in Gethsemane, we can take God at His Word—even when it costs us dearly—knowing the Father makes the potential worth the sacrifice. Our choices can produce good beyond imagination.[5]

As we examine the wilderness tabernacle, Solomon's temple,

Herod's temple, and the rebuilt temple in Ezra and Nehemiah's day, we will also look more closely at the similarities between these places of worship and the garden of Eden. Just as there are types and shadows of the coming Messiah and His work of redemption throughout the Old Testament, so in the construction of the central places of worship we see similarities with the garden of Eden. The garden and the tabernacle were places of great fluidity—the wind whispered through the trees, swaying the branches, rustling the leaves and spreading the perfume of flowers like a sweet-smelling savor. The hangings in the tabernacle were also swayed by the winds, and the aroma of spices from the altar of incense wafted through the camp. And the very presence of the structure within the camp of the Israelites would point man back to God with whom fellowship had been broken by sin.

In Genesis 3:15, Jehovah pronounces judgment on the serpent (Satan) while pointing toward the cross and the ultimate sacrifice for the sin of mankind:

> "And I will put enmity between you and the woman, and between your offspring and hers; he will crush your head, and you will strike his heel."

Christ, the Redeemer, would be born of a woman. In an attempt to destroy the Son of God, Satan would shout with triumph at the sight of Christ on the cross. I can easily imagine that Satan and all the demons in hell were dancing with glee. The Son of God was near death; the heel of the Son of Man had been bruised. The Enemy was certain he had won! Other bystanders bowed their heads in shame and compassion. Their beloved friend and companion hung exposed to the world. Tears rolled down those faces, and sobs could be heard echoing from the hillside. Little did Satan know that the final pages of the book had already been written in heaven. It would be delivered to John on the Isle of Patmos:

> And the devil, who deceived them, was thrown into the lake of burning sulfur, where the beast and the false prophet had been thrown. They will be tormented day and night for ever and ever. (Revelation 20:10)

In *The Genesis Record*, author Henry M. Morris wrote of the promised Seed who would

> ... one day be born of a human woman, but Satan was left in the dark as to which woman and at what time. Both he and Eve may have thought initially it would be her firstborn son. Later on, as the centuries passed, Satan continued his attacks against all the males born in the promised line, particularly those who were objects of special prophetic interest (e.g., Noah, Abraham, Jacob, David), in case one of them might be the promised Seed.[6]

Judgment was now pronounced on Adam and Eve. Genesis 3:23–24 (NKJV) gives us in graphic detail the ultimate punishment they would bear for their sin:

> Therefore the LORD God sent him [Adam] out of the garden of Eden to till the ground from which he was taken. So He drove out the man; and He placed cherubim at the east of the garden of Eden, and a flaming sword which turned every way, to guard the way to the tree of life.

Adam and Eve would be driven from the home they had enjoyed

since creation. No longer would they be able to walk from tree to tree to pluck the fruit; no longer would they be fed by the hand of God. Now they would have to endure the harsh reality of providing for themselves. They would be subject to the whims of the natural growth cycle. They would have to till the land for every bite of their food. Their fellowship with Jehovah in the cool of the day had been broken and the chasm left in their spirits could not be crossed—until Calvary. At the foot of a wooden tree in the shape of a cross, the promised Seed would give His life to span the gulf between God and man. But there in the garden, the cherubim gripping flaming swords were posted at the entrance.

When Jehovah gave Moses the design for the tabernacle, these same cherubim would be replicated in gold over the mercy seat. The slab of pure gold covered the ark of the covenant, which symbolized the very presence of Jehovah in the midst of His people. The garden was replete with trees and flowers, and that symbolism continued within the tabernacle, which boasted lampstands with branches and bowls, which represented the almond tree. The ready abundance of food in the garden was signified in the tabernacle by the shewbread on the table. These very instruments were also a foreshadowing of the One who was to come to reconcile fallen man with a righteous God.

4

GENESIS:

SACRIFICIAL OFFERINGS

Although the sacrifice by God in the garden was the first shedding of blood, it would surely not be the last sacrifice offered. One of the earliest examples of an acceptable sacrifice to Jehovah was that of Abel, the second son of Adam and Eve. In Hebrew, Abel means "breath, or vapor," perhaps an indication of the shortness of his life. James wrote: "Your life is like the morning fog—it's here a little while, then it's gone" (James 4:14 NLT).

Cain, the older brother, was a tiller of the ground—a farmer; Abel was a shepherd. Genesis does not tell us exactly how the two brothers knew what was considered a proper sacrifice to the most Holy God, but clearly they did.

The story of God's grace to their parents must have been told over and over to Cain and Abel. Both worshiped God and brought sacrifices to present to Him—but each brought a different offering. Genesis 4:3 says that "Cain brought ... the fruit of the ground" (NKJV). He approached the altar of sacrifice with whatever he could pluck from his garden. His gift was one of convenience—for show, one given not in faith, but in haste, a last-minute effort. Though he gave lip service to Jehovah, he was not a godly man; instead, he was quick to anger, self-indulgent, and jealous. Cain's wrathful response when God rejected his spur-of-the-moment offering was indicative of his character:

> But [the Lord] did not accept Cain and his gift. This made Cain very angry, and he looked dejected.
>
> "Why are you so angry?" the LORD asked Cain. "Why do you look so dejected?" (Genesis 4:5–6 NLT)

Cain was angry that God dared to reject his sacrifice. He was so indignant that he stood boldly at the altar and argued with the Creator of the universe. His anger coupled with his appalling attitude could not mask his realization that Jehovah's requirements had not been met. Even before Christ offered grace to everyone through His death on the cross, God offered Cain a second chance:

> "You will be accepted if you do what is right. But if you refuse to do what is right, then watch out! Sin is crouching at the door, eager to control you. But you must subdue it and be its master." (Genesis 4:7 NLT)

Cain could have reviewed the requirements for an acceptable offering, humbled himself before God, and returned with a proper sacrifice. Instead, his choice was to stomp angrily away with Jehovah's warning ringing in his ears. Sin became his master and he responded accordingly.

Abel had made preparation for his offering by choosing a first-born from his flock. He did not choose a skinny, lame, marred lamb; rather, it was the best he had to offer. Abel approached the altar humbly and penitently, bowed low in the presence of Almighty God,

and presented his gift with faith that his obedience would be honored—his gift accepted.

Abel's offering of a sheep was his way of acknowledging what
God had done in the garden when He wrapped Abel's mother and
father in animal skins. He presented an animal from his flock as
both a thank offering and a sin offering. In essence, he was saying,
"I want to be obedient. I am thanking You for showing grace to my
parents, and I am asking You to show the same grace to me."

The two brothers walked away from the altar with totally
different countenances. Abel's was radiant with God's love and
approval; Cain's was dark, his face infused with rage, his heart filled
with jealousy and murderous intent.

Noted Christian pastor, author, and teacher Charles Swindoll
wrote of jealousy:

> This was Cain's sin. He was jealous of Abel. He
> resented God's acceptance of his brother. No doubt
> his face was red with emotion and his eyes filled with
> rage as God smiled on Abel's sacrifice. Not until Abel's
> warm blood poured over Cain's cruel hands did jeal-
> ousy subside.[7]

Solomon, the wise king, defined the effects of such jealousy
when he wrote, "Jealousy is cruel as the grave. Its flashes are flashes
of fire" (Song of Solomon 8:6 RSV).

Abel's hands were raised in praise to Jehovah; Cain's fists were
clenched in fury. He was so filled with resentment that he lured his
brother into the field and murdered him.

Suddenly God called to Cain, "Where is Abel, your brother?"

A sullen Cain replied, "I don't have any idea. Why are you asking
me, anyway? Am I my brother's keeper?" (Genesis 4:9, paraphrased.)

The punishment for Cain's crime was swift and severe. God stripped him of the land that he had tilled and banished him from His presence. He was thrust out of Eden and consigned to be a vagrant and wanderer. And God warned:

> "Therefore, whoever kills Cain, vengeance shall be taken on him sevenfold." And the LORD set a mark on Cain, lest anyone finding him should kill him (Genesis 4:15 NKJV).

When the horror of Cain's sin gripped him, he cried, "My punishment is greater than I can bear!" (Genesis 4:13 NKJV).

Of the lives of Cain and Abel, noted Christian minister and author John MacArthur wrote:

> Abel's sacrifice was accepted because he knew what God wanted and obeyed. Cain's was rejected because he knew what God wanted, yet disobeyed. To obey is righteous; to disobey is evil. Abel was of God; Cain was of Satan (1 John 3:12) . . . Abel offered a better sacrifice because it represented the obedience of faith. He willingly brought God what He asked, and he brought the very best that he had. In Abel's sacrifice, the way of the cross was first [foreshadowed.] The first sacrifice was Abel's lamb—one lamb for one person. Later came the Passover [Pesach]—with one lamb for one family. Then came the Day of Atonement—with one lamb for one nation. Finally came Good Friday—one Lamb for the whole world.[8]

Abel's obedience won him a place in the Bible's Heroes Hall of Fame:

> By faith Abel offered God a better sacrifice than Cain
> did. By faith he was commended as righteous, when
> God spoke well of his offerings. And by faith Abel still
> speaks, even though he is dead. (Hebrews 11:4)

Abel responded to the call of God. His decision to obey regardless of the circumstances or outcome led to his death, but it also produced great faith and an even greater reward. His sacrifice was an act of reverence, respect, reliance, and supplication.

✧　✧　✧

Following the flood, Noah offered a sacrifice to Jehovah. "Then Noah built an altar to the LORD, and took of every clean animal and of every clean bird, and offered burnt offerings on the altar" (Genesis 8:20 NKJV).

Day after day Noah and his family lived with the pounding of waves against the hull of the huge vessel, the sound of rain pounding on the deck, and the noises of a boatload of animals. This does not take into account the smells that must have emanated from various levels where the creatures were housed. Finally one morning Noah must have been awakened—not by the noise but by the quiet that reigned. Throwing on his robe, he raced to the uppermost level of the craft, threw open a window, and realized that the rains had stopped, the forty days had come to an end, and now the waters would begin to recede. How Noah and his family must have praised Jehovah, the One who had saved them from certain destruction!

The day came when the huge boat came to rest atop Mount Ararat and Noah and his family cautiously made their way down the gangplank onto dry ground. Noah began to fully comprehend what

God had done in providing animals for food, clothing, and their very sustenance. In gratitude, Noah gathered stones and built an altar—the first mention of an altar in the Old Testament. He brought forth one of every type of clean animal and offered it as a sacrifice unto Jehovah.

Dr. Henry M. Morris, founder of the Institute of Creation Research, wrote:

> The clean animals included a few "beasts" and "birds," but apparently no "creeping things." It seems likely that the clean animals were those adjudged suitable for domestication ... and thus also suitable for sacrificial offerings in atonement for man. Since no previous categorization of animals as "clean" or "unclean" is given in Genesis, it is perhaps reasonable to believe that God allowed Noah to use his own judgment on this [or perhaps these categories had been revealed earlier to Adam, Abel and others, but not recorded in Genesis, only inferred]. The three pairs were to encourage the relatively greater numerical proliferation of the clean animals after the Flood ... The seventh animal in each [clean] group clearly was intended for sacrificial purposes (Genesis 9:20). Much later, the Mosaic law plainly spelled out which animals were to be regarded as clean in the Israelite system (Leviticus 11, etc.), though all such distinctions were to be removed altogether in the Christian dispensation, [See Acts 10:9-15; I Timothy 4:4.][9]

Noah had simply given back to God what he had been given, an offering in acknowledgment of Jehovah's gracious provision.

✧   ✧   ✧

Genesis reveals that Abraham, the patriarch, was a man who sacrificed to Jehovah on countless occasions. His first sacrifice was made upon his arrival in Shechem (see Genesis 12:7). The late Dr. Boushra Mikhael, surgeon and biblical scholar, wrote of Abraham:

> Having lingered for a long while in Haran, Abraham finally made it into the land to which the Lord had called him. It was totally unknown to him, yet it became the sphere of his obedience. He moved through the land guided only by his faith in God and his desire to obey Him. This 'obedience of faith' showed how he trusted God implicitly and without questioning, for he believed that God would give him the land for an inheritance. The altar he built was to the 'Lord who appeared to him'.[10]

God promised Abram a son from whom would descend a people that numbered as many as the stars even before him and Sarai set out from Ur of the Chaldees:

> But Abram said, "LORD GOD, what will You give me, seeing I go childless, and the heir of my house is Eliezer of Damascus [a servant]?" Then Abram said, "Look, You have given me no offspring; indeed one born in my house is my heir!" And behold, the word of the LORD came to him, saying, "This one shall not be your heir, but one who will come from your own body shall be your heir." Then He brought him outside and said, "Look now toward heaven, and count the stars if

you are able to number them." And He said to him, "So shall your descendants be." (Genesis 15:2–6 NKJV)

And then God fulfilled His promise to Abram and Sarai. He said to Abram (loosely translated), "It's time for you to step up to the plate and walk uprightly before me. No more delayed obedience. I want your undivided attention." God then made another stipulation:

> "No longer shall your name be called Abram, but your name shall be Abraham [father of a multitude]; for I have made you a father of many nations . . . . As for Sarai your wife, you shall not call her name Sarai, but Sarah [noble-woman] shall be her name. And I will bless her and also give you a son by her." (Genesis 17:5, 15–16 NKJV)

Soon Abraham reached the age of ninety-nine and Sarah eighty-nine, both obviously well past normal childbearing age. Then came the day when Sarah awoke to find that she was pregnant in her old age. She who had laughed at the pronouncement that she would bear a child—she who had intervened and proposed her own plan for an heir—Sarah was now carrying Isaac, the son of promise. Not only had God taken away her barrenness, He provided the strength to carry the child to term and to bring him forth. God had fulfilled his vow, and the child of promise had finally arrived. Abraham began to teach God's covenant promises to his son. But suddenly, horror descended into Abraham's life:

> Then [God] said, "Take now your son, your only son Isaac, whom you love, and go to the land of Moriah, and offer him there as a burnt offering on one of the mountains of which I shall tell you." (Genesis 22:2 NKJV)

We often underestimate just how outrageous, how despicable this must have seemed to Abraham. Dr. Henry M. Morris says of this verse:

> This first mention of "love" in Scripture ... calls attention to the fact that the love of a godly father for his only son is a miniature picture of the love existing among the persons of the Holy Trinity, and in particular the love of the Father for the Son. This love ... existed long before the world was created, and from eternity past. Therefore, this love must be the root and foundation of all other types of love. The love of man and woman, the love of mother for child—and indeed all love—has its source in God's love.[11]

This earthly depiction of love between a father and his beloved son is repeated in heavenly fashion in the New Testament following the baptism of Jesus by John the Baptist:

> And suddenly a voice came from heaven, saying, "This is My beloved Son, in whom I am well pleased." (Matthew 3:17 NKJV)

The finite mind finds it impossible to believe that Abraham didn't question God's directive, but the biblical narrative doesn't suggest that. Abraham knew only what God had demanded of him. Verse 3 says:

> So Abraham rose early in the morning and saddled his donkey, and took two of his young men with him, and Isaac his son; and he split the wood for the burnt offering, and arose and went to the place of which God had told him. (Genesis 22:3 NKJV)

Abraham did not argue or try to bargain with God. Instead, he immediately made arrangements for the three-day journey to Mount Moriah. I believe he did so with a heavy heart, and was puzzled about God's plan. Abraham was not some Superman—a spiritual hero with mystical powers; he was "everyman" and he was about to offer up his child of promise. How would you feel if you knew you were about to lose a beloved son or daughter? Abraham surely felt no differently.

So off they set on a trek across the desert terrain—a journey of some sixty miles—to the place designated by God. When they arrived at the foot of Mount Moriah, Abraham asked the servants to wait while "the lad and I will go yonder and worship." Then he added what might well be a hint to the strength of his faith, "and we will come back to you" (Genesis 22:5 NKJV).

Abraham was assured that God would provide. As he unloaded the wood from the donkey and laid it on Isaac's back, the lad asked, "Look, the fire and the wood, but where is the lamb for a burnt offering?" (Genesis 22:6–7 NKJV). And in verse 8 with great conviction and complete assurance, his father replied, "My son, God will provide for Himself the lamb for a burnt offering." And father and son continued their ascent to what was to be the place of sacrifice. As Isaac willingly bore the wooden burden on his back to the place of sacrifice, we can picture yet another type of Christ upon whose back the wooden cross was laid as He staggered toward Golgotha. Abraham had no way of knowing just how God would provide—a lamb wandering by, Isaac raised from the dead, a last-minute stay of execution—but he was convinced that provide God would!

When the two arrived at their destination, Abraham and Isaac set about gathering stones to erect an altar to Jehovah. Abraham carefully laid the wood and knelt before his son. He gently bound Isaac's hands and feet and laid him on the altar. Isaac was old enough to run for his life (some scholars think he could have been twenty-five to thirty-five years old), but instead, he obeyed the instruction of his father.

And Abraham stretched out his hand and took the knife to slay his son.

> But the angel of the Lord called to him from heaven and said, "Abraham, Abraham!" So he said, "Here I am."
>
> And He said, "Do not lay your hand on the lad, or do anything to him; for now I know that you fear God, since you have not withheld your son, your only son, from Me." (Genesis 22:10–12 NKJV)

I believe Abraham heard something rustling in a bush near the altar. He looked around, and held fast in the thicket was a ram caught by its horns. With unparalleled gratitude, Abraham untied his son, bound the ram, and laid it on the altar as a sacrifice to his faithful Jehovah-Jireh—his provider. The angel then goes one step further; he reiterates the pact God made with Abraham:

> "By Myself I have sworn, says the Lord, because you have done this thing, and have not withheld your son, your only son—blessing I will bless you, and multiplying I will multiply your descendants as the stars of the heaven and as the sand which is on the seashore; and your descendants shall possess the gate of their enemies. In your seed all the nations of the earth shall be blessed, because you have obeyed My voice." (Genesis 22:16–18 NKJV)

This extraordinary happening—the first instance of Abraham having made a blood sacrifice—took place about two thousand years before Christ was born, and yet it's a perfect picture of God's offering of a substitute for our sins. He would offer up His own Son for our redemption.

✧   ✧   ✧

Certainly Job was another of the Old Testament patriarchs who offered sacrifices to Yahweh. In his book *The Remarkable Record of Job*, Dr. Henry M. Morris opined:

> There is no hint in the book [of Job] of the nation of Israel—no mention of Moses, or Abraham, or any of the judges, kings, or prophets of Israel … Even more significant is the fact that there is no mention of the Ten Commandments or any of the Mosaic Laws … Divine laws were given to men and women long before Moses … Exactly how these primeval laws were given, and in what form we do not know, for they have not been preserved …. They were known by Abraham, however, and no doubt by his ancestors. They were also known by Job.[12]

As the head of his household, Job regularly offered sacrifices to Jehovah on behalf of his sons and daughters. Job 1:4–5 (NKJV) records:

> And his sons would go and feast in their houses, each on his appointed day, and would send and invite their three sisters to eat and drink with them. So it was, when the days of feasting had run their course, that Job would send and sanctify them, and he would rise early in the morning and offer burnt offerings according to the number of them all. For Job said, "It

may be that my sons have sinned and cursed God in their hearts." Thus Job did regularly.

Morris explains Job's actions:

> Job was "the greatest of all the men of the east" (Job 1:3), known far and wide for his wisdom and God-honoring righteousness. He believed all of God's Word, in whatever form he knew it, and sought to obey all God's laws . . . He never claimed to be sinless (Job 7:20-21), and he knew that he could only come to God by a substitutionary sacrifice. As head of the family, he offered sacrifices not only for himself but also for his children.[13]

Job lived before the Mosaic Covenant was given, before the order of sacrifices was laid out for the children of Israel. Yet he fully understood that only by the innocent dying for the guilty could sin be pardoned and a relationship between God and man be established. Job somehow knew that God would provide a sacrificial Lamb to redeem mankind. This law would be given to Moses on Mount Sinai, and plans for the tabernacle would establish a central place for people to come together to offer worship and sacrifices to Jehovah God. Pastor and teacher Bob Deffinbaugh wrote of the structure:

> The purpose of the tabernacle was to provide a place where God may dwell in the midst of men. All of the furnishings facilitate ministries and ceremonies which contribute to this one place of providing a "tent of meeting."[14]

5

EXODUS:
INTO *the* WILDERNESS

xodus, the second book of the Pentateuch, is the story of deliverance from bondage and restoration—the establishing of a special relationship between Jehovah and the children of Israel. After the death of Joseph and during the next 430 years, the offspring of his father, Jacob, lived under Egyptian bondage. As the Israelites multiplied, hatred for them grew exponentially and the burdens placed upon them by their Egyptian taskmasters became unbearable.

In Exodus 2 we meet the person whom God had ordained to deliver His people out of bondage—Moses. His story begins with his mother, Jacobed, who hid him from the Egyptians for three months after his birth. Because of the explosive birth rate among the Israelites, Pharaoh had issued a decree that every Hebrew male child was to be slaughtered. He instructed the midwives to kill every child as soon as he emerged from the womb. Instead, they united to save as many children as possible, one of them being Moses. When Jacobed's son became too old to hide at home, she took reeds and wove a basket. She waterproofed it, set it among the bulrushes on the bank of the Nile, and entrusted her baby boy to Yahweh. She stationed her daughter, Miriam, nearby to watch over her baby brother.

The first miracle of Moses' young life was that the child was not consumed by the crocodiles that inhabited the Nile. The second miracle was that Pharaoh's daughter came down to the water's edge to bathe and spotted the basket with the child inside floating on the water. She sent one of her handmaidens to fetch it and recognized immediately that it was a Hebrew child. Miriam crept from her hiding place and with great fear and trembling approached the princess. She timidly offered the services of her mother, Jacobed, as a wet nurse for the baby. Then a third miracle: The mother of Moses was able to nurse her own son:

> And the child grew, and [Jacobed] brought him to Pharaoh's daughter, and he became her son. So she called his name Moses, saying, "Because I drew him out of the water." (Exodus 2:10 NKJV)

So Moses was reared in the household of Pharaoh, a family of wealth and privilege. Nothing else is recorded of Moses' life until he was a young man, but as suddenly as he disappeared from the pages of the Bible, he reappeared. Moses was out walking one day when he happened upon an Egyptian taskmaster beating a Jewish slave. So incensed was Moses that he killed the Egyptian and hid the body. The following day, he saw two Hebrew men fighting. He adopted the role of intermediary, but one of the men challenged him:

> "Who made you a prince and a judge over us? Do you intend to kill me as you killed the Egyptian?" So Moses feared and said, "Surely this thing is known!" (Exodus 2:14 NKJV)

Moses quickly realized that his relationship with his foster mother, an Egyptian princess, would not spare him from the wrath of Pharaoh. He had murdered a man who was carrying out a direct order from the king. Moses, having heard that Pharaoh had placed a price on his head, packed his knapsack and headed for the far reaches of the desert.

Three separate incidents marked Moses' early life, yet in all three he exhibited an almost compulsive need to combat wickedness. His intervention was limited to the underdog: He championed the Hebrew slave; he intervened when two Jews were fighting and again when a group of Gentiles was oppressing another like group on the backside of the desert.

When fleeing Pharaoh, Moses had no idea he would meet his future wife, Zipporah, at a watering trough out in the middle of nowhere. Her father, Reuel, offered Moses the job of sheepherder as well as Zipporah's hand in marriage. Now Moses had a job, a wife, and soon a child, Gershom. He didn't know that he was about to face the challenge of a lifetime—greater than leaving home and family, greater than the daily grind of taking care of the sheep. God was about to intervene in Moses' life in a unique way.

One day as he led the sheep to the far reaches of Mount Horeb, he stumbled upon a bush that burned brightly but was not consumed. This was totally against the laws of nature, and Moses turned aside to see this phenomenon. He must have been stunned when from the midst of the bush the Lord spoke to him:

> "Do not come any closer," God said. "Take off your
> sandals, for the place where you are standing is holy
> ground." Then he said, "I am the God of your father,
> the God of Abraham, the God of Isaac and the God

of Jacob." At this, Moses hid his face, because he was afraid to look at God. The LORD said, "I have indeed seen the misery of my people in Egypt. I have heard them crying out because of their slave drivers, and I am concerned about their suffering. So I have come down to rescue them from the hand of the Egyptians and to bring them up out of that land into a good and spacious land, a land flowing with milk and honey— the home of the Canaanites, Hittites, Amorites, Perizzites, Hivites and Jebusites. And now the cry of the Israelites has reached me, and I have seen the way the Egyptians are oppressing them. So now, go. I am sending you to Pharaoh to bring my people the Israelites out of Egypt." (Exodus 3:5–10)

The Pharaoh from whom Moses fled had died. Moses could have let fear rule his life, and while he did argue about his ability to sway both the current king and the children of Israel, he ultimately chose to obey the call of God upon his life. God had captured his attention and dealt with Moses' concerns—he was to find his older brother, Aaron, and demand that Pharaoh "Let my people go!"

You shall speak all that I command you. And Aaron your brother shall tell Pharaoh to send the children of Israel out of his land . . . . And the Egyptians shall know that I am the LORD, when I stretch out My hand on Egypt and bring out the children of Israel from among them." (Exodus 7: 2, 5 NKJV)

In essence, God was telling Moses that his obedience would bring deliverance to the entire Hebrew nation in bondage in Egypt.

After Moses encountered his blood brother, Aaron, in the desert, the two men made their way to the palace to challenge Pharaoh. With his refusal to let the Israelites go, God began to visit ten plagues on the land. Each plague was in direct opposition to one of the gods worshiped by the Egyptians:

1. Water turned to blood: Hapi, the god of the Nile River, the source of water

2. Frogs: Heqt, god of the frogs

3. Gnats (lice): Kheper, god of insects

4. Flies: Kheper, god of insects

5. Cattle: Apis, the Egyptian bull god

6. Boils: Imhotep, god of medicine

7. Hail and fire: Nut, goddess of the sky

8. Locusts: Seth, god of crops

9. Darkness: Ra, the sun god[15]

Jehovah visited judgment upon the taskmasters who had treated His people so vilely; but to the children of Israel He offered grace and great mercy. Rather than persuade the ruler to comply with Moses' request, this did the opposite: the burdens that had been heaped upon the children of Jacob were intensified. The last and tenth plague, the death of all of Egypt's firstborn, was the final straw for the rebellious Pharaoh and an eye-opening event for the

Egyptians. The king and his son were considered gods to be wor-shiped. When the death angel took the life of the firstborn male child, it was a formidable message: El Elyon—God Most High—was more powerful than any manmade god—wood, stone, metal, or flesh. Not only was it the ultimate defeat for Pharaoh, but the lamb that was to be sacrificed, according to internationally known scholar and theologian Dr. Douglas K. Stuart

> ... served as a reminder of the eventual deliver-ance that a perfect God perfectly provided for his people as part of the process of making them holy like himself. Proper relating to God requires perfection... Jesus of Nazareth was to be young at the time of his death, male of course, and perfect—free from defect before God. His sinlessness qualified him alone to be the lamb of God, a human lamb rather than an animal of the flock, and yet a lamb in the sense of meeting the criteria for the Passover meal.[16]

Beginning in Exodus 11:4, Moses and Aaron were sent to warn the Egyptian ruler of what was to come:

> "Thus says the LORD: 'About midnight I will go out into the midst of Egypt; and all the firstborn in the land of Egypt shall die, from the firstborn of Pharaoh who sits on his throne, even to the firstborn of the female servant who is behind the handmill, and all the firstborn of the animals. Then there shall be a great cry throughout all the land of Egypt, such as was not like it before, nor shall be like it again. But against none of the children of Israel shall a dog move

its tongue, against man or beast, that you may know
that the LORD does make a difference between the
Egyptians and Israel.' And all these your servants
shall come down to me and bow down to me, saying,
'Get out, and all the people who follow you!' After
that I will go out." Then he went out from Pharaoh in
great anger. (vv. 4–8 NKJV)

Moses and Aaron willingly complied with God's directives; they
did just as He had instructed. Together, they went before the king
and demanded that he release the children of Israel to go into the
desert and worship Jehovah God.

Moses was vitally aware of what was about to befall the Egyptian
people. As a baby he was saved by Pharaoh's daughter because of an
edict that demanded the deaths of all male babies born to the children of Israel. The king's disobedience would exact a dire penalty,
not only upon his household but also each one in the land of Egypt.
Harsh, yes, but Pharaoh had been given numerous opportunities to
heed the voice of Jehovah. Because He is a God of love, a way was
made for the Israelites to escape the sentence of death that had been
pronounced, but the Egyptians chose instead to ignore the warnings—all ten of them in the form of various plagues visited upon the
land. The use of the number ten in the Bible points to the "number
of completion based on God's order AND human responsibility."[17]
Yahweh had ordered ten divine interruptions in the lives of the
Egyptian people; it was their responsibility to heed His warnings
in order to escape judgment. Exodus 11:1 tells us that the children of
Israel were literally forcefully ejected from Egypt by Pharaoh.

Shortly after their departure from Egypt, the Israelites again
encountered Pharaoh's troops on the banks of the Red Sea. This is

a fascinating study in itself, but we will forego that at this time and simply say that God's deliverance of His people was both divine and faith-building. Despite their miraculous escape from the Egyptian army, human nature soon reasserted within the ranks of the delivered. By the third day of freedom, the Israelites began to grumble about a lack of water. When at last they happened upon the wells at Marah, it was only to discover that the waters were bitter, a cause for agitation, apprehension, and accusations:

> When they came to Marah, they could not drink its water because it was bitter. (That is why the place is called Marah.) So the people grumbled [murmured, complained] against Moses, saying, "What are we to drink?" (Exodus 15:23–24)

This is the first instance in the Old Testament of the use of the word *murmured* but certainly not the last in the narrative concerning the freed Israelites. Jehovah sweetened the bitter waters at Marah, fed them with quail and manna (Exodus 16), and provided water from a rock (Exodus 17). Then, after three long months of trekking through the wilderness, He led the children of Israel to the foot of Mount Sinai. For the following ten months and nineteen days, the Israelites would encamp at the foot of the mountain of God. Moses would be called to climb the mountain into the clouds symbolic of the very presence of Jehovah to commune with God. It was that scaling of the heights that would inspire Dr. Martin Luther King Jr. to great oratory on April 3, 1968, in Memphis, Tennessee:

> Well, I don't know what will happen now. We've got some difficult days ahead. But it really doesn't matter with me now, because I've been to the mountaintop.

And I don't mind. Like anybody, I would like to live a long life. Longevity has its place. But I'm not concerned about that now. I just want to do God's will. And He's allowed me to go up to the mountain. And I've looked over. And I've seen the Promised Land. I may not get there with you. But I want you to know tonight, that we, as a people, will get to the promised land![18]

In Exodus 19 and 20, Jehovah began to set forth the code of conduct for His people even as He reminded them of all that had gone before in the land of Egypt. Jehovah began the conversation with Moses by laying out the conditions for His covenant with the children of Israel. Robin Fish, pastor of Shaped by the Cross Lutheran Church in Laurie, Missouri, wrote regarding Exodus 19:1–6:

We are going to see God giving guidance to His people. He has never left His Chosen People without direction, and He has never left them without hope. He not only rescued them from cruel slavery, and set them free to be His holy people, He showed them the way in which they should walk, a way of health and sanity and peace. He made them something when they were nothing. He offered them a future and a hope, just as He has done for us.

God gave Moses a message for the people. His first words from the mountain were invitation and welcome. He said, in effect, 'Look at what I did for you . . . . You have seen My power and you have seen My love. I have chosen you and shown you how good it can be to have a God like Me." That was "Welcome!'

> Then came the invitation . . . . That was like saying
> 'Trust Me and love Me and I will keep you, and I will
> make you something special among all the people of
> the earth.' The nature of the relationship, and the way
> that they were to express their faith and love was laid
> out for them in the content of the Law.
>
> The Law of God was the love of God, expressed in
> guidance.[19] (Punctuation as it is in original quote.)

When Moses stood at the foot of Mount Sinai and looked skyward into the swirling clouds filled with thunder and lightning, he had no way of knowing that he would not lead his people into the Promised Land. He just knew that he had been summoned to prepare the people to hear from Jehovah, and soon thereafter he would sit down with his Creator, an honor he had never imagined as he led Jethro's sheep on the backside of the desert all those years before.

After Jehovah delivered the commandments to the people, they begged Moses not to let God speak to them lest they die. In Exodus 20:22–26 (NLV), God ended His audible message to the people:

> Then the Lord said to Moses, "Say this to the people of Israel: 'You have seen for yourselves that I have spoken to you from heaven. Do not make any gods other than Me. Do not make for yourselves gods of silver or gods of gold. Make an altar of earth for Me, and on it give your burnt and peace gifts in worship, your sheep and cattle. In every place where My name is to be remembered, I will come to you and bring good to you. If you make an altar of stone for Me, do not build it of cut stones. For if you use an object to cut it, it will be unclean. And do not go up on steps to

My altar, so no part of your body may be seen without being covered.'"

The one thing many remember about the Ten Commandments is the "Thou shalt nots." All too often, those are shunned in favor of the Gospels. Our human nature would prefer to know the "dos" rather than the "don'ts" and all too often we focus on the latter when studying the ten laws handed down on Mount Sinai. Upon looking more closely, we see that, as one writer opined:

> The Ten Commandments teach us how to first love God, and then love our neighbor. When God is first in our lives, the rest comes naturally .... The first commandment says, "You shall have no other gods before me" (Exodus 20:3). In other words, love God above everything .... God wants us to use his name positively, not in vain. He wants us to concentrate on his word and his ways, on remembering the Sabbath day by honoring God with our choices. It is good to honor our father and mother; we should always treat family members with respect. Do not kill, do not commit adultery, and do not steal. Those three commandments value life and relationship and respecting others. Not bearing false witness against your neighbor, and not coveting what belongs to your neighbor applies to men and women, young and old—everyone .... Each commandment is a separate rule but together they offer directions on how to live without sin .... Jesus did not do away with the moral law at the cross, but his sacrifice for mankind revealed the grace and forgiveness available to us.[20]

Jehovah is concerned about the lives of His people; thus, He gave instructions for every aspect of our relationship with Him— from how we are to love Him to how we are to treat our next-door neighbor. He did not set us on this journey and then abandon us. Even more compelling: Jehovah still offers His unfathomable grace to those who have transgressed His laws through the shed blood of His Son, Jesus Christ.

6

JEHOVAH:
The TABERNACLE ARCHITECT

n Exodus 24, Jehovah summoned Moses to climb the mountain, along with Aaron, and his first two sons, Nadab and Abihu. Hur plus seventy elders of Israel also accompanied Moses. Stationing the other leaders in a specific place on the mountainside, Moses sat for six long days, waiting for direction. And then further instructions for his companions were given to Moses:

> "Wait here until we return to you. See, Aaron and Hur are with you. Let whoever has a problem go to them." Then Moses went up on the mountain, which was covered with a cloud. The shining-greatness of the Lord rested on Mount Sinai. And the cloud covered it for six days. On the seventh day He called to Moses from the cloud. To the people of Israel, the shining-greatness of the Lord looked like a fire that destroys on the mountain top. Moses went into the cloud as he went up on the mountain. And Moses was on the mountain forty days and forty nights. (Exodus 24:14–18 NLV)

From Exodus 25–40 and through Leviticus 1–17 Moses was given very specific plans for the tabernacle—the symbol of God's dwelling that was to be the central place of worship for His people. As Moses sat in silent awe and listened to the voice of El-Elyon—the Lord Most High—he was surely consumed with joy. He was in the presence of the One who had delivered the People of the Book from the brutal hand of Pharaoh and was now delivering the law by which they would not only survive but thrive. Now, the greatest glory of all, that the King of all kings, the Lord Creator, the God of the universe would abide in the very midst of His people.

Popular Bible expositor David M. Levy wrote of the tabernacle:

> The Tabernacle is of such great importance to God's redemptive program that 50 chapters in the Bible are given to explaining its pattern, construction, and service. Nothing was left to Moses' speculation; God revealed to him in minute detail every aspect of the Tabernacle . . . which stood as a testimony to Israel and the world of God's truth and glory.[21]

The intrinsic holiness of Jehovah was to be set forth in the instructions governing His tabernacle. Every aspect of the tabernacle recorded in the book of Exodus in some way reflected the coming Messiah about whom Adam and Eve were told in the garden of Eden. It was to be a visual representation of the ongoing presence of God in the midst of His children—one that runs through the Bible from Genesis to Revelation.

After Moses sat in the presence of Jehovah for forty days and nights, God warned him of the betrayal of the people left waiting at the bottom of the mountain. Moses hefted the tablets written by the very finger of God and made his way back down to the Israelite encampment. Charles Swindoll wrote of that monumental treasure:

> Remember, these tablets, written by Almighty God Himself, were the most precious documents man ever had in his possession. Think of having a book written by the very finger of God! Imagine possession of a document that God personally penned, signed, and deposited to your trust. That is what Moses had. In his own hands he held the precious documents of the inspired Torah.[22]

He rejoined Joshua as he neared the foot of the mountain:

> And when Joshua heard the noise of the people as they shouted, he said to Moses, "There is a noise of war in the camp."
> But he said:
> "It is not the noise of the shout of victory,
> Nor the noise of the cry of defeat,
> But the sound of singing I hear."
> So it was, as soon as he came near the camp, that he saw the calf and the dancing. So Moses' anger became hot, and he cast the tablets out of his hands and broke them at the foot of the mountain. Then he took the calf which they had made, burned it in the fire, and ground it to powder; and he scattered it on the water and made the children of Israel drink it. And Moses said to Aaron, "What did this people do to you that you have brought so great a sin upon them?" (Exodus 32:17–21 NKJV)

Moses might have turned to Aaron and demanded, "What were you thinking?!" Aaron's answer would have won an Oscar for his response and lame excuse. Can you picture him with arms upraised and a shrug of his shoulders?

> "Do not be angry, my lord," Aaron answered. "You know how prone these people are to evil. They said to me, 'Make us gods who will go before us. As for this fellow Moses who brought us up out of Egypt, we don't know what has happened to him.' So I told them, 'Whoever has any gold jewelry, take it off.' Then they gave me the gold, and I threw it into the fire, and *out came this calf*!" (Exodus 32:22–24, emphasis mine.)

Aaron didn't bow in contrition and take responsibility for his actions; he tried to justify going along with the crowd. How often does that happen—drifting into disobedience instead of taking a stand? We all too often chuckle at Aaron's disingenuous reply, but haven't we been guilty of the same? We excuse our own behavior while pointing a finger at someone else's fall into sin.

So distraught was Moses that he literally drew a line in the sand:

> Then Moses stood in the entrance of the camp, and said, "Whoever is on the LORD's side—come to me!" And all the sons of Levi gathered themselves together to him. (Exodus 32:26 NKJV)

At that moment, the Israelites had no comprehension of how close they had come to having been totally wiped out by the hand of God. Yet in the months and years ahead, they would execute the plans that Jehovah had given Moses on the mountain and erect the tabernacle—a constant God-sanctioned reminder that He was in their midst.

Not only did God give a detailed pattern for the tabernacle, He also gave instructions as to how the building materials and furnishings were to be amassed:

> "Tell the Israelites to bring me an offering. You are
> to receive the offering for me from everyone whose
> heart prompts them to give." (Exodus 25:2)

In Matthew 10:8, Jesus had instructed His disciples, "Freely you have received; freely give." Jehovah wanted the same from the Israelites. He knew it had only been a matter of days since they had willingly offered their golden earrings to fashion an idol in the form of a calf.

The list of items required for the tabernacle was long: While traversing the Sinai, they collected acacia wood. They were to give of the gold, silver, brass, jewels, fine linens, and dyes donated by their Egyptian captors; from their flocks the hair of goats and the hides of rams, and sealskins—to provide a waterproof covering. Maps outlining the path taken by the Israelites from Egypt to the Sinai show they were most often near the shores of the Red Sea. According to *Easton's Bible Dictionary*:

> The dugong, very plentiful in the shallow waters
> on the shores of the Red Sea, is a marine animal from
> 12 to 30 feet long, something between a whale and a
> seal, never leaving the water, but very easily caught.[23]

It is conceivable that men were sent out to capture, kill, and skin the animals for the materials necessary for the tabernacle. Jehovah did not require anything of the children of Israel that was not readily available; His plan is always built around dedicated and wholehearted individuals.

As amazing as God's directions were for the symbol of His presence at the heart of the Exodus, He also gave instructions for the placement of the twelve tribes around the structure. The tribes of Issachar, Judah, and Zebulun were to be on the east side; Asher, Dan, and Naphtali on the north; Manasseh, Ephraim, and Benjamin on the west, and Simeon, Reuben, and Gad on the south. The placement did not include Moses, Aaron, and the priestly tribe of the Levites who were scattered throughout the encampment. It has been estimated that the men, women, and children totaled between two and a half to three million people. Dick Harfield of Answers.com has estimated the sheer volume of food and water required to sustain this massive group:

> To feed 2.5 million people just two pounds of food and four pints of water per day would require around 2250 tons of food, excluding bones and scraps, plus around 1.25 million gallons of water. This excludes fodder and water for their livestock. Over the forty years that the Exodus was said to have taken, it would have required at least 33 million tons of food and 18,000 million gallons of water just to sustain the people.[24]

It has also been estimated that the train of people and livestock would have stretched through the desert dunes for approximately forty miles.

The tabernacle was divided into three main segments—the Courtyard, the Holy Place, and the Most Holy Place. Each area was set aside for varying consecrated activities. Hovering over the structure was the cloud by day and the pillar of fire by night, signifying God's presence.

In Exodus 25:9, Jehovah was precise with His command:

> "Make this tabernacle and all its furnishings *exactly* like the pattern I will show you" (emphasis mine).

Why? The various components of the place of worship were to be a complex pictorial to exemplify the relationship between Jehovah and His people. First and foremost, God required total compliance—absolute conformity—to His commands. Researchers at The Tabernacle Place reveal that:

> The whole compound was surrounded by a high fence with only one entrance. A person could not simply come from any direction into the tabernacle as he pleased—he had to enter through the one gate, which was always located to the east (so that people were facing west when they entered the tabernacle— a direct opposition to the pagan sun worshipers of the day who always faced east) .... This setup informed the Israelites that they could only come to God in the way He prescribed. There was no other way.[25]

There the gate by which those seeking forgiveness could enter was thirty feet wide and covered with a heavy drape fashioned from fine linen in blue, purple, and scarlet—the colors often associated with royalty.

Jesus made it very clear to His disciples that He would become the only way one could achieve close fellowship with the Father. He said:

"I am the gate; whoever enters through me will be saved." (John 10:9)

And in John 14:6:

"I am the way and the truth and the life. No one comes to the Father except through me."

Per God's directives, the courtyard into which one entered after passing through the gate was to be precisely fifty cubits by one hundred cubits, or approximately 75 feet by 150 feet (a cubit is thought to have been eighteen inches in length). The tent of the tabernacle was protected by a fence of twenty bronze posts on the north and south sides. The fence on the west and east sides was comprised of ten bronze posts. Suspended between the posts surrounding the courtyard were seven and a half feet high screens of the finest linen held in place by silver hooks (see Exodus 27:9–11). The four middle posts on the east side of the enclave held a special embroidered panel of "blue, purple and scarlet yarn and finely twisted linen—the work of an embroiderer" (Exodus 27:16).

It was the courtyard that held the seven and a half feet by seven and a half feet bronze altar and the bronze laver. Bronze was symbolic of judgment, and the Israelites supplied approximately 6,700 pounds. Because it has a very high melting point (well over 1,500 Degrees), it was to be used in those places where heat resistance was essential.[26]

When a sacrificial animal was to be offered, it was presented to the priest before the altar. If approved for sacrifice, it was lifted onto the altar and bound to the four horns or corners. In Old Testament times, horns were symbolic of strength and power. The owner would then place his hands on the animal in identification with the

animal and as a sign of the transference of sin to the offering. After
the animal was sacrificed, its blood was applied to the horns, representative of ability of the blood to make atonement for sin. As the
Lamb of God, Jesus fulfilled the shedding of blood once for all. The
purpose of the bronze altar in the tabernacle courtyard would be
realized on a wooden cross on the hill of Golgotha in the person of
Jesus Christ:

> "This is my blood of the covenant, which is poured
> out for many." (Mark 14:24)

> The blood of goats and bulls and the ashes of
> a heifer sprinkled on those who are ceremonially
> unclean sanctify them so that they are outwardly
> clean. How much more, then, will the blood of Christ,
> who through the eternal Spirit offered himself
> unblemished to God, cleanse our consciences from
> acts that lead to death, so that we may serve the living
> God! (Hebrews 9:13–14)

The altar was the place of sacrifice where the following was
offered:

- ✧ meal offering, free will, firstfruits offerings—
  a portion incinerated; a portion presented to
  the priests for consumption

- ✧ burnt offering—the entire offering was incinerated by fire

- ✧ peace offering—the one presenting the sacrifice consumed a portion

✧   sin offering—a portion was burned; a portion
     given to the priests

From the sacrificial altar, the priest walked over to the bronze laver—a large basin filled with water. It was constructed from bronze mirrors donated by the women of Israel and polished to a highly reflective state. It was there that the priests bathed their hands and feet before entering the tabernacle to present an offering to Jehovah. At the laver, the priests would wash away the blood and dirt that stained their hands and feet, a sign of sanctification, or purity, before entering into God's presence. The apostle Paul reminds us in Hebrews 13:12 (ESV), "So Jesus also suffered outside the gate in order to sanctify the people through his own blood."

After the purification ritual, the priest would enter the tabernacle, where he could have communion with Jehovah. The Tent of Meeting measured 45 feet in length, 15 feet in width, and stood 15 feet high. It consisted of two areas: the Holy Place (15 feet by 30 feet), where priests were allowed and the Holy of Holies (a 15-foot square), where only the high priest was permitted entrance. To enter the Holy Place, the priest must access a curtain comprised of four layers. The first was of porpoise skin for waterproofing the structure; the next layer was of goat hair; the third layer was fashioned from the skins of rams that had been dyed red; and the interior layer was of finely woven, embroidered linen.

The Holy Place contained three specific furnishings: the table of shewbread; the golden, seven-branched lampstand; and the altar of incense, which occupied the place of honor before the veil into the Holy of Holies. Each was used in a very specific way and was indicative of the relationship between the Believer and Christ, the supreme offering.

7

BREAD, LIGHT,
PRAYERS *of the* PEOPLE

The table of shewbread in the Holy Place fashioned of acacia (shittim) wood was overlaid with pure gold. Gold was symbolic of the deity and divinity of Jehovah, while silver used in the edifice symbolized redemption. The Israelites offered up approximately 2,800 pounds of gold and 9,600 pounds of silver to be used in the construction of the tabernacle.

Jehovah's instructions to Moses on the mountaintop were very specific according to Exodus 25:23–30:

> "Make a table of acacia wood—two cubits long, a cubit wide and a cubit and a half high. Overlay it with pure gold and make a gold molding around it. Also make around it a rim a handbreadth wide and put a gold molding on the rim. Make four gold rings for the table and fasten them to the four corners, where the four legs are. The rings are to be close to the rim to hold the poles used in carrying the table. Make the poles of acacia wood, overlay them with gold and carry the table with them. And make its plates and

dishes of pure gold, as well as its pitchers and bowls for the pouring out of offerings. Put the bread of the Presence on this table to be before me at all times."

It would have measured three feet by one and a half feet, and was two feet, three inches tall. The golden utensils resting on the "table of the bread of presence" held the shewbread—twelve loaves, each representing one of the tribes of Israel. The holy bread was baked with "2/10 of an ephah of fine flour, such as was used for honored guests and for the king's table"[27] before being placed on the table for one week. According to the *Jewish Encyclopedia*:

> Upon the rows of cakes [shewbread] cups of frank-incense were placed; this frankincense constituted the "azkarah," or memorial, and was offered upon the altar . . .[28]

When the Sabbath arrived, the priests in service in the tabernacle would remove the bread, break it, and eat it in the Holy Place. Twelve loaves of freshly baked bread were then placed on the table—and so the cycle would continue week after week. The bread was representative of the covenant between Jehovah and the children of Israel—a reminder of God's promise to feed His people. It was also a foreshadowing of Christ, who would be born in Bethlehem, the house of bread:

> Jesus said to them, "I am the bread of life; he who comes to Me will not hunger, and he who believes in Me will never thirst." (John 6:35 NASB)

The shewbread was sometimes referred to as the "bread of the presence" or the *lechem ha'panim,* as it remained in the Holy Place as a symbol of Jehovah's relationship and intimacy with His creation. The priests as representatives of the people were welcome to enjoy the presence of God and partake of the shewbread. At the last supper, Jesus introduced breaking of bread as a sign of covenant, not just for the Levitical priesthood, but for all Believers. In 1 Peter 2:9, we read:

> But you are a chosen people, a royal priesthood, a holy nation, God's special possession, that you may declare the praises of him who called you out of darkness into his wonderful light.

Jehovah had pledged to protect and guide Israel, to be her God. He would fight Israel's battles for her and lead the offspring of Abraham, Isaac, and Jacob to a land flowing with milk and honey. The shewbread was an outward indication of the promise—of the covenant—between Jehovah-Jireh—the God who provides—and Israel. God had promised to lead His people to a place of rest and provision.

As beautiful today as when first written are the words of the old Welsh hymn by John Hughes:

> Guide me, O thou great Redeemer,
> Pilgrim through this barren land;
> I am weak, but thou art mighty;
> Hold me with thy powerful hand:
> Bread of heaven, bread of heaven
> Feed me till I want no more.
> Feed me till I want no more.[29]

The shewbread typified the sinless life of the Sinless One. Jesus, the Bread of Life, was without sin. "God made him who had no sin to be sin for us, so that in him we might become the righteousness of God" (2 Corinthians 5:21). Christ walked through the fires of persecution, rejection, and death for you and me to offer salvation to all who place their trust in Him. Songwriter Charles B. Widmeyer, penned the words to this invitation:

> "Come and dine," the Master calleth, "Come and dine";
> You may feast at Jesus' table all the time;
> He Who fed the multitude, turned the water into wine,
> To the hungry calleth now, "Come and dine."[30]

✧   ✧   ✧

The Holy Place, which housed the table of shewbread, also held the seven-branched golden lampstand (menorah), which was a source of light for the priests. (Seven is the number of completeness in the Bible.) Jehovah's instruction to Moses was:

> "You shall make a lampstand of pure gold. The lampstand shall be made of hammered work: its base, its stem, its cups, its calyxes, and its flowers shall be of one piece with it." (Exodus 25:31 ESV)

> The lampstand was to be hammered from a solid talent (seventy-five pounds) of gold—not pieced together from fragments. It might have been symbolic of the deity of the Messiah. As the apostle Paul wrote in Colossians 2:9, "For in Him dwells all the fullness of the Godhead bodily" (NKJV).

Some Bible scholars believe that the design in the form of a tree was to remind the Israelites of the Tree of Life in the garden of

Eden—a sign that life can only be found in the presence of Jehovah-
'Ori—God, my Light. Almonds in early Mediterranean times signified
hope and abundance. Jewish tradition indicates the lampstand was
about five feet high and three and a half feet wide. Its actual shape is
not known, but the menorah configuration is usually accepted.

The menorah was positioned on the left side of the Holy Place
and was fashioned as a central branch with three additional branches
reaching outward from each side. Each bowl held olive oil with a
wick extending upward from the oil. The instruction to the priests
was to keep the light from going out in the tabernacle:

> The LORD said to Moses, "Command the Israelites
> to bring you clear oil of pressed olives for the light
> so that the lamps may be kept burning continually.
> Outside the curtain that shields the ark of the cov-
> enant law in the tent of meeting, Aaron is to tend
> the lamps before the LORD from evening till morn-
> ing, continually. This is to be a lasting ordinance for
> the generations to come. The lamps on the pure gold
> lampstand before the LORD must be tended continu-
> ally." (Leviticus 24:1–4)

The light was positioned so that it illuminated the table of
shewbread and the altar of incense. Without it, the priests would
have been stumbling around in the darkness while trying to worship Jehovah. Such a practice would have been anathema to the
very nature of God, as light is a simile for righteousness. In Proverbs
4:18, we read, "The path of the righteous is like the morning sun,
shining ever brighter till the full light of day." And Psalm 76:4 says of
Jehovah, "You are radiant with light, more majestic than mountains
rich with game."

Conversely, darkness is a simile for evil and sin. Isaiah 9:2 tells us, "The people walking in darkness [sin, evil] have seen a great light [Jehovah's righteousness]; on those living in the land of deep darkness a light has dawned." And in 1 John 1:5 we read, "This is the message we have heard from him and declare to you: God is light; in him there is no darkness at all."

Of course, Jesus said in John 8:12:

> "I am the light of the world. Whoever follows me will never walk in darkness, but will have the light of life."

Dr. John MacArthur wrote:

> And so when Jesus said I am the light, He is claiming to be Messiah. And John the author of the book made the same claim in the first chapter. In verse 5 he says, "And the light shines in darkness and the darkness overcame it not." Verse 9, "That was the true light," see. Christ came as that light that Messianic prophecy said God would send.
>
> You say, "Why is He called light?" Huh, to the darkness of falsehood He is the light of truth. To the darkness of ignorance He is the light of wisdom. To the darkness of impurity He is the light of holiness. To the darkness of sorrow He is the light of joy. To the darkness of death He's the light of life. He is called light because the world is dark and the antithesis of darkness is what? Is light. He is everything the world isn't. And Jesus is saying nothing more and nothing less at this point than I am your Messiah.[31]

The menorah is a symbol of Believers' relationship to Christ. In John 15:5, Jesus said, "I am the vine; you are the branches." If we abide in the vine, we can draw on the hope and abundance provided for us in Him.

✧　✧　✧

Standing in the center of the Holy Place before the curtain into the Holy of Holies rested the altar of incense, or the golden altar. Smaller than the brazen altar that occupied the courtyard, it was constructed of acacia wood with an overlay of pure gold. The one-and-a-half-feet square table stood three feet high. Jehovah gave Moses the specifications for this special piece of furniture in Exodus 30:1–6:

> "Make an altar of acacia wood for burning incense. It is to be square, a cubit long and a cubit wide, and two cubits high—its horns of one piece with it. Overlay the top and all the sides and the horns with pure gold, and make a gold molding around it. Make two gold rings for the altar below the molding—two on each of the opposite sides—to hold the poles used to carry it. Make the poles of acacia wood and overlay them with gold. Put the altar in front of the curtain that shields the ark of the covenant law—before the atonement cover that is over the tablets of the covenant law—where I will meet with you."

The tabernacle priests were required to burn incense on the altar twice daily—morning and evening—as an offering to Jehovah. Burning incense on the altar required taking fire from the bronze altar in the courtyard to light the incense. The rising, sweet-smelling smoke was indicative of the prayers and intercessions from God's people. The psalmist wrote, "Let my prayer be counted as incense before you, and the lifting up of my hands as the evening sacrifice!" (Psalm 141:2 ESV)

The special incense was a compound of four spices and salt. From the website "God as a Gardener," Professor Carolyn Adams Roth relates:

> When God listed offerings for the Tabernacle, he included spices for fragrant incense (Exodus 25:6). Specifically, a perfumer was to blend the holy incense out of equal proportions of gum resin (stacte), onycha, galbanum, and pure frankincense. The incense was to be salted and pure and sacred (30:35). Several scholars have commented on what "salted" meant. One idea was that salt was a preservative in the incense. A second idea was related to the ancient's belief that sharing salt between two people was considered to bind them in a covenant. In the incense, the Israelites offered salt to God, which set Israel's seal on the covenantal relationship that God offered. Finally, directing the incense to be salted could have meant it was to be well prepared. The Tabernacle incense was to be "most holy" to the Israelites, and the Israelites were to consider the Tabernacle incense "holy to the Lord" (Exodus 30:36, 37).[32]

The tabernacle, and later the temple, were to be a house of prayer. When Jesus drove the moneychangers from the temple in Jerusalem, He quoted the prophet Isaiah in chapter 56, verse 7, "For My house will be called a house of prayer for all nations."

In Revelation, 8:3–4, John wrote:

> Another angel, who had a golden censer, came and stood at the altar. He was given much incense to offer, with the prayers of all God's people, on the golden altar in front of the throne. The smoke of the incense, together with the prayers of God's people, went up before God from the angel's hand.

Believers enter into the presence of God through prayer. The difference today is that we are not separated from our heavenly Father by a veil, but are allowed free access to the throne room. The writer of Hebrews tells us:

> Let us then approach God's throne of grace with confidence, so that we may receive mercy and find grace to help us in our time of need. (Hebrews 4:16)

Dr. W. A. Criswell, noted pastor of First Baptist Church, Dallas, said in his sermon "The Golden Altar of Prayer":

> Wherever there is somebody that needs God, there God is. Wherever somebody bows his heart to pray, there God bows His ear to hear. Wherever needed, there God is. And wherever in the wilderness wanderings the people went, there was the altar of sacrifice, and there was the golden altar of intercession. . . .
>
> There is no greater thing or meaningful thing than to remember one another in our prayers. To give him money, that is good if he needs it, to pay a debt for him, to help him, all of these things, but, ah, nothing, nothing [is] ever comparable to remembering somebody in

prayer. There at the golden altar, to call his face. Ah, what a privilege! What an invitation! And the Lord seeketh such; come.[33]

8

THE HOLY OF HOLIES
AND THE ARK *of the* COVENANT

The tent of the tabernacle held two areas—each with a very specific purpose. The Holy Place held the golden lamp stand, the table of shewbread, the altar of incense, and the Holy of Holies, a sacred abode where the ark of the covenant resided. As noted in a previous chapter, it was a perfect fifteen-foot cube.

The ark was built of acacia wood, every surface completely enshrouded in pure gold. The box was three feet, nine inches in length by two feet, three inches in height and width. Jehovah had instructed Moses to place inside the ark a golden vessel containing manna, the stone tablets on which had been inscribed the Ten Commandments, and Aaron's rod that had budded. Why was the rod significant? At one point in their journey, the Israelites rebelled against the leadership of Moses and Aaron—thinking erroneously that the two men had declared themselves leaders. Jehovah ended the argument once and for all time when He instructed:

> "Speak to the Israelites and get twelve staffs from
> them, one from the leader of each of their ancestral

tribes. Write the name of each man on his staff. On the staff of Levi write Aaron's name, for there must be one staff for the head of each ancestral tribe. Place them in the tent of meeting in front of the ark of the covenant law, where I meet with you. The staff belonging to the man I choose will sprout, and I will rid myself of this constant grumbling against you by the Israelites." So Moses spoke to the Israelites, and their leaders gave him twelve staffs, one for the leader of each of their ancestral tribes, and Aaron's staff was among them. Moses placed the staffs before the LORD in the tent of the covenant law. The next day Moses entered the tent and saw that Aaron's staff, which represented the tribe of Levi, had not only sprouted but had budded, blossomed and produced almonds. Then Moses brought out all the staffs from the LORD's presence to all the Israelites. They looked at them, and each of the leaders took his own staff. The LORD said to Moses, "Put back Aaron's staff in front of the ark of the covenant law, to be kept as a sign to the rebellious. This will put an end to their grumbling against me, so that they will not die." (Numbers 17:2–10)

The lid of the ark was known as the "atonement cover," or the mercy seat. It held two cherubim, one at each end, fashioned from pure gold, wings outspread and meeting at the center of the cover. It symbolized God's seat of authority and His presence in the tabernacle. It was Jehovah's meeting place with the high priest as stated in Exodus 25:22: "There, above the cover between the two cherubim that are over the ark of the covenant law, I will meet with you and give you all my commands for the Israelites." Some scholars believe there is a correlation between the lid for the ark of the covenant and the positioning of the two angels in the tomb following the resurrection of Jesus: "And she [Mary Magdalen] saw two angels in white, sitting where the body of Jesus had lain, one at the head and one at the feet (John 20:12 ESV).

The ark of the covenant was, as I mentioned, a symbol of God's power and presence in the midst of His people, Israel; it was also, however, symbolic of His wrath and judgment. It was to be treated with the utmost respect and handled only in accordance with the instructions given to Moses:

> "When the camp is to move, Aaron and his sons are to go in and take down the shielding curtain and put it over the ark of the covenant law. Then they are to cover the curtain with a durable leather, spread a cloth of solid blue over that and put the poles in place." (Numbers 4:5)

The penalty for mishandling the holy items was severe: "After Aaron and his sons have finished covering the holy furnishings and all the holy articles, and when the camp is ready to move, only then are the Kohathites to come and do the carrying. But they must not touch the holy things or they will die" (Numbers 4:15).

This family was descended from Kohath, a son of Levi, the patriarch of the priestly tribe. The offspring who followed Moses from Egypt were positioned around the tabernacle and given roles of great importance. They were to transport the contents of the Holy Place and the Holy of Holies when Jehovah directed the Israelites to move forward. The Kohathites were to encamp on the south side of the Tent of Meeting. They were charged with moving the ark of the covenant, the lampstand, altars, vessels of the sanctuary, and the curtain—but only after the furnishings had been properly prepared by the high priest. They were forbidden to touch the objects upon sentence of death.

This was proven in 1 Samuel when the Israelites ignorantly disregarded Jehovah's laws regarding the handling of the ark and carried it into battle—as a talisman, a lucky charm. It was captured by the Philistines and placed in close proximity to their idol, Dagon. So alarming was the loss that upon hearing the news, the daughter-in-law of the high priest went into labor, bore a son, and then succumbed. With her dying breath, she whispered that her newborn child was to be named Icabod, meaning "the glory has departed."

The Philistines were jubilant! They thought they had captured the God of the Israelites—the one who had led them across the Jordan River on dry ground; the one who had caused the walls of Jericho to fall down flat. Conversely, the Israelites believed Jehovah had forsaken them, that He was little more than a golden treasure hidden away in the Holy of Holies of the tabernacle. They wrung their hands in horror because for them, evil had triumphed. But God was still sitting on His throne, and none of this was a surprise to Him.

The capture of the ark by the Philistine hoard was taken too lightly. The symbol of Jehovah's presence in the midst of His people was not magical; it was not a graven image. It did not place the Ruler of the Universe at their disposal to do their bidding. No mystical powers would be made available. God would only do what He had promised.

Former US Army Chaplain Lt. Col. Robert Leroe in his sermon "Dwelling in Dagon's Tent" said of this dark day in Israel's history:

The Ark was placed within the temple of Dagon, in Ashdod, put on display as a trophy of victory. At this point the Philistines were clapping each other on the back and claiming that Dagon was more powerful than the God of Israel. The name Dagon means, "grain"; he was their agriculture-god, prominent in pagan farming and fertility rituals. Yet Dagon fell prost[r]ate before the Ark. The Philistines hurriedly set their idol back up, only to find him the next morning not just on the ground, but with his head and hands lopped off, incapacitated. He had to be sent out for repairs! It became quite evident that this god held no power, no wisdom. Psalm 95 describes God as "the great King above all gods" (vs 3). The demise of Dagon was no act of vandalism; it was the wrath of God Almighty. Dagon fell, humbled, just as one day every knee shall bow before the Lord Jesus Christ.[34]

It soon became obvious to the Philistine leaders that the ark taken from the Israelites was the cause of their problems—from the destruction of their idol to the deaths in their towns and villages. It became of paramount importance to dispose of the article. Magicians and psychics were summoned for advice. They suggested making images of gold of the tumors (or nodules) and rats that had plagued the people and sending them home with the ark as an offering to the God of the Israelites.

Wanting definitive proof that the ark was the cause of all their problems, the Philistines devised an ingenious plan to make that determination:

"Now then, get a new cart ready, with two cows that have calved and have never been yoked. Hitch the cows to the cart, but take their calves away and pen them up. Take the ark of the LORD and put it on the cart, and in a chest beside it put the gold objects you are sending back to him as a guilt offering. Send it on its way, but keep watching it. If it goes up to its own territory, toward Beth Shemesh, then the LORD has brought this great disaster on us. But if it does not, then we will know that it was not his hand that struck us but that it happened to us by chance." So they did this. They took two such cows and hitched them to the cart and penned up their calves. They placed the ark of the LORD on the cart and along with it the chest containing the gold rats and the models of the tumors. Then the cows went straight up toward Beth Shemesh, keeping on the road and lowing all the way; they did not turn to the right or to the left. The rulers of the Philistines followed them as far as the border of Beth Shemesh. (1 Samuel 6:7–12)

The absolute truth is, "For our God *is* a consuming fire" (Hebrews 12:29 KJV). And He calls His people to be holy, ". . . for I the LORD your God *am* holy" (Leviticus 19:2 KJV). God demands respect, for He is omnipotent—all-powerful; omniscient—all-knowing; and omnipresent—everywhere, all the time. Do we give Him the glory, honor, and reverence He deserves?

The ark, handled according to God's ordinances, was returned to the land of Israel. It resided in the home of Abinadab for twenty years before David had it returned it to its rightful place. Once again, it was safeguarded from the prying eyes of sinful man by the thick veil—both in the tabernacle and in the temple that followed—until the crucifixion of Jesus.

After a twenty-year sojourn in Kiriath-jearim, King David resolved to bring the ark to his new capital city, Jerusalem. Totally unprepared to transport the sacred symbol of Jehovah's presence, those moving the ark slid it unceremoniously onto a newly prepared ox cart, the first mistake. Accompanying the group was Uzzah, a priest of the Kohath tribe. He should have known the ritual for handling the holy implements of the tabernacle, and that the ark was to be lifted only by poles inserted through the rings on the piece; but a second and fatal mistake was made. When crossing the threshing floor of Nakon, the cart tilted precariously, causing its contents to slide. Uzzah reached out with his hand to steady the ark and was immediately slain—not by the men in attendance, but by the hand of Almighty God. Fear gripped the entourage, and David called an abrupt halt to the mission. Perhaps Uzzah had disregarded, or simply disobeyed, Jehovah's instructions for the proper handling of the symbol of His divine presence. In his book *The Holiness of God*, author and theologian Dr. R. C. Sproul wrote:

> Not only was Uzzah forbidden to touch the ark, he was forbidden to even look at it. He touched it anyway. He stretched out his hand and placed it squarely on the ark, steadying it in place lest it fall to the ground. An act of holy heroism? No! It was an act of arrogance, a sin of presumption. Uzzah assumed that his hand was less polluted than the earth. But it wasn't the ground or the mud that would desecrate the ark; it was the touch of man. The earth is an obedient

creature. It does what God tells it to do. It brings forth
its yield in its season. It obeys the laws of nature that
God has established.[35]

After Uzzah's death the ark was taken for safekeeping to the
home of a Gentile, Obed-Edom, for three months. While there,
Jehovah's blessings rested on the dwelling place of the Gittite. (See 2
Samuel 6:10–11.) When David heard of the windfall that had settled
on the household, he "went to bring up the ark of God from the house
of Obed-Edom to the City of David with rejoicing" (v. 12). I believe
we can determine from David's later success in moving the ark to
Jerusalem that God was not opposed to the relocation; He objected to
the method of transportation. He sent David home to do his research
and learn the proper way to handle the holy things of Jehovah. Once
he had been apprised of Mosaic Law regarding the relocation of the
ark, David returned to the home of Obed-Edom with a designated
priestly contingent. Second Samuel 6:12b–15 paints the scene for us:

> So David went to bring up the ark of God from the
> house of Obed-Edom to the City of David with rejoic-
> ing. When those who were carrying the ark of the
> LORD had taken six steps, he sacrificed a bull and a
> fattened calf. Wearing a linen ephod, David was danc-
> ing before the LORD with all his might, while he and
> all Israel were bringing up the ark of the LORD with
> shouts and the sound of trumpets.

David's delight in having the representation of the presence of
God in the midst of Jerusalem took the form of dancing. The noble
king of Judah cast aside his dignity to celebrate the return of the ark
of the covenant.

In the tabernacle, the Holy of Holies had been separated from the Holy Place by a thick, woven curtain—or veil—fashioned from fine linen and embroidered with purple and blue yarns. The figures on the veil mimicked the cherubim that Jehovah had stationed outside the garden of Eden after Adam's sin. They were indicative of the power and majesty that enshrouded the throne of God, and the veil was the instrument that separated sinful, mortal man from a holy Creator—El Elyon, the Most High God. In the New Testament, the cherubim are again seen in Revelation 4:6–9 proclaiming the majesty of God:

> Day and night they never stop saying: "'Holy, holy, holy is the Lord God Almighty,' who was, and is, and is to come." (Revelation 4:8b)

The high priest was the only individual allowed to enter the Holy of Holies, and only once each year on Yom Kippur, the Day of Atonement. The curtain divided the priests who performed the daily activities in the Holy Place from the Holy of Holies. It was a barrier so that man would not casually, rashly, or disrespectfully enter into the presence of El Hakkadosh, the Holy God, who could not tolerate sin. Habakkuk 1:13 says of Jehovah, "Your eyes are too pure to look on evil; you cannot tolerate wrongdoing."

Although specially chosen to minister in the Holy of Holies, there were exact steps that had to be undertaken by the high priest before he could safely step through the veil into the overwhelming presence of God. (We will examine the various priestly duties in an ensuing chapter.) Once inside the veil, the high priest stood before the only item in the chamber: the ark of the covenant. Although it occupied the innermost chamber of the tabernacle, the ark was the first piece assembled after Moses was given the plans for the structure and its furnishings. Before approaching the veil, the high priest had washed himself and donned the clothing indicated by Jehovah for the mission. In his hand he carried a censer filled with coals from the altar of incense in the Holy Place and a golden bowl containing two handfuls of incense, which, once inside the Holy of Holies, was sprinkled on the burning coals. As the thick, sweet-smelling fragrance from the incense rose before the ark of the covenant, the eyes of the high priest were obscured by the smoke to forestall any possibility that he would see God. The smoke represented the prayers of the children of Israel wafting upward on the most holy of days—the Day of Atonement.

The high priest slipped back through the curtain to the brazen altar, lifted a golden basin of blood taken from the bullock offered for the sins of the people, and returned to the Holy of Holies. He then dipped his finger into the blood seven times, each time sprinkling it on the mercy seat to signify the finished atonement, and entreating Jehovah to accept the sacrifice and grant mercy to His people.

The task of the high priest is outlined simply in Hebrews: "But only the high priest entered the inner room, and that only once a year, and never without blood, which he offered for himself and for the sins the people had committed in ignorance" (9:7).

Moses had been instructed in Leviticus 16:2, "Tell your brother Aaron that he is not to come whenever he chooses into the Most Holy Place behind the curtain in front of the atonement cover on the ark, or else he will die. For I will appear in the cloud over the atonement cover."

Waiting patiently and fearfully outside the courtyard, the Israelites watched for the high priest to exit the tabernacle and signal that God had accepted the sin offering that would postpone the sins of the people for another year.

In 1828, Anglican minister and poet Hugh Stowell wrote:

> From every stormy wind that blows,
> From every swelling tide of woes,
> There is a calm, a sure retreat;
> 'Tis found beneath the mercy seat.
>
> There is a place where Jesus sheds
> The oil of gladness on our heads;
> A place than all besides more sweet;
> It is the blood bought mercy seat.[36]

The mercy seat is a place of grace; more so because sinners can now boldly approach the throne of God due to the shed blood of Jesus Christ, the ultimate sacrifice of atonement for sin.

9

THE PRIESTLY GARMENTS:
CLOTHED *for* SERVICE

I n my book *Living in the FOG (Favor of God)* is a glimpse of the first priest mentioned in the Bible, a man by the name of Melchizedek. Certainly Melchizedek, at the very least, foreshadowed our Lord, as that is made apparent in Hebrews 7:1–3:

> This Melchizedek was king of Salem and priest of God Most High. He met Abraham returning from the defeat of the kings and blessed him, and Abraham gave him a tenth of everything. First, the name Melchizedek means "king of righteousness"; then also, "king of Salem" means "king of peace." Without father or mother, without genealogy, without beginning of days or end of life, resembling the Son of God, he remains a priest forever.

As you can see, the writer of Hebrews described Melchizedek as having no father or mother. He seemed to come from out of nowhere, for his genealogy is unknown. Secondly, he was said to be a priest of the Most High God and yet he was born before both Aaron and

Levi. He asked Abraham for nothing. The Scriptures declare that it was Melchizedek who offered bread and wine—symbols of Christ's perfect sacrifice and obedience—to the weary warrior.

Humbled by the presence of the unassuming king of Salem, Abraham was constrained to offer him one-tenth of his personal wealth. He chose to break bread with the King of Righteousness, Melchizedek, and honor him with an offering. He allied himself with the one who worshiped El Elyon—God Most High—the one who followed after the Supreme Ruler of the Universe. Along with the bread and wine, Melchizedek offered a blessing:

> "Blessed be Abram by God Most High, Creator of
> heaven and earth. And praise be to God Most High,
> who delivered your enemies into your hand." (Genesis
> 14:19–20)

When God chose Moses to lead His children out of Egyptian bondage, He also chose Aaron, his brother, to be Moses' spokesman. It was he who made the impassioned speeches to Pharaoh and delivered—at Moses' behest—the word of God to the Egyptian ruler. We know little of Aaron's early life other than that he was a fourth-generation offspring of Levi, the third son of Jacob. Aaron wed Elisheba, the daughter of Amminadab and sister to Nahshon, a forebear of King David. Elisheba bore Aaron four sons, Nadab, Abihu, Eleazar, and Ithamar. Aaron would eventually assume the role of founder of the Levitical priesthood and serve as high priest.

Aaron and his descendants were to be kohen (priests) and hold positions of spiritual leadership:

> The Holy One chose these men to be in a position
> of spiritual leadership. In the days of the Temple, they

were responsible for the sacred service. The Hebrew word kohen actually means *"to serve,"* and a deeper linguistic connection can be found in the word ken, meaning *"yes,"* itself related to kivvun, *"to direct."* Thus a kohen is called upon to direct himself, and others, in the proper service of God ... [See Exodus 28:1][37]

As the God-appointed high priest, Aaron was consecrated for service in the tabernacle. Hebrews 5:1–4 clearly explains that this was not an office of choice:

Every high priest is selected from among the people and is appointed to represent the people in matters related to God, to offer gifts and sacrifices for sins. He is able to deal gently with those who are ignorant and are going astray, since he himself is subject to weakness. This is why he has to offer sacrifices for his own sins, as well as for the sins of the people. And no one takes this honor on himself, but he receives it when called by God, just as Aaron was.

The role of the priests in tabernacle—and later temple—service was to function as intermediaries between Jehovah and His children. It was Levites who were not direct offspring of Aaron who offered the sacrifices of the people. The high priest of the lineage of Aaron was charged with representing the entirety of Israel before the mercy seat. The priests were also charged with the upkeep of the tabernacle, and later the temple, preparing the daily sacrifices, performing the duties of the cantors/musicians, and acting as doorkeepers to the house of God. They were also responsible for maintaining the exact weights and measures employed throughout the nation of Israel.

Barnes' Bible Charts gives us the qualifications for the priesthood:[38]

> ✧ Must be a male. (Exodus 28:1)
>
> ✧ Must be a descendant of Aaron (Exodus 28:1) with a documented linage.
>
> ✧ Must be between 30 and 50 years old. (Numbers 4:3)
>
> ✧ Must be unblemished (not lame or blind). (Lev. 21:16–23)
>
> ✧ Must have a proper marriage. (Leviticus 21:9, 14)
> 1. Not married to a harlot.
> 2. Not married to a divorced woman.
> 3. Not married to a widow other than a priest's widow. (Ezekiel 44:22)
> 4. The high priest must marry a virgin of his own people.

The high priest was to be the mediator between God and man, the individual who would offer up the sacrifices for the sins of the Israelites. That role was bestowed upon Christ, "For there is one God and one mediator between God and mankind, the man Christ Jesus, who gave himself as a ransom for all people" (1 Timothy 2:5–6a).

For Aaron and his progeny, it would be a position of holy obligation, set apart by the very clothing designed for their service to the people in the tabernacle and later in the temple in Jerusalem. The clothing of the high priest was constructed to give an aura of dignity to the office.

Next to his body, the high priest wore a one-piece tunic woven of fine linen. Over that he donned a dark blue, knee-length robe with a hole incorporated for his head and arms. The hem of the garment was bedecked with alternating pomegranates of blue, purple, and scarlet and bells of gold. The third layer was an ephod, an apron-like piece of fine linen also embroidered with blue, purple, and scarlet. It was bound at the waist by a girdle of the same material and was fastened at the shoulders by onyx stones wrapped with pure gold on which was engraved the names of the twelve tribes of Israel in accordance with their birth. On the right shoulder were the names of Reuben, Simeon, Levi, Judah, Dan, and Naphtali. On the left was written Gad, Asher, Issachar, Zebulun, Joseph, and Benjamin.

Over the three layers, the high priest wore a four-inch-square breastplate upon which was fastened four rows of three jewels each set in gold and containing the name of one of the twelve tribes. (Instead of the names of Levi and Joseph, the names of Joseph's sons—Mannasseh and Ephraim—were engraved on two of the stones.) It was suspended from the shoulder pieces of the ephod by chains of gold secured by golden rings. The breastplate also contained a pocket for the Urim and Thummim, where they rested securely over the heart of the high priest. Urim is translated *lights* and Thummim *perfections*, and the two instruments—perhaps precious stones—were employed to determine Jehovah's divine guidance in a situation. David M. Levy wrote of the pieces:

> The Urim was a beautiful picture of Christ, who is the believers' light. He said, "I am the light of the world; he that followeth me shall not walk in

darkness, but shall have the light of life," (John 8:12, KJV.) ... The Thummim speaks of the perfection found in Christ ... He is our perfect counselor ... and lights the path we are to tread as He guides us along the way.[39]

Only the high priest could verify the will of God or employ the Urim and Thummim to determine truth from falsehood. In Numbers 27:18–23, we see a reference to the ability of the high priest to obtain decisions from Jehovah:

> So the LORD said to Moses, "Take Joshua son of Nun, a man in whom is the spirit of leadership, and lay your hand on him. Have him stand before Eleazar the priest and the entire assembly and commission him in their presence. Give him some of your authority so the whole Israelite community will obey him. He is to stand before Eleazar the priest, who will obtain decisions for him by inquiring of the Urim before the LORD. At his command he and the entire community of the Israelites will go out, and at his command they will come in." Moses did as the LORD commanded him. He took Joshua and had him stand before Eleazar the priest and the whole assembly. Then he laid his hands on him and commissioned him, as the LORD instructed through Moses.

Upon his head, the high priest wore a miter or turban of fine linen with an engraving fastened to the front by blue cords and engraved with the words, "Holy to the Lord." Exodus 28:38 gives us the purpose of the miter:

It will be on Aaron's forehead, and he will bear the guilt involved in the sacred gifts the Israelites consecrate, whatever their gifts may be. It will be on Aaron's forehead continually so that they will be acceptable to the LORD.

The inscribed band attached to Aaron's turban was more than a decoration; it was a perpetual token of Jehovah's endless and compassionate forgiveness. It was symbolic of Aaron's faithfulness to perform the duties of his office as high priest, and of Jehovah's trustworthiness to honor His sacred word. In his commentary on the book of Exodus, Douglas Stuart wrote of a future date when "Holy to the Lord" would take on a new connotation as outlined in Zechariah 14:20–21, which reads:

On that day HOLY TO THE LORD will be inscribed on the bells of the horses, and the cooking pots in the LORD's house will be like the sacred bowls in front of the altar. Every pot in Jerusalem and Judah will be holy to the LORD Almighty, and all who come to sacrifice will take some of the pots and cook in them.

Stuart exposited:

Zechariah depicts the democratization of holiness with the wording of the inscription (as originally used on Aaron's forehead but in the latter days on every horse), bells (as originally on Aaron's robe but in the latter days adorning even horses as expansion of the function of their usual bells), and cooking pots (as originally used for secular purposes but in the latter days used for holy sacrifices because so many people will worship the true God in spirit and truth that every pot in Jerusalem will be needed . . . holiness that results from obedience in faith . . . surpasses what could ever be accomplished by a human high priest, no matter how many sacrifices he might try to make on behalf of the people.[40]

With the inclusion of the miter, the high priest was clothed with dignity and honor for service before a holy God. The question has been asked: Did it actually matter what the high priest, or any of the priests, wore when in service in the tabernacle? The answer is an unequivocal yes! Why? The clothing of the priestly office was not something Moses dreamed up while waiting to hear from God on Mount Sinai; Jehovah had given comprehensive instructions for each separate article to be donned by the high priest. They were to be exquisitely constructed because Aaron and his descendants were to be set apart for service to the King of Kings. They were to be worn only when the high priest was employed within the tabernacle. They were to be garments of beauty to honor the holiness of God. Psalm 96:9 (NKJV) reminds us, "Oh, worship the LORD in the beauty of holiness! Tremble before him, all the earth."

Not only were the garments special, but those who fashioned them were especially gifted by God:

> "Make sacred garments for your brother Aaron to give him dignity and honor. Tell all the skilled workers to whom I have given wisdom in such matters that they are to make garments for Aaron, for his consecration, so he may serve me as priest." (Exodus 28:2–3)

The garments worn by the general population of priests who served daily in the tabernacle were comprised of breeches, girdle, coat, and miter—all made of fine linen. They were much simpler than those worn by the high priest—except for the clothing worn on the Day of Atonement (Yom Kippur).

Leviticus 16:4 tells us that on the High Holy Day:

> "He is to put on the sacred linen tunic [woven from six-ply white flax], with linen undergarments next to his body; he is to tie the linen sash around him and put on the linen turban. These are sacred garments; so he must bathe himself with water before he puts them on."

At sundown on Yom Kippur, the garments were discarded:

> "Then Aaron is to go into the tent of meeting and take off the linen garments he put on before he entered the Most Holy Place, and he is to leave them there. He shall bathe himself with water in the sanctuary area and put on his regular garments." (vv. 23–24)

Just as the high priest laid aside the splendid garments of his office to don the more practical garments of service, so did Christ. He donned the robe of flesh to be born of woman and live among men. Philippians 2:8 reveals, "And being found in appearance as a man, he humbled himself by becoming obedient to death—even death on a cross!"

The priesthood of Jesus Christ resonates through the book of Hebrews. In chapter 3, verse 1, He is called "apostle and high priest." Again in chapter 4, verse 15, the writer refers to our Lord as "high priest." The commission of the high priest was to offer atonement for the sins of man—to bring man into a place of communion with God. Jesus took on the role of high priest in order to open the way for man to approach Jehovah through a new covenant—the blood covenant of the cross. As our High Priest, Jesus is superior to Aaron, Moses, even Melchizedek, of whom the psalmist wrote, "You are a priest forever after the order of Melchizedek" (Psalm 110:4 ESV).

Christ presented not offerings but Himself—the sinless Lamb of God—as a sacrifice to redeem fallen man. He had none of the frailties of earlier high priests; no need to slay sheep and bullocks for forgiveness of sin. He was the sinless Son of God sent to take away the sins of the world—not to postpone them for another year. "For I will forgive their wickedness and will remember their sins no more" (Hebrews 8:12). When Jesus whispered, "It is finished," on Golgotha, the work that He had been sent to do had been completed. Philippians 2:9–11 reveals what happened afterward:

> Therefore God exalted him to the highest place and gave him the name that is above every name, that at the name of Jesus every knee should bow, in heaven and on earth and under the earth, and every tongue acknowledge that Jesus Christ is Lord, to the glory of God the Father.

Jesus is the perfect High Priest:

- ✧ He is the Door into the Holy of Holies, allowing Believers into the presence of the Father (John 10:9);

- ✧ At the brazen altar, He is our Reconciliation (2 Corinthians 5:18);

✧ At the bronze laver, He is our Sanctifier (1 Corinthians 6:11);

✧ At the golden candlestick, He is the Light of the World (John 8:12);

✧ At the altar of incense, He is our Mediator (1 Timothy 2:5);

✧ At the table of shewbread, He is the Bread of Life (John 6:35);

✧ Before the ark of the covenant, He is the perfect Sacrifice (Hebrews 9:12).

10

SWEET SAVOR SACRIFICES

The tabernacle had been completed. The furnishings were in position, and every golden vessel had been fashioned and was in its rightful place of service. The only question that remained was: Would Jehovah set His stamp of approval on the work that had been done?

The *Pulpit Commentary* gives us a brief glimpse of the events that followed the final stitch of embroidery on the veil and the priestly garments:

> The cloud, which had gone before the Israelites from Succoth onward (Exodus 13:20-22), and which had recently settled upon the extemporised "Tent of Meeting" (Exodus 33:9), left its place, and "covered" the newly-erected structure externally (ver. 34), while an intensely brilliant light—here called "the glory of God"—filled the whole interior of the tabernacle .... Moses, it appears, would fain have re-entered the tabernacle—to see the great sight (Exodus 3:3); but he could not—the "glory" was too dazzling (ver. 35).

Thus a distinct approval was given to all that had been done. God accepted his house, and entered it. The people saw that he had foregone his wrath, and would be content henceforth to dwell among them and journey with them. Henceforth, throughout the wanderings, the cloud and tabernacle were inseparable. If the cloud was lifted a little off it and moved in front, the tabernacle had to follow (ver. 36)—if it settled down on the roof, the people stopped and remained until it moved again (ver. 37). The appearance was as of a cloud by day, and as of fire by night, so that all could always see where the tabernacle was, and whether it was stationary or in motion (ver. 38). After the first descent, it would seem that "the glory" withdrew into the Holy of Holies, so that both Moses and the priests could enter the holy place, and minister there.[41]

Now the time had come for the offering of sacrifices to take place in the courtyard and be presented in the Holy Place and the Holy of Holies. As we have read, the first sacrifice took place in the garden of Eden—the life of an animal to clothe the sin-ravaged bodies of Adam and Eve. The second instances of sacrifice were those offered by Cain and Abel—with tragic results. We have seen how Noah offered a sacrifice when he stepped from the ark onto dry ground, and that Job made atonement for the sins of his children. Abraham, too, built altars during his journey from Ai to the land promised to him by Jehovah, as did his son Isaac and grandson Jacob. Once the children of Israel moved into Egypt and became slaves to Pharaoh, there is no record of sacrificial offerings by the descendants of Abraham.

Not until the night the death angel was to pass over the land of Egypt do we see the Israelites offering a sacrifice to Jehovah—an act that was to become a memorial to the salvation of the people through the generations. This, too, was to be a picture of the work of the Messiah—the paschal lamb who would make atonement for sin one time for all time.

Once miraculously freed from the strictures of slavery under Pharaoh, the Israelites stopped at Mount Sinai, where Moses met with Jehovah. It was there he received the instructions, not only for the tabernacle, but for the furnishings, priestly garments, and sacrificial offerings that were to be presented to Jehovah.

In the book of Leviticus, chapters 1–7, we read of the five very distinct offerings that were to be presented to Jehovah:

- ✧ The Burnt Offering (chapter 1)

- ✧ The Grain Offering (chapter 2)

- ✧ The Peace Offering (chapter 3)

- ✧ The Sin Offering (chapter 4)

- ✧ The Trespass Offering (chapter 5)

The first three offerings were presented when in fellowship with Jehovah. They are also sometimes referred to as sweet-savor sacrifices. They presented a pleasant odor to God, giving Him delight. They were indicative of relationship, adoration, submission, acknowledgment, and fulfillment. Each was an offering freely presented simply for the joy of giving.

The other two sacrifices were offered for the forgiveness of sin and to restore intimacy with Jehovah. The smoke that rose from those two offerings was a stench in the nostrils of God, for they spoke of iniquity, debauchery, immorality, and self-indulgence. They were offered, not on the bronze altar in the courtyard, but were burned outside the camp. The one who made the offering came before the priests to confess the sin in his life and to seek God's forgiveness.

The burnt offering or *olah* was to be just that—completely consumed by the fire on the altar, which was never to be extinguished (see Leviticus 6:13). None of this offering was to be eaten. The sacrifice was to be a male—a bull, goat, or lamb. If a pigeon or turtledove was offered, it was not required to be without blemish and was killed by the priest. The male animal was brought to the priest and the one making the offering placed his hands on the head of the creature. The penitent one would then ask Jehovah's forgiveness for his sin and immediately slay the animal. It was skinned, cut into pieces, washed, and its blood sprinkled on the altar. Then it would be burned as a sacrifice to Jehovah. The olah remained on the altar all night. The following morning, the priest would change into his linen garments, then remove the ashes and place them beside the altar. The linen garments would be removed, the priest would don his regular garments and carry the ashes outside the camp (see Leviticus 6:10–11). Although not permitted to eat a portion of the offering, the priest was allowed to keep the skin from the sacrificial animal.

✧ ✧ ✧

The *minchah* or grain offering was given to the priest who took a portion of the grain to the bronze altar. It was offered to Jehovah as a memorial, and the remainder was presented to the priests:

"Aaron's sons are to bring it [the grain] before the LORD, in front of the altar. The priest is to take a handful of the finest flour and some olive oil, together with all the incense on the grain offering, and burn the memorial portion on the altar as an aroma pleasing to the LORD. Aaron and his sons shall eat the rest of it, but it is to be eaten without yeast in the sanctuary area; they are to eat it in the courtyard of the tent of meeting." (Leviticus 6:14–16)

S. Michael Houdmann, founder of Gotquestions.com, provided this information regarding the observance:

The grain offering is described as "a most holy part of the food offerings presented to the Lord" (Leviticus 2:10b). Grain offerings would often be presented after a burnt offering, which required an animal sacrifice for the atonement of sin. Blood had to be shed for the remission of sins to take place, so a grain offering would not serve the same purpose as a burnt offering. Instead, the purpose of a grain offering was to worship God and acknowledge His provision.[42]

The grain offering could be considered a sacrifice of praise that followed the burnt offering. This offering, instituted during the wanderings in the desert, was particularly sacrificial. The Israelites had been promised a land the flowed with "milk and honey," but that certainly wasn't true of their Sinai surroundings of rocks and sand. They had been promised a land of abundance, but their travels took them through a barren and unproductive land. Their journey left no time to plant crops and harvest grain, so to surrender a portion of their supply for an offering spoke of unselfish dedication. And the offering represented so much more than a simple handful of flour: As the grain was presented, oil, symbolizing the Holy Spirit's anointing, was poured over the grain. Incense was added to represent the sweet savor of the prayers of the people offered to Jehovah. Salt was sprinkled over the offering, a reminder of God's eternal covenant with His people.

The third of the offerings to be presented to Jehovah was a peace offering, delineated in Leviticus 7:11–21. It was a freewill donation, a thank-you gift for God's unmerited favor and unsolicited bounty—a doxology, perhaps akin to the one written by Thomas Ken in 1674:

> Praise God, from Whom all blessings flow;
> Praise Him, all creatures here below;
> Praise Him above, ye heavenly host;
> Praise Father, Son, and Holy Ghost.[43]

Author C. W. Slemming wrote of the grain offering:

> Christ is seen as the kernel of wheat that fell into the ground and died that He might bring forth much fruit. He was also the kernel of wheat which went through the crushing mill of Gethsemane and the fierce oven of Calvary to become the Bread of Life, the sustainer of His people on a pilgrim journey. He gave His all. He knew no reservation. He came not to be served but to serve and to give His life a ransom for many, and now upon Him we feed and in Him find our source of strength.[44]

The grain offering was also symbolic of the price Jesus paid for our sins. He took upon himself the sins of the world—every awful thing imaginable was laid on our Lord. He was contaminated body (the flesh), soul (mind, emotions, and will), and spirit. Grain was first offered on an open fire, which corresponds with the outwardly visible agony of our Lord.

The second method of offering the grain was in a pan or skillet. Emotional or psychological pain is only partially visible to those around us. The article being consumed in the skillet could only be seen from a distance. Isaiah prophesied in chapter 53 that the suffering Savior would be a man of sorrows and acquainted with grief (v. 3). Not only would He suffer physically but emotionally as well. The burden of sin must have been devastating to One who knew no sin. The mental anguish was Jesus' "travail of his soul." (See Isaiah 53:11 KJV.)

The third method was for the grain to be burned in the oven, out of sight. As Jesus hung on the cross, wracked with horrific pain, in travail of soul, something even more punishing happened. Matthew 27:46 (NKJV) tells us, "And about the ninth hour Jesus cried out with a loud voice, saying, "Eli, Eli, lama sabachthani?" that is, "My God, My God, why have You forsaken Me?" Jesus had been spiritually separated from His Father because of my sin and your sin. While in the oven of terrible adversity, the relationship between Father and Son had been severed. As excruciating as the physical pain had been, as distressing as the anguish of soul had been, the spiritual detachment was worse. Dr. John MacArthur wrote:

> In the midst of being willingly engulfed in our sins and the sins of all men of all time, He [Jesus] writhed in anguish not from the lacerations on His back or the thorns that still pierced His head or the nails that held Him to the cross but from the incomparably painful

loss of fellowship with His heavenly Father that His becoming sin for us had brought.[45]

But that separation would not last. Jesus would be taken from the cross, His body anointed for burial, and three days later:

> But God raised him from the dead, freeing him from the agony of death, because it was impossible for death to keep its hold on him. (Acts 2:24)

✧ ✧ ✧

Often the peace offering was in honor of a vow to God that had been fulfilled, i.e., Hannah's gift to Jehovah when she brought her son, Samuel, to the temple. In the first chapter of 1 Samuel, a heart-broken and barren woman made her way to the temple to offer a sacrifice and pray. She pleaded with God to grant her request for a child. Hannah covenanted with Jehovah to rear her son only until he was old enough to be weaned from her breast and then to present the child to the Lord for service in the temple. Along with her child, Hannah brought a peace offering to express her gratitude to Jehovah and to indicate that she held no resentment in her heart. God had answered her prayer, and in so doing she birthed Samuel, a righteous prophet, to serve Him.

The majority of sacrifices offered to Jehovah in Old Testament times were not consumed by those making the offering. The peace offering was to be eaten after a portion had been burnt on the altar. The remainder of the offering was returned to the presenter and then distributed to the poor. It is a perfect illustration of Jehovah's provision—physically and spiritually; a picture of His matchless grace and kindness. The peace offering was a wonderful way to thank Jehovah-Jireh, our Provider whose grace is sufficient.

Ernie Brown, contributor to Biblecentre.org, wrote of the peace offering:

> A prime feature of the Peace Offering is that it is a voluntary offering. It is offered willingly. It is not obligatory. It is also a sweet savour offering. That indicates that what is being offered is rising up to God as a sweet savour. That is, what is being done is acceptable to God. It pleases Him, it gives Him pleasure.[46]

The peace offering was a foreshadowing of the One to come—the Messiah:

> For He Himself is our peace, who has made both one, and has broken down the middle wall of separation, (Ephesians 2:14 NKJV)

The consistent instruction given throughout the Scriptures—beginning in Leviticus—is that praise springs forth from an offering that is completely satisfactory to Jehovah. Our freedom of worship flows from the one truly acceptable offering: Jesus Christ our Lord, the matchless Son of God, the Lamb slain before the foundation of the world (see Revelation 13:8). Because of that sacrifice, not only can we worship God in "spirit and in truth" (John 4:24 KJV), we can receive forgiveness of sin through the blood of Christ.

GUILT *and* SIN OFFERINGS

The Israelites were also required to present a fourth offering—a sin offering, not for any and all unspecified sins but for a definite sin that demanded atonement. It could have been an unintentional mistake—a sin committed through ignorance, perhaps—but once the person was aware that sin was present, an immediate offering was necessary. This specific offering was not an option for a deliberate sin. We read in Numbers 15:27–29:

> "But if just one person sins unintentionally, that person must bring a year-old female goat for a sin offering. The priest is to make atonement before the LORD for the one who erred by sinning unintentionally, and when atonement has been made, that person will be forgiven. One and the same law applies to everyone who sins unintentionally, whether a native-born Israelite or a foreigner residing among you."

Unlike the sin offering for the entire camp of the Israelites, the body of the animal offered—a female goat or sheep—was taken to the doorway of the tabernacle. There it was slain by the individual making the presentation to Jehovah. The blood was drained into a basin and the priest then sprinkled some of the blood on the horns of the bronze altar where the sacrifice was burned. The remaining blood was poured out at the base of the altar. The priest who offered the animal was allowed to consume the remainder of the sheep or goat in the courtyard of the tabernacle. The person who had presented the offering was not allowed to eat any part of it.

The sin offering was instituted to educate the Israelites about sin. What lessons, then, can we take away from Leviticus chapter 4?

1) God sets the parameters for sin, and that is defined as anything contrary to His Word and instructions. Psalm 136:1 (ESV) reminds us that we are to "Give thanks to the LORD, for he is good, for his steadfast love endures forever." Pastor and teacher Dr. Bob Deffinbaugh said this of the definition of sin:

> Obedience is best evidenced by our willingness to do something which we would rather not do, for reasons we don't understand, simply because God says so.[47]

2) Mosaic Law made a definite distinction between intentional and unintentional sin for which this sacrifice was instituted. Numbers 15:30–31 reveals that there was no recompense for intentional sin, only separation from fellowship:

> "But anyone who sins defiantly, whether native-born or foreigner, blasphemes the LORD and must be cut off from the people of Israel. Because they have despised the LORD's word and broken his commands,

they must surely be cut off; their guilt remains on them."

Transgressions are a direct blow against a righteous God. It matters not whether the sin is done in the open for all to see, or in the secret place of the heart. First Samuel 16:7 (NKJV) reminds us, "For the LORD does not see as man sees; for man looks at the outward appearance, but the LORD looks at the heart."

3) Spiritual defilement takes many forms. God warned the Israelites to avoid intermingling with the peoples who inhabited the Promised Land:

> Do not defile yourselves with any of these things [see Leviticus 18 verses 1–24]; for by all these the nations are defiled, which I am casting out before you. For the land is defiled; therefore I visit the punishment of its iniquity upon it, and the land vomits out its inhabitants.

The prophet Ezekiel outlined the sins that defiled the Israelites in chapter 23, verses 37–39 (NKJV):

> "For they have committed adultery, and blood is on their hands. They have committed adultery with their idols, and even sacrificed their sons whom they bore to Me, passing them through the fire, to devour them. Moreover they have done this to Me: They have defiled My sanctuary on the same day and profaned My Sabbaths. For after they had slain their children for their idols, on the same day they came into My

sanctuary to profane it; and indeed thus they have
done in the midst of My house."

The Israelites' deliberate sins had ultimately caused them to be
carried off to other lands as captives. It was a devastating punishment, but one of which they had been warned repeatedly.

The apostle Paul intoned in Romans 6:23 (KJV), "For the wages
of sin is death." But he didn't leave us hopeless, for he continued,
"But the gift of God is eternal life through Jesus Christ our Lord."

Just as God had shown Adam and Eve in the garden that the
shedding of blood was necessary to cover their nakedness—their
sin exposed—so He made it abundantly clear to the Israelites that
a blood sacrifice was necessary to cleanse the damage caused
by sin. The writer of Hebrews penned this warning in chapter
9, verse 22, "And almost all things are by the law purged with
blood; and without shedding of blood is no remission" (KJV).
Jesus Christ was our sin offering, assuring forgiveness by the Father.
This was reinforced by John the Baptist, who cried out to the people
amassed at the Jordan for baptism, "Look, the Lamb of God, who
takes away the sin of the world!" (John 1:29)

Robert Lowry penned a mighty hymn of the church, "Nothing
But the Blood":

> What can wash away my sin?
> Nothing but the blood of Jesus;
> What can make me whole again?
> Nothing but the blood of Jesus.[48]

Jesus paid an exorbitantly high price so that "whosoever
believed" could experience forgiveness and grace. Knowing the
wages of sin, God sent forth His only begotten Son to cover our

transgressions and give the gift of eternal life. The author of Hebrews penned this warning:

> For if we sin willfully after we have received the knowledge of the truth, there no longer remains a sacrifice for sins, but a certain fearful expectation of judgment, and fiery indignation which will devour the adversaries. Anyone who has rejected Moses' law dies without mercy on the testimony of two or three witnesses. Of how much worse punishment, do you suppose, will he be thought worthy who has trampled the Son of God underfoot, counted the blood of the covenant by which he was sanctified a common thing, and insulted the Spirit of grace? (Hebrews 10:26–29 NKJV)

The sin offering was a means to present a sacrifice to the priest for unintentional sins, ignorantly committed. Today, we have a "great High Priest" who has made it possible for us to "come boldly to the throne of grace, that we may obtain mercy and find grace to help in time of need" (Hebrews 4:16 NKJV).

✧   ✧   ✧

The fifth offering required by Jehovah was the trespass, sometimes called the guilt offering. The guilt or trespass offering was based on two aspects of an individual's life—the lawful or ethical and the emotional or that based on the conscience.

God created man with a conscience, an innate sense of right and wrong. It is intended to cause us to feel internal remorse when we break the laws established by Jehovah. The concept of sin and guilt are so intertwined that Jehovah made provisions for both. That the conscience can be overridden is evident by all around us. The great British statesman Winston Churchill said:

> The only guide to man is his conscience; the only shield to his memory is the rectitude and sincerity of his actions. It is very imprudent to walk through life without this shield, because we are so often mocked by the failure of our hopes and the upsetting of our calculations; but with this shield, however the fates may play, we march always in the ranks of honor.[49]

It is our honed conscience that causes us to feel God's pain when we reject His standards. Hebrews 5:14 (ESV) reminds us:

> But solid food is for the mature, for those who have their powers of discernment trained by constant practice to distinguish good from evil.
>
> Feelings of guilt are as common today as they were in the days of Moses. God knew that guilt would plague mankind through the ages and made provision with the trespass offering. It was true of Adam and Eve; from the sin of disobedience sprang the guilt that prompted the pair to cover their nakedness. An old Indian proverb defines conscience as "a three-cornered thing in my heart that stands still when I am good, but when I am bad, it turns around and the corners hurt a lot. If I keep on doing wrong, the corners wear off and it does not hurt anymore."[50]

In the book of Leviticus chapters 5, 6, and 7 outline the trespass offering as follows:

1. A trespass offering is necessitated should an individual violate the holy things of God (Leviticus 5:14–16). This would include

   a. taking the Lord's name in vain or dishonoring the name of Jehovah;

   b. violating the Sabbath;

   c. desecrating the rites and offerings of the tabernacle or temple—especially by the priests;

   d. failing to heed the instructions implemented by God, i.e., worshiping false gods and intermarrying with those who did.

2. A trespass offering was obligatory when one realized he/she had sinned unknowingly (Leviticus 5:17–19).

3. When guilty of extortion or theft, a trespass offering was essential, but more was required.

   a. In Leviticus 6:1–7 (NLT), Moses instructed the people regarding the circumstances that necessitated a trespass offering:

      "Suppose one of you sins against your associate and is unfaithful to the LORD. Suppose you cheat in a deal involving a security deposit, or you steal or commit fraud, or you find lost property and lie about it, or you lie

while swearing to tell the truth, or you commit any other such sin. If you have sinned in
any of these ways, you are guilty. You must
give back whatever you stole, or the money
you took by extortion, or the security deposit,
or the lost property you found, or anything
obtained by swearing falsely.

You must make restitution by paying the
full price plus an additional 20 percent to the
person you have harmed. On the same day
you must present a guilt offering. As a guilt
offering to the LORD, you must bring to the
priest your own ram with no defects, or you
may buy one of equal value. Through this
process, the priest will purify you before the
LORD, making you right with him, and you
will be forgiven for any of these sins you have
committed."

   b. To simplify the above passage, trespass offerings were required when a neighbor was
cheated or if property found and unreturned.
The guilty party must return what was taken,
along with compensation of 20 percent.

4. Leviticus 7:1–6 (NLT) defines the details of how
the guilt or trespass offering is to be made:

"These are the instructions for the guilt offering. It is most holy. The animal sacrificed as a guilt
offering must be slaughtered at the place where the

burnt offerings are slaughtered, and its blood must be splattered against all sides of the altar. The priest will then offer all its fat on the altar, including the fat of the broad tail, the fat around the internal organs, the two kidneys and the fat around them near the loins, and the long lobe of the liver. These are to be removed with the kidneys, and the priests will burn them on the altar as a special gift presented to the LORD. This is the guilt offering. Any male from a priest's family may eat the meat. It must be eaten in a sacred place, for it is most holy."

The ultimate guilt offering was made at Golgotha. The prophet Isaiah wrote of the suffering Savior in chapter 53, verses 10–11 (ESV):

Yet it was the will of the LORD to crush him; he has put him to grief; when his soul makes an offering for guilt, he shall see his offspring; he shall prolong his days; the will of the LORD shall prosper in his hand. Out of the anguish of his soul he shall see and be satisfied; by his knowledge shall the righteous one, my servant, make many to be accounted righteous, and he shall bear their iniquities.

Through the offering of Christ on Calvary, Believers were justified—declared "not guilty." The writer of Hebrews 10:10 (ESV) penned:

And by that will [the will of God] we have been sanctified through the offering of the body of Jesus Christ once for all.

The question of sin and guilt was settled when Jesus uttered, "It is finished." All that is required of you and me is to admit that we are sinners in need of a Savior and then accept the offering Christ made for our sin and guilt.

12

FOLDING *the* TENT

T he departure of the children of Israel from Egypt took them to the foot of Mount Sinai where Jehovah gave Moses instructions regarding the tabernacle and its furnishings. All were constructed according to minute detail and erected at Sinai. Exodus 40:2–3 describes the culmination of the work on the edifice. As the pieces were brought together to complete the tabernacle, Moses received instructions from God:

> "Set up the tabernacle, the tent of meeting, on the first day of the first month. Place the ark of the covenant law in it and shield the ark with the curtain."

It was at that moment that the symbol of the presence of God came to dwell in the midst of the children of Israel. Though they would wander for forty years through the barren wilderness, Jehovah would never leave them, and the congregation would not go forward from the site of their camp until the cloud moved from its resting place over the tabernacle. Numbers 10:11–13 informs us:

> On the twentieth day of the second month of the second year, the cloud lifted from above the tabernacle of the covenant law. Then the Israelites set out

from the Desert of Sinai and traveled from place to place until the cloud came to rest in the Desert of Paran. They set out, this first time, at the LORD's command through Moses.

Paran was south of the Negev in southern Canaan, near the northern edge of the Gulf of Aqaba, an extension of the Red Sea. (Today it is bordered on the east by Saudi Arabia and on the west by Egypt. Its north-northeastern tip touches the southernmost border of Israel at Eilat.)

As the twelve tribes followed the cloud, the leaders watched carefully for signs that it was time to stop and erect the tabernacle. When the cloud moved along the banks of the Jordan River, the Israelites followed—engaging and defeating enemies as God led. When His precepts and directions were obeyed, Jehovah's people were victorious; when disobedience entered the ranks, the people suffered sorely.

Under Moses' leadership, the ark of the covenant stopped at many places: Kadesh, Mount Gerizim, and the land of Moab among them. It was later during a stop at Mount Nebo that Moses died. During their trek through the Desert of Zin (see Numbers 20) the children of Israel grumbled because they had no water to drink. God had instructed Moses to speak to a rock and water would be provided. Moses' anger with the Israelites for their grumbling caused him to strike the rock not once but twice. For his disobedience, Jehovah informed Moses that he would no longer be eligible to lead the Israelites into the Promised Land. It was not the first time that water had come from a rock. At Horeb the people had complained about the lack of water. God told Moses, "Strike the rock, and water will come out of it for the people to drink" (Exodus

17:6). This time, Jehovah wanted to teach His people a valuable lesson—one missed because of Moses' anger with the congregation. He wanted them to see a picture of the Messiah who, ultimately, would have a spear thrust into His side from which would flow water and blood. He would not have to suffer the pain of crucifixion again in order to allow His children access to God the Father. Now we need only speak to Him to have our petitions met. Jesus issued the invitation in John 7:37: "Let anyone who is thirsty come to me and drink."

Barred from entering the land of Canaan, Moses would see the end of his life, but not before a glimpse at what awaited his followers in Deuteronomy 34:1–6:

> Then Moses climbed Mount Nebo from the plains of Moab to the top of Pisgah, across from Jericho. There the LORD showed him the whole land— from Gilead to Dan, all of Naphtali, the territory of Ephraim and Manasseh, all the land of Judah as far as the Mediterranean Sea, the Negev and the whole region from the Valley of Jericho, the City of Palms, as far as Zoar. Then the LORD said to him, "This is the land I promised on oath to Abraham, Isaac and Jacob when I said, 'I will give it to your descendants.' I have let you see it with your eyes, but you will not cross over into it." And Moses the servant of the LORD died there in Moab, as the LORD had said. He buried him in Moab, in the valley opposite Beth Peor, but to this day no one knows where his grave is.

Thus, the tabernacle rested below Mount Nebo in the land of Moab when Moses died. At last, the time had come for Joshua and the ark of the covenant to lead the people into the Promised Land. Moses' successor had followed in the footsteps of God's chosen leader since the twelve tribes settled at the foot of Mount Sinai. He had been chosen as one of the twelve to survey the land and was one of only two who had brought back a good report. In Joshua 3:1–4, we see:

> Early in the morning Joshua and all the Israelites set out from Shittim and went to the Jordan, where they camped before crossing over. After three days the officers went throughout the camp, giving orders to the people: "When you see the ark of the covenant of the LORD your God, and the Levitical priests carrying it, you are to move out from your positions and follow it. Then you will know which way to go, since you have never been this way before. But keep a distance of about two thousand cubits between you and the ark; do not go near it."

What a sight that must have been—a sea of humanity accompanied by livestock, oxcarts, and more took up their burdens and fell into line behind Joshua. They all followed the Levites who bore the ark of the covenant—the symbol of God's presence. With Jehovah's admonition to stay 2,000 cubits behind (approximately half a mile), the Israelites marched forth. After forty years of wandering in the desert, they were ready to see the land God had promised to Abraham, Isaac, and Jacob.

The people must have been astonished as the feet of those bearing the ark stepped into the Jordan, and the waters ceased to flow. The men moved forward to the middle of the riverbed and the people passed over. Once the last straggler had set foot in Canaan, the bearers moved forward to the other side and the Jordan resumed its flow. The Israelites halted at Gilgal, where they were instructed to set up camp. The tabernacle was erected in the center and the tribes arranged according to Moses' directives. The ark would have been placed in the Holy of Holies, as Jehovah commanded all the males born during the wilderness trek to be circumcised and given time to heal. The people were then ordered to prepare for Passover.

Afterward, the Israelites set out to conquer the southern reaches of the Promised Land. The ark was carried forth from the Holy of Holies at God's command and circled the walls once a day for six days. The Levites followed seven priests carrying seven trumpets. The people were told to keep silent, and after the march the ark was returned to its resting place. Joshua 6:15–16, gives us a picture of the events that followed:

> On the seventh day, they got up at daybreak and marched around the city seven times in the same manner, except that on that day they circled the city seven times. The seventh time around, when the priests sounded the trumpet blast, Joshua commanded the army, "Shout! For the LORD has given you the city!"

The tabernacle remained at Gilgal during the entire conquest of both the northern and southern regions of Canaan. It was then moved to Shiloh where the portions of land were meted out. Joshua instructed:

> "Appoint three men from each tribe. I will send them out to make a survey of the land and to write a

description of it, according to the inheritance of each. Then they will return to me. You are to divide the land into seven parts. Judah is to remain in its territory on the south and the tribes of Joseph in their territory on the north. After you have written descriptions of the seven parts of the land, bring them here to me and I will cast lots for you in the presence of the LORD our God. The Levites, however, do not get a portion among you, because the priestly service of the LORD is their inheritance. And Gad, Reuben and the half-tribe of Manasseh have already received their inheritance on the east side of the Jordan. Moses the servant of the LORD gave it to them." (Joshua 18:4–7)

Joshua possibly chose Shiloh as a tactical position. It lay to the west of Jericho and was at the bottom of a sheer plunge from the mountainous area above. Defending the tabernacle and the people would have been simpler than on the open plain on which Gilgal lay. Although the Israelites had entered the Promised Land, there were still battles to fight and the tabernacle to protect and preserve. The late Rev. Dan Snaddon, Plymouth Brethren pastor and author, wrote of the importance of the tabernacle:

> The great lesson of the tabernacle is that God came down to dwell with His people. From Genesis to Deuteronomy we have accounts of God visiting men. These visits culminated in God's dwelling with men in the Tabernacle or tent. John picks up the same thought and uses the same word "tabernacled," to describe God dwelling among men in the person

of Christ. John 1:14 says, "The Word became flesh
and tabernacled [or pitched His tent] among us." The
Tabernacle served as God's dwelling place for 500
years among the children of Israel . . . .

The Word of God makes it quite plain that there is
a twofold purpose for the divine conception and the
human construction of the Tabernacle. There was
an immediate and ultimate purpose. The immediate
purpose was to wean the children of Israel away from
the base idolatry of Egypt and set before them a pure
and noble ideal of worship and witness. The natural
tendency of these ancient pilgrims was downward
and backward. We see a clear example of this with
the worship of the golden calf in Exodus 32.

The worship of the unseen God was something
new. All heathen religions had their visible gods.
Thus, the immediate purpose of the Tabernacle was
the provision of a place of worship. The Israelite came
to the door of the Tabernacle to worship God. He
could not see Him. He brought his offering— the visible expression of his reverence and awe.[51]

The Bible gives us no further reference to the tabernacle until
we read in Judges 20:27 that the ark was in Bethel. It appears that
it was moved several times from Shiloh to Bethel and back before
Solomon built the temple. The importance of the tabernacle was as a
covering for the ark of the covenant. It was at Shiloh, however, that
disaster struck. The children of Israel had assembled to fight the
Philistines—a perennial foe. Eli was high priest, and his two sons,
Phinehas and Hophni, discharged the office of priest when their

aging father was unable. According to Fausset's Bible Dictionary, the two men:

> "Sons of Belial," who, though knowing externally and professionally, "knew not the Lord" experimentally and practically (1 Samuel 2:12, compare Jeremiah 22:16; Titus 1:16). Greediness, violent rapacity, wherewith they made themselves fat with the chiefest of the offerings of God's people, (and this in the sanctuary itself, so that "men abhorred the offering of the Lord,") and even lust indulged with the women assembling at the door of the tabernacle, were their crying sins. These in accordance with the prophecies of a man of God, and of Samuel, brought on both a violent death in one day.[52]

Eli's boys were guilty of four forbidden faults:

1. Iniquity—the two treated the Lord's offerings with sinful contempt.

2. Insolence—taking whatever they wanted, rather than the portions allotted the priests. "But even before the fat was burned, the priest's servant would come and say to the person who was sacrificing, 'Give the priest some meat to roast; he won't accept boiled meat from you, but only raw'" (1 Samuel 2:15).

3. Intimidation—demanding that their needs be met before the sacrifice had been offered (see verse 16).

4. Immorality—the two brought prostitutes into the tabernacle: "Now Eli, who was very old, heard about everything his sons were doing to all Israel and how they slept with the women who served at the entrance to the tent of meeting" (verse 22).

Apparently, the two men viewed the ark as something of a lucky charm—a rabbit's foot—symbolic of Jehovah for whom they had little, if any, respect. They thought it would cause the Philistines to turn and run from sheer terror. They soon realized the truth: that God could not be manipulated, and Israel would suffer the consequences for their bad behavior. The ark was captured, the two priests slain, and when Eli heard the news of the deaths of his sons, he fell backward and his neck was broken. With the ark in enemy hands, the tabernacle became just another tent.

After the Israelites had been in the Promised Land for a time, a clamor went up from the people for a king; they wanted to be like everyone else. The prophet Samuel urged them to reconsider by laying out to them all the burdens a king would place upon them. When he saw that they refused to listen, Samuel capitulated:

[He said to the Israelites,] "This is what the LORD, the God of Israel, says: 'I brought Israel up from Egypt, and I delivered you from the power of Egypt and all the kingdoms that oppressed you.' But you have now rejected your God, who saves you out of all your disasters and calamities. And you have said, 'No,

appoint a king over us.' So now present yourselves
before the LORD by your tribes and clans." (1 Samuel
10:18–19)

As the men filed before Samuel tribe by tribe, the Lord pointed
out Saul, who was "as handsome a young man as could be found anywhere in Israel, and he was a head taller than anyone else" (1 Samuel
9:2). During Saul's rule, the ark rested in the house of Abinadab, but
only a form of worship continued. With no tabernacle and no ark,
no central place for worship, the people drifted away from Jehovah-
Shammah—the Lord who is Present. Irish pastor and author George
Kirkpatrick said of the loss of the ark and the subsequent demand
for a king, "The presence, power, promises, protection, praise,
peace, and provision had been removed from Moses' tabernacle,
but their form of worship continued."[53] The apostle Paul referred to
this practice as "having a form of godliness but denying its power"
(2 Timothy 3:5).

After the ark was returned to the Israelites and the time arrived
for David to return the ark of the covenant to Jerusalem, it was
housed in an ordinary tent unlike its former dwelling. But nothing
can remain pedestrian for long when God's presence takes up
residence. It became a holy place where the ark resided until after
David became king and then shared his plan with his son, Solomon.
In David's tent, the priests were silent. With the ark gone from the
Holy of Holies, there was no reason to sacrifice or to praise. Smoke
from the altar of incense still drifted heavenward, but the trumpets
were silent, and the blood sacrifice was missing. The priests, who
had brought the ark to Jerusalem offered, not incense, but unceasing
praise and worship to Jehovah.

The specter of "Ichabod" hung over the curtain that separated the Holy of Holies from the Holy Place, for the presence of God had departed. The high priest was barred from the Holy of Holies, for it no longer had a purpose—the ark was gone. Sacrifices were not possible, for the ark was gone. The sins of the people could not be postponed for another year, for the ark was gone! The people would have to wait until the son of David could erect a permanent place of worship and sacrifice—the temple. Moses' tabernacle had been folded away; David's tabernacle was no longer in use. The finely crafted instruments that had been lovingly placed in the tabernacle in the wilderness would be employed again in Solomon's temple. All the worship of God came together in Solomon's temple. Once again, the presence of the Lord, as a cloud, filled the temple, "and the priests could not perform their service because of the cloud, for the glory of the LORD filled the temple of God" (2 Chronicles 5:14).

13

THE BUILDING *of* SOLOMON'S TEMPLE

When King Solomon wrote in Proverbs 22:1 (NKJV), "A *good* name is to be chosen rather than great riches, loving favor rather than silver and gold," perhaps he was thinking of his father, David. A good name and favor would be of paramount importance as David planned his life's work and heart's desire: building a temple to house the ark of the covenant. The shepherd who had slain Goliath and then had run for his life from King Saul had finally consolidated Judah and Israel into one united kingdom.

The ark had been captured by the Philistines, and even the defeat of Goliath and the rout of the enemy did not secure a return of the symbol of God's presence. The ark had been paraded throughout the Philistine territory with trouble and disease following the desecration of the holy emblem. Finally, with the lesson learned, the ark was returned to the Israelites and housed at Kirjath Jearim, a village west of Jerusalem. First Samuel 7:1 (NKJV) tells us, "Then the men of Kirjath Jearim came and took the ark of the LORD, and brought it into the house of Abinadab on the hill, and consecrated Eleazar his son to keep the ark of the LORD." It resided there until after the deaths of Samuel and King Saul. After an initial aborted attempt to move the ark to Jerusalem (see 2 Samuel 6), it was left in the home of Obed-Edom. We then read in 2 Samuel 6:12–15 (NKJV):

> Now it was told King David, saying, "The LORD has blessed the house of Obed-Edom and all that belongs to him, because of the ark of God." So David went and brought up the ark of God from the house of Obed-Edom to the City of David with gladness. And so it was, when those bearing the ark of the LORD had gone six paces, that he sacrificed oxen and fatted sheep. Then David danced before the LORD with all his might; and David was wearing a linen ephod. So David and all the house of Israel brought up the ark of the LORD with shouting and with the sound of the trumpet.

The ark of the covenant had been returned to the City of David. Pondering the place of the presence of God, David realized that while he lived in a palace constructed of the finest cedars from Lebanon and built by the most talented craftsmen provided by his friend King Hiram of Tyre—a Phoenician city north of Carmel—Jehovah's dwelling place was a tent! How ludicrous that must have seemed to a man who had risen through the ranks from sheep pen to palace.

With that realization, David began to make plans to build a temple for Jehovah. When he shared his building proposal with Nathan, the prophet, Nathan gave him a hearty thumbs-up—at least before he went home and retired for the night. As he slept, the Spirit of God spoke to him and said:

> "Go and tell my servant David, 'This is what the

LORD says: Are you the one to build me a house to dwell in? I have not dwelt in a house from the day I brought the Israelites up out of Egypt to this day. I have been moving from place to place with a tent as my dwelling. Wherever I have moved with all the Israelites, did I ever say to any of their rulers whom I commanded to shepherd my people Israel, "Why have you not built me a house of cedar?"'

"Now then, tell my servant David, 'This is what the LORD Almighty says: I took you from the pasture, from tending the flock, and appointed you ruler over my people Israel. I have been with you wherever you have gone, and I have cut off all your enemies from before you. Now I will make your name great, like the names of the greatest men on earth. And I will provide a place for my people Israel and will plant them so that they can have a home of their own and no longer be disturbed. Wicked people will not oppress them anymore, as they did at the beginning and have done ever since the time I appointed leaders over my people Israel. I will also give you rest from all your enemies.

"'The LORD declares to you that the LORD himself will establish a house for you: When your days are over and you rest with your ancestors, I will raise up your offspring to succeed you, your own flesh and blood, and I will establish his kingdom. He is the one who will build a house for my Name, and I will establish the throne of his kingdom forever. I will be his father, and he will be my son. When he does wrong,

I will punish him with a rod wielded by men, with floggings inflicted by human hands. But my love will never be taken away from him, as I took it away from Saul, whom I removed from before you. Your house and your kingdom will endure forever before me; your throne will be established forever.'" (2 Samuel 7:5–16)

God wanted David to know that He really didn't need a house made of cedar and stone. He wanted His dwelling to be within the hearts of His people Israel. Never had Jehovah asked for a place of residence; He had asked for commitment, honesty, kindness, loyalty, mercy. He required His people to honor their parents, to remember the Sabbath day and keep it holy. He commanded that they not commit adultery, murder, covet, lie, or steal; but never had He demanded, "I want an opulent palace."

Author and pastor, Eugene Peterson wrote:

> But there are times when our grand human plans to do something for God are seen, after a night of prayer, to be a huge human distraction from what God is doing for us. That's what Nathan realized that night: God showed Nathan that David's building plans for God would interfere with God's building plans for David.[54]

Peterson then boils it down to the nitty-gritty:

> The message that Nathan delivers to David is dominated by a recital of what God has done, is doing, and will do. God is the first-person subject of twenty-three verbs in this message, and these verbs carry the

action. David, full of what he's going to do for God, is
now subjected to a comprehensive rehearsal of what
God has done, is doing, and will do for and in David.
What looked yesterday like a bold Davidic enterprise
on behalf of God now looks picayune.[55]

David's leadership acumen and favor with those surrounding
him enabled him to build a united country with Jerusalem as its
center of religious influence. It became a shining inspiration as a
city, but God was more interested in the holiness of its inhabitants.
The easy part was the building; the more difficult proposition was its
people. All these centuries later, the first and second temples are in
ruins, the beautiful implements lost to the Jews. There is, however,
a remnant to this day—spiritual descendants—of the house of David.

While David was king and even after God had forbidden him
to begin work on the temple, he began to gather and stockpile the
materials that would be needed by Solomon to build the house of
God in Jerusalem. It would be years later before God revealed to
David the reason He withheld the task of building the temple from
the "man after God's own heart" (see 1 Samuel 13).

In 1 Chronicles 28:3 (NKJV) God admonished David, "You shall
not build a house for My name, because you have been a man of war
and have shed blood."

After the death of his father, David, King Solomon issued the
mandate for construction and work began on the temple site. Actually,
it was King Hiram of Tyre who first reached out to Solomon. In 1
Kings 5:1–7 (NKJV):

Now Hiram king of Tyre sent his servants to
Solomon, because he heard that they had anointed
him king in place of his father, for Hiram had always

loved David. Then Solomon sent to Hiram, saying: You know how my father David could not build
a house for the name of the LORD his God because
of the wars which were fought against him on every
side, until the LORD put his foes under the soles of his
feet. But now the LORD my God has given me rest on
every side; there is neither adversary nor evil occur-
rence. And behold, I propose to build a house for the
name of the LORD my God, as the LORD spoke to my
father David, saying, "Your son, whom I will set on
your throne in your place, he shall build the house for
My name." Now therefore, command that they cut
down cedars for me from Lebanon; and my servants
will be with your servants, and I will pay you wages
for your servants according to whatever you say. For
you know there is none among us who has skill to
cut timber like the Sidonians. So it was, when Hiram
heard the words of Solomon, that he rejoiced greatly
and said, Blessed be the LORD this day, for He has
given David a wise son over this great people!

Solomon replied to Hiram by telling him that he desired to
build a house for the Lord. Hiram responded by honoring David
for raising such a wise son, and the two covenanted together to
build. Tyre, the city-state homeland of the Phoenicians, lay to the
north of Israel. It was a narrow sliver of seacoast situated between
the Lebanon Mountains, which run parallel to the Mediterranean
for 240 kilometers (150 miles). Rather than become isolated by the
strictures of its location, the Phoenicians put out to sea in merchant
ships. According to author and historian Patricia Berlyn:

The wares the Phoenicians produced and sold were luxury goods for rich customers, among them the splendid cedars of Lebanon that far-off kings sought for their palaces and temples. They also long held a virtual monopoly on making purple dyes, an industry prodigiously profitable, for the wearing of purple was held to confer such dignity that it is even today the royal color. The Phoenicians were resourceful and successful, but Plutarch describes them as "a grim people, averse to good humor." Homer deems them to be master mariners but greedy and tricky.[56]

One day, King Hiram of Tyre looked around and realized that the upstart shepherd of Israel was flourishing. David had been crowned king and established his headquarters in the city of Jerusalem. Second Samuel 5:9–12 (NLT) relates:

> So David made the fortress his home, and he called it the City of David. He extended the city, starting at the supporting terraces and working inward. And David became more and more powerful, because the LORD God of Heaven's Armies was with him. Then King Hiram of Tyre sent messengers to David, along with cedar timber and carpenters and stonemasons, and they built David a palace. And David realized that the LORD had confirmed him as king over Israel and had blessed his kingdom for the sake of his people Israel.

The two leaders quickly established a symbiotic relationship—David was the warrior king, gifted in battling the enemies of Israel;

Hiram's expertise was in naval dominance. The two rulers were harmonious rather than hostile. Hiram's contribution would be in the area of construction and technological expertise unknown to the bucolic Israelites. Plans for a temple to house the symbol of the presence of God in Jerusalem were an opportunity for the two men, and later Solomon, to become comrades, confederates, and quite possibly related at some point. (According to other Phoenician historians {quoted by Tatian, "Contra Græcos," § 37}, Hiram gave his daughter in marriage to Solomon.[57])

After David's death, Solomon reached out to Hiram for help with the temple architecture as we see in 1 Kings 5:6–9:

> "So give orders that cedars of Lebanon be cut for me. My men will work with yours, and I will pay you for your men whatever wages you set. You know that we have no one so skilled in felling timber as the Sidonians." When Hiram heard Solomon's message, he was greatly pleased and said, "Praise be to the LORD today, for he has given David a wise son to rule over this great nation." So Hiram sent word to Solomon: "I have received the message you sent me and will do all you want in providing the cedar and juniper logs. My men will haul them down from Lebanon to the Mediterranean Sea, and I will float them as rafts by sea to the place you specify. There I will separate them and you can take them away. And you are to grant my wish by providing food for my royal household."

So began the flotilla of cedars launched in Tyre and taken ashore by the Israelites, and vessels laden with grains, wine, and olive oil were sent to the Phoenicians. Hiram also provided a skilled artist, a man who also bore the name Hiram (see 1 Kings 7) to ply his artistry in the erection of the temple:

> King Solomon sent to Tyre and brought Huram, whose mother was a widow from the tribe of Naphtali and whose father was from Tyre and a skilled crafts-man in bronze. Huram was filled with wisdom, with understanding and with knowledge to do all kinds of bronze work. He came to King Solomon and did all the work assigned to him. (1 Kings 7:13–14)

The interpretive design of the temple furnishings bore a decid-edly more Phoenician style than had Moses' wilderness tabernacle. With Hiram's assistance, Solomon tapped the vast supplies of gold from Ophir, a highly sought pure product mentioned by Isaiah in chapter 13, verse 12, "I will make people scarcer than pure gold, more rare than the gold of Ophir."

The alliance between Solomon and Hiram would eventually lead to a cursed marriage between Ahab, the ruler of Israel after the death of Solomon, and Jezebel, a Phoenician worshiper of Baal—altogether a match made in the fiery regions of hell. Even as the sins of these two wanton individuals set the pace for the destruction of Israel, so would the sins of the people bring about the destruction of the once-glorious temple.

LAND *for the* TEMPLE:
ARANUAH'S THRESHING FLOOR

The land on which the temple was built was purchased by David at a dire moment in Israel's history. In 2 Samuel 24, we read that King David made a disastrous decision to take a census of the men in Israel. Although he had studied the proper etiquette for transporting the ark back to Jerusalem, David failed God's instructions in Exodus 30:11–16 (NLT):

> Then the LORD said to Moses, "Whenever you take a census of the people of Israel, each man who is counted must pay a ransom for himself to the LORD. Then no plague will strike the people as you count them. Each person who is counted must give a small piece of silver as a sacred offering to the LORD. (This payment is half a shekel, based on the sanctuary shekel, which equals twenty gerahs.) All who have reached their twentieth birthday must give this sacred offering to the LORD. When this offering is given to the LORD to purify your lives, making you right with

him, the rich must not give more than the specified
amount, and the poor must not give less. Receive this
ransom money from the Israelites, and use it for the
care of the Tabernacle. It will bring the Israelites to
the LORD's attention, and it will purify your lives."

What prompted David to defy Jehovah's commands? The answer
is found in 1 Chronicles 21:1, "Satan rose up against Israel and incited
David to take a census of Israel." Israel's king was about to discover
that the true Monarch, the Righteous Ruler of the people, was El
Elyon—the Most High God. He alone claimed ownership of the children of Israel; He alone had the authority to number His people. Only
Jehovah could issue the command to institute a census, and if done
by anyone else, it should follow the prescribed protocol.

Joab, David's nephew and commander of the armies of Israel,
fearlessly objected to the king's move:

"May the LORD your God multiply the troops a
hundred times over, and may the eyes of my lord the
king see it. But why does my lord the king want to do
such a thing?" (2 Samuel 24:3)

David had enjoyed peace in the kingdom during his reign. Did
he want to know if his army was large enough to repel any invasion?
Had he given thought to what Jehovah required of him? Or was ego-
driven pride behind David's desire to number the people? Dr. John
Maxwell wrote, "'Bad pride' is the deadly sin of superiority that reeks
of conceit and arrogance."[58]

For "nine months and twenty days" (see 2 Samuel 24:8), Joab
followed the king's edict to number the people. He then returned to
Jerusalem and presented the figures to David. His announcement

was followed almost immediately by David's conviction. He knew he had sinned against Jehovah:

David was conscience-stricken after he had counted the fighting men, and he said to the LORD, "I have sinned greatly in what I have done. Now, LORD, I beg you, take away the guilt of your servant. I have done a very foolish thing." (2 Samuel 24:10)

Even as the king arose the following morning, the prophet, Gad, was receiving a word from the Lord to deliver to David:

> "Go and tell David, 'This is what the LORD says: I am giving you three options. Choose one of them for me to carry out against you.'" So Gad went to David and said to him, "Shall there come on you three years of famine in your land? Or three months of fleeing from your enemies while they pursue you? Or three days of plague in your land? Now then, think it over and decide how I should answer the one who sent me." (vv. 12–13)

God gave David three choices:

- ✧ Dearth—seven long years of famine, of dependence on others for provisions;

- ✧ Discord—three months at the hands of his enemies, the nations that abhorred Israel;

- ✧ Disease—three days in the hands of Jehovah.

David chose to throw himself on the mercy of God. In verse 14, he responds to Gad's message, "Let us fall into the hands of the LORD, for his mercy is great; but do not let me fall into human hands." The king knew that under God's judgment even he and his family were at risk. He also realized that Jehovah was infinitely more merciful than man. David knew that Psalm 84:11 (NKJV) was true that "The Lord will give grace and glory."

Theologian G. Campbell Morgan wrote of David's decision:

> David's choice of his punishment once more revealed his recognition both of the righteousness and tenderness of Jehovah. He willed that the stroke which was to fall, should come directly from the divine hand rather than through any intermediary.[59]

With David's selection, a great tragedy struck the heart of the nation. Plague claimed the lives of 70,000 inhabitants. As the angel of the Lord reached the threshing floor of Araunah, the Jebusite, near the city of Jerusalem, the Lord said, "It is enough!" He stayed the hand of His emissary. That same day, Gad came to David to deliver further instructions from Jehovah. David was to build an altar at Araunah's threshing floor on Mount Moriah and offer a sacrifice to the Lord. It was there that David met the angel of death and would now worship. It was the same mountain where one thousand years earlier, Abraham had been sent to offer his only son, Isaac, and it was there that Solomon would build the temple.

At Araunah's threshing floor, the wheat was divided from the chaff and the faithful were separated from the fickle. Its owner offered the site to David:

> "Let my lord the king take whatever he wishes and offer it up. Here are oxen for the burnt offering, and here are threshing sledges and ox yokes for the wood.

Your Majesty, Araunah gives all this to the king." (2 Samuel 24:22–23)

Realizing the sanctity of the locale and the price that had been exacted for his rebellion, David declined the generous offer:

> "No, I insist on paying you for it. I will not sacrifice to the LORD my God burnt offerings that cost me nothing." So David bought the threshing floor and the oxen and paid fifty shekels of silver for them. David built an altar to the LORD there and sacrificed burnt offerings and fellowship offerings. Then the LORD answered his prayer in behalf of the land, and the plague on Israel was stopped. (vv. 24–25)

David realized he could not offer a sacrifice that had cost him nothing—such was the nature of a ransom. Not only did he offer a burnt offering for his sin, he offered a peace offering, a sign of fellowship with Jehovah. First Chronicles 21:26 shows us God's response to David's sacrifice: "The LORD answered him with fire from heaven on the altar of burnt offering."

Author and pastor, Dr. Charles Swindoll, wrote of David's dilemma and its resolution:

1. To live an unaccountable life is to flirt with danger. Accountability is one of the things God uses to keep His people pure. We all need to be held accountable by someone. Had David listened to Joab he would never have numbered the people . . . or been the cause of such devastation. To ignore accountability is to flirt with danger.

2. To ignore sin's consequences is to reject God's
   truth . . . . Sin is really a selfish act. It's all about
   bringing ourselves pleasure, caring little about the
   toll it will take on someone else.

3. To fail to take God seriously is to deny His lordship
   . . . it is tempting to go too far and take the edge off
   His holiness . . . when it comes to God, we need to
   take Him *very* seriously, not play games with Him
   . . . . If asked what one thing [David] would want us
   to remember, I think he would mention this segment from his own experience and warn against
   falling under the subtle spell of pride.[60]

When 2 Samuel 24 opens, David is focused on self and ego; when it
closes, his eyes and heart are centered solely on God. Satisfying David's
wants had taken a backseat to serving God and making Him the pri-
ority in his life. Moments before, David had been a totally broken man.
How do we know this? He cried out to God:

> "Was it not I who ordered the fighting men to be
> counted? I, the shepherd, have sinned and done wrong.
> These are but sheep. What have they done? LORD my
> God, let your hand fall on me and my family, but do not
> let this plague remain on your people." (1 Chronicles
> 21:17)

The king was broken, bowed low in abject repentance and humili-
ation, acknowledging the holiness of Jehovah. David, the man after
God's own heart, then offered praise to Jehovah God and had been
restored and renewed.

15

PLANNING, PREPARATION,
and PRESENTATION

K ing David's dream was to build a permanent resting place for the ark of the covenant in Jerusalem, but he had been banned from building the temple when the prophet Nathan delivered the following message from Jehovah:

> "When your days are over and you rest with your ancestors, I will raise up your offspring to succeed you, your own flesh and blood, and I will establish his kingdom. He is the one who will build a house for my Name, and I will establish the throne of his kingdom forever. I will be his father, and he will be my son. When he does wrong, I will punish him with a rod wielded by men, with floggings inflicted by human hands. But my love will never be taken away from him, as I took it away from Saul, whom I removed from before you. Your house and your kingdom will endure forever before me; your throne will be established forever." (2 Samuel 7:12–16)

During the last days of his life David began to gather workers and materials for the temple:

> So David gave orders to assemble the foreigners residing in Israel, and from among them he appointed stonecutters to prepare dressed stone for building the house of God. He provided a large amount of iron to make nails for the doors of the gateways and for the fittings, and more bronze than could be weighed. He also provided more cedar logs than could be counted, for the Sidonians and Tyrians had brought large numbers of them to David. (1 Chronicles 22:2–4)

David enlisted approximately 70,000 men to cut the massive stones that would be used for the foundation of the temple and to forge the iron nails for the gates. He stockpiled bronze, and from Lebanon, cedar in massive quantities. He desired only the best for the house of God. David had come to terms with the truth that he would not be the one to fulfill his dream to build the edifice in Jerusalem.

The late Teddy Kollek, former mayor of Jerusalem, and Moshe Pearlman wrote of King David:

> David emerges from the biblical record as a very human individual, with human foibles and weaknesses. We see him in temptation and in penitence, in grief and in ecstatic joy as he dances in front of the ark. He is the self-made man, rough, rugged, volatile.[61]

As former Michigan governor Jennifer Granholm said, "Sometimes leadership is planting trees under whose shade you'll never sit."[62] David was well aware he would never enter the temple courtyard; he would never offer a sacrifice to Jehovah; he would never see the temple dedicated. His love for Jehovah overshadowed his disappointment, and rather than pout and shout about his loss of opportunity, David accepted the Lord's decision and set to work.

Can you visualize the father and son, David and Solomon, standing side by side and intensely studying the design for the temple? The father is pointing out the plans that Jehovah had entrusted to him, the young man absorbing the contents. David said to his son:

> "Now, my son, the LORD be with you, and may you have success and build the house of the LORD your God, as he said you would. May the LORD give you discretion and understanding when he puts you in command over Israel, so that you may keep the law of the LORD your God. Then you will have success if you are careful to observe the decrees and laws that the LORD gave Moses for Israel. Be strong and courageous. Do not be afraid or discouraged. I have taken great pains to provide for the temple of the LORD a hundred thousand talents of gold, a million talents of silver, quantities of bronze and iron too great to be weighed, and wood and stone. And you may add to them. You have many workers: stonecutters, masons and carpenters, as well as those skilled in every kind of work in gold and silver, bronze and iron—craftsmen beyond number. Now begin the work, and the LORD be with you." (1 Chronicles 22:11–16)

The vision and the mantle were passed from king to prince, and Solomon assumed the sacred responsibility to fulfill David's dream. This was to be Solomon's legacy, his paramount achievement. The magnitude of the promise of God was this miraculous promise: If Solomon was obedient and put God first, Jehovah would take care of him and the people of Israel.

Rev. Charles Spurgeon said of David's charge to Solomon:

> I revere the man who, in his old age, when there is weight in every syllable that he utters, concludes his life by urging others to carry on the work of Christ. It is something to gather about your last bed young men who have years of usefulness before them, and to lay upon their consciousness and their heart the duty of preaching Christ crucified, and winning the souls of men for the Lord.[63]

It is amazing that David did so much of the work—from planning to provision—and yet the temple is never referred to as "David's Temple." It speaks to the king being a "man after God's own heart" that he allowed Solomon to receive the recognition for the work. Spurgeon continued:

> It is well to have an ambition not to build upon another man's foundation; but do not carry that idea too far. If there is a good foundation laid by another man, and you can finish the structure, be thankful that he has done his part, and rejoice that you are permitted to carry on his work. It is God's way of striking a blow at your personal pride by allowing one man's work to fit on to another's.[64]

David did not stop with his instructions to Solomon; he also charged the elders and leaders of the land to assist his son with the overwhelming task at hand:

"Is not the LORD your God with you? And has he not granted you rest on every side? For he has given the inhabitants of the land into my hands, and the land is subject to the LORD and to his people. Now devote your heart and soul to seeking the LORD your God. Begin to build the sanctuary of the LORD God, so that you may bring the ark of the covenant of the LORD and the sacred articles belonging to God into the temple that will be built for the Name of the LORD." (1 Chronicles 22:18–19)

David would be a hard act to follow, yet Solomon had been given every advantage in order to succeed: Jehovah had promised favor; the country was at peace; Solomon had asked for and been granted wisdom with which to rule the people. His charge was to be a faithful and obedient servant of God. From David, Solomon had been taught commitment and enthusiasm. At the inauguration of the late president John F. Kennedy, the newly elected leader said:

Let the word go forth from this time and place, to friend and foe alike, that the torch has been passed to a new generation of Americans—born in this century, tempered by war, disciplined by a hard and bitter peace, proud of our ancient heritage . . . United, there is little we cannot do in a host of cooperative ventures. Divided, there is little we can do—for we dare not meet a powerful challenge at odds and split asunder.[65]

The Israelites were to devote themselves totally to serving Jehovah, to following His precepts and edicts. The temple built in Jerusalem would be vastly different from every other edifice in the land—it would house no idol. It would hold only the ark of the covenant in the Holy of Holies. Isaiah the prophet challenged Israel with these words from Jehovah:

> "Heaven is my throne, and the earth is my footstool. Where is the house you will build for me? Where will my resting place be? Has not my hand made all these things, and so they came into being?" (Isaiah 66:1–2)

It must have been difficult for Solomon to follow in his father's footsteps, yet for a time he was on a par with him. While David was a warrior king, Solomon (whose name means "His peace") was endowed by God with great wisdom. As Kollek and Pearlman wrote:

> David emerges from the biblical record as a very human individual, with human foibles and weak- nesses .... Solomon is the suave heir, aloof, sophis- ticated, viewed always through his majesty and grandeur.[66]

David inspired Solomon with optimism, enthusiasm, and dedi- cation so that he was prepared to build the temple.

Then David rested with his ancestors and was buried in the City of David. He had reigned forty years over Israel—seven years in Hebron and thirty-three in Jerusalem. So Solomon sat on the throne of his father David, and his rule was firmly established. (1 Kings 2:10–12)

16

SOLOMON'S TEMPLE

I n the thirteenth century BCE, the children of Israel entered the Promised Land. For the next four centuries they went about the work of setting boundaries, subduing enemies, and waiting for the God-appointed men who would accomplish His purposes—Saul, David, and finally Solomon. Not until then could the temple be erected in the heart of Jerusalem. In 1 Kings 6:1, we read:

> In the four hundred and eightieth year after the Israelites came out of Egypt, in the fourth year of Solomon's reign over Israel, in the month of Ziv, the second month, he began to build the temple of the LORD.

The construction was a massive undertaking. Solomon employed 80,000 stonemasons, 3,600 supervisory personnel, and 30,000 laborers conscripted from the twelve tribes.[67] Solomon engaged the progeny of a woman from the tribe of Dan and a man from Tyre. Huram-Abi, their son, was a brilliant craftsman who, according to 2 Chronicles 2:14, was "trained to work in gold and silver, bronze and iron, stone and wood, and with purple and blue and crimson yarn and fine linen. He is experienced in all kinds of engraving and can execute any design given to him."

It is difficult to imagine a building being erected without the sound of hammer striking stone or nail. Jehovah wanted no reminders of the bloody battles of David's reign, the sounds of sword clashing with sword. Solomon was a ruler of peace, not of war, and it was he whom God had selected to oversee the construction.

In his book *Jerusalem: The Biography*, British journalist and historian Simon Sebag Montefiore wrote of the structure:

> There had to be silence in God's house ... His [Solomon's] Phoenician craftsmen dressed the stones, carved the cedar and cypress, and crafted the silver, bronze and gold decorations in Tyre before shipping them to Jerusalem. King Solomon fortified Mount Moriah by expanding the old walls: henceforth the name "Zion" described both the original citadel and the new Temple Mount.[68]

For seven (the biblical number of completion) long years, the work was diligently undertaken day after day. The huge stones that defy description were chiseled out of the quarries and prepared before transportation to the building site. In *Come Before Winter and Share My Hope*, Dr. Charles Swindoll wrote of Solomon's work:

> And the temple that Solomon had built? One of the famed wonders of the world! First Kings chapter 6 will blow your mind. Artistic frames for the windows. Beams and timbers—in fact, "the whole house"—overlaid with gold. Stones quarried to such

a precise size they slipped into place on site. In fact, while the temple was being built, no sound of a hammer or ax or any other iron tool was heard in the place (I Kings 6:7). Wall beams were dovetailed and "inserted" together, and each piece of furniture was a choice carving, a dazzling and unduplicated work of original art.

Why not? God's reputation was at stake. God's name was on display.[69]

The Jerusalem's Insider's Guide website describes the majesty of the temple construction:

The dimensions for the Temple of Jerusalem were staggering: 460 meters to the east, 315 m to the north, 280 m to the south, and the western wall was 485 meters long. The walls above ground rose 30 meters (ten stories tall), and their foundations were as deep as 20 meters in some places in order to reach bedrock. Each layer of the wall was recessed about 3 centimeters from the layer beneath it. This was to avoid the optical illusion created whenever you look up a tall, straight object, that it is about to fall over you. Some of the quarried stones used in the Western Wall are so large that, to this day, archaeologists have trouble understanding how they could possibly have been transported. The smallest stones weight between 2 to 5 tons and the largest stone of them all— possibly the largest building stone in antiquity— is 13.6 meters long, 4.6 meters thick and 3.3 meters high, and is estimated to weigh 570 tons. The builders used dry construction— there is no cement between the stones. In fact, there's nothing holding the stones together except their own weight.[70]

The one feature of the temple that caused such awe was its magnificent furnishings set in an interior overlaid with pure gold. Its architects were on loan from King Hiram of Tyre, therefore the design was typically Phoenician. The design of the Holy of Holies and the mercy seat—the throne of Jehovah—were borrowed from the tabernacle. The portico of the structure held two columns that bordered the entrance into the Holy Place. Rabbi Emeritus of the Great Synagogue in Sydney, Australia, Dr. Raymond Apple gives more insight into the columns:

> The Bible deals with the pillars in three main passages: I Kings 7:15-22, 41-42 (cf. II Kings 25:17); II Chronicles 3:17; and Jeremiah 52:20-23. The version in I Kings reads, "He [Hiram] set up the columns at the portico of the Great Hall; he set up one column on the right and named it Jachin, and he set up the other column on the left and named it Boaz. Upon the top of the columns there was a lily design. Thus the work of the columns was completed" (verses 21-22). The text in II Chronicles states: "He erected the columns in front of the Great Hall, one to its right and one to its left; the one to the right was called Jachin, and the one to the left, Boaz" .... Jewish commentators tend to treat both the pillars themselves and their duality as symbols .... Suggestions include the notion that they represent two trees of life; the pillars of cloud and fire in the wilderness; the two *keruvim* (cherubs)

in the Sanctuary; ... the two eyes placed high above in the human body; or the two copper mountains (Zion and Scopus) from which Divine judgment goes forth (Zech. 6:1).[71]

The hollow pillars of bronze stood twenty-seven feet tall and each held a decorative capital described in 1 Kings 7:17–20:

A network of interwoven chains adorned the capitals on top of the pillars, seven for each capital. He made pomegranates in two rows encircling each network to decorate the capitals on top of the pillars. He did the same for each capital. The capitals on top of the pillars in the portico were in the shape of lilies, four cubits high [about 6 feet]. On the capitals of both pillars, above the bowl-shaped part next to the network, were the two hundred pomegranates in rows all around.

As with the tabernacle, the temple was divided into three distinct sections: the courtyard, the Holy Place, and the Holy of Holies—which was completely secreted from prying eyes. It could only be accessed by the high priest. Sitting directly before the entrance to the temple was the brazen altar. It would have dwarfed the altar made by Moses' artisans for the tabernacle courtyard, as it stood fifteen feet high with steps leading up to the place of sacrifice. The first altar was only four and a half feet high and required no steps. Randall Price, author of *Rose Guide to the Temple*, explains that the entire altar was most assuredly not made completely of bronze, "particularly the steps which the priests would have had to climb barefoot in the hot sun."[72]

The laver of the tabernacle used for ritual bathing was replaced by a "Molten Sea" placed near the bronze altar in the temple courtyard. Its circumference was 45 feet with a height of 7.5 feet and a thickness of 3 inches. The large cast metal bowl held about 11,000 gallons of water.[73] Second Chronicles 4:2–3 describes the temple laver:

> He made the Sea of cast metal, circular in shape, measuring ten cubits [fifteen feet] from rim to rim and five cubits high. It took a line of thirty cubits to measure around it. Below the rim, figures of bulls encircled it—ten to a cubit. The bulls were cast in two rows in one piece with the Sea.

The Molten Sea was flanked on two sides by ten basins of bronze—five to the north side and five to the south. They were used for the washing of various sacrifices. The basins were set on wheeled carts and were used to move water from place to place. Also prepared for the priests to offer daily sacrifices were the necessary "pots, shovels, and sprinkling bowls" (1 Kings 7:45).

While the accoutrements were being prepared for the courtyard, artisans were busy working on the interior furnishings of the temple:

> The golden altar; the golden table on which was the bread of the Presence; the lampstands of pure gold (five on the right and five on the left, in front of the inner sanctuary); the gold floral work and lamps and tongs; the pure gold basins, wick trimmers, sprinkling bowls, dishes and censers; and the gold sockets for the doors of the innermost room, the Most Holy

Place, and also for the doors of the main hall of the
temple. (1 Kings 7:48–50)

While the tabernacle held one golden lampstand, Solomon outfitted the temple with ten lampstands, which stood within the gold-
overlaid cedar panels that formed the Holy Place. Again, they sat five
on the north and five on the south sides of the room (2 Chronicles
4:8). Each of the ten tables of the bread of the Presence sat alongside the lampstands and held the shewbread formed from the finest
of flours. One hundred sprinkling bowls were divided among the
tables, along with other dishes of pure gold that were used in service
to Jehovah.

The altar of incense, also covered with pure gold, held a prominent place in the room. On it special incense was burned as a savor
to the Lord Most High. It was outfitted with ten gold censers used by
the high priest when he entered the Holy of Holies during the Day of
Atonement (Yom Kippur).

Separating the Holy Place from the Holy of Holies was the
temple veil, a replica of the one in the tabernacle. Second Chronicles
3:14 is the only description provided by scripture: "He made the curtain of blue, purple and crimson yarn and fine linen, with cherubim
worked into it."

The Holy of Holies was a perfectly fashioned cube measuring
about thirty feet on all sides. Within the room sat a platform covering the Foundation Stone atop Mount Moriah. It is believed to
have been the site where Adam was formed by the Creator, and atop
that dais rested the ark. On either side of the ark rested two long,
golden poles used by the high priest to guide his way to the mercy
seat. Overshadowing the holy symbol of God's presence with Israel
were two cherubim that stood fifteen feet tall. Made of olive wood,

the two angels were covered with pure gold. What a magnificent sight that must have been to see the golden sculptures spanning the interior of the Holy of Holies and standing guard over the ark! Just as God was dominant in the garden of Eden, in the tabernacle, in David's tent, and now in the temple, the ark of the covenant was the dominant furnishing. First Kings 8:9 discloses that the only relic remaining in the ark when it was transported into the gilded room was "two stone tablets that Moses had placed in it at Horeb, where the LORD made a covenant with the Israelites after they came out of Egypt."

The ultimate purpose of the temple is revealed in Isaiah 56:6b–7:

> ". . . all who keep the Sabbath without desecrating it and who hold fast to my covenant—these I will bring to my holy mountain and give them joy in my house of prayer. Their burnt offerings and sacrifices will be accepted on my altar; for my house will be called a house of prayer for all nations."

A house of prayer: This designation was reiterated by Jesus in Matthew 21:13: "My house will be called a house of prayer." The temple was also to be the place where Jehovah heard the cries of His people, as we read in 1 Kings 8:28–30:

> "Yet give attention to your servant's prayer and his plea for mercy, LORD my God. Hear the cry and the prayer that your servant is praying in your presence this day. May your eyes be open toward this temple night and day, this place of which you said, 'My Name shall be there,' so that you will hear the prayer your servant prays toward this place. Hear the

supplication of your servant and of your people Israel
when they pray toward this place. Hear from heaven,
your dwelling place, and when you hear, forgive."

First Kings 8:41–43 tells us the temple was to be a safe haven for
Jews and strangers alike:

> "As for the foreigner who does not belong to your
> people Israel but has come from a distant land because
> of your name—for they will hear of your great name
> and your mighty hand and your outstretched arm—
> when they come and pray toward this temple, then
> hear from heaven, your dwelling place. Do whatever
> the foreigner asks of you, so that all the peoples of the
> earth may know your name and fear you, as do your
> own people Israel, and may know that this house I
> have built bears your Name."

Even though El Elyon could not be contained in a mere building,
yet as a symbol of God's presence with His people, Israel, the temple
stood in all the earthly magnificence that could be summoned. It
was made of the best materials that could be found and would be a
constant reminder the of Jehovah-'Immeku—the Lord Who is with
You. It symbolized another promise that Jehovah, "has given rest to
his people Israel just as he promised" (1 Kings 8:56).

Perhaps the psalmist best described the purpose of the temple
in chapter 132, verses 13–14:

> For the LORD has chosen Zion, he has desired it
> for his dwelling, saying, "This is my resting place for
> ever and ever; here I will sit enthroned, for I have
> desired it."

17

DEDICATION

The dedication of a building or the launching of a ship is always a great occasion. Dignitaries assemble and deliver hyperbole-filled speeches. Champagne flows; food is consumed; and millions of dollars can sometimes be spent just on the celebration surrounding the event. It matters little to those who erected the building or built the ship whether anyone approves of their efforts. This was not the case with King Solomon; he desired not the approval of the people, but the blessing of Jehovah.

The building rising from the top of Mount Moriah was not just an ordinary house; it was *God's* house. It was the site from which sacrifices would be made; the covering for the ark of the covenant that would rest inside the Holy of Holies. This was the place where God would communicate with man. It was the temple, and Solomon wanted to know that God was pleased with his efforts.

The king sent out invitations to all the elders of Israel—the statesmen, heads of tribes, and family patriarchs. Once assembled, he called for the Levites. Gently, reverently, they prepared the ark of the covenant according to Mosaic law and then transported it to the new edifice. All things were in readiness—ten golden candlesticks each with seven lighted candles, the table of shewbread laden with the loaves prepared for the occasion, each of the golden utensils lovingly sculpted and set in their respective places ready for use. The treasuries were overflowing with riches from the tabernacle and from King David's coffers.

Carefully, the Levites bore the most treasured possession of all into the Holy of Holies and rested it between the wings of the two golden cherubim. First Kings 8:10–11 gives us a dramatic picture of Jehovah's response when the ark reached its new resting place:

> When the priests withdrew from the Holy Place, the cloud filled the temple of the LORD. And the priests could not perform their service because of the cloud, for the glory of the LORD filled his temple.

Outside in the temple courtyard could be heard the lowing of cattle and oxen, the bleating of sheep and goats, and the cooing of doves brought to Jerusalem for the multitude of sacrifices that were taking place. Priests in white linen filed from the Holy Place just inside the temple doors. They joined musicians, also clad in white linen, as the trumpets began to resound. Soon they were accompanied by cymbals, harps, and psalteries as the assembled choir began to sing what could have been Psalm 136 (KJV):

> O give thanks unto the LORD; for he is good: for his mercy endureth for ever. O give thanks unto the God of gods: for his mercy endureth for ever. O give thanks to the Lord of lords: for his mercy endureth for ever. (See entire psalm.)

As the voices rose toward the heavens, something inexplicable happened—the *shekinah* glory of God Almighty settled on the mountaintop and filled the temple so that the priests were unable to perform their duties. All came to a standstill. Instruments were silenced; the people fell prostrate to the ground in overpowering awe. Only when God fills the house can there be such unity, such accord.

Solomon mounted a small platform and addressed the people, and then he dropped to his knees, stretched his hands heavenward, and began to invoke a prayer perhaps unequaled in all the Old Testament. Beginning in 1 Kings 8:23, he addressed the prayer to Jehovah:

> "LORD, the God of Israel, there is no God like you in heaven above or on earth below—you who keep your covenant of love with your servants who continue wholeheartedly in your way."

Solomon then reminded God of His promises to "your servant David," and asked for fulfillment of these assurances. On his face before Jehovah, the earthly king asked the King of Kings to

> "Hear the cry and the prayer that your servant is praying in your presence this day. May your eyes be open toward this temple night and day, this place of which you said, 'My Name shall be there,' so that you will hear the prayer your servant prays toward this place. Hear the supplication of your servant and of your people Israel when they pray toward this place. Hear from heaven, your dwelling place, and when you hear, forgive." (vv. 28–30)

Solomon petitioned for all who would need help from Jehovah, and ended his prayer with:

"May your eyes be open to your servant's plea and
to the plea of your people Israel, and may you listen to
them whenever they cry out to you. For you singled
them out from all the nations of the world to be your
own inheritance, just as you declared through your
servant Moses when you, Sovereign LORD, brought
our ancestors out of Egypt." (vv. 52–53)

Then Solomon blessed the people who had assembled and wit-
nessed the glory of God in that place. He challenged them to know
that there was no other like Jehovah and to walk in obedience, faithfulness, and commitment to Him.

The altar was laden with sacrificial animals prepared for the
dedication. When Solomon ended his petition to the God of glory,
fire fell from heaven and consumed the offerings, and once again the
shekinah glory of God filled the sanctuary.

Dr. Bob Deffinbaugh made several annotations regarding
Solomon's magnificent prayer:

- ✧ The petition was predominately Solomon's
  prayer of dedication (1 Kings 8:10–11, 23).

- ✧ The prayer and the Mosaic Covenant were
  closely related. (See Deuteronomy 28.)

- ✧ The passage in 1 Kings 8 is not just *a* prayer;
  it is *about* prayer, a word or its derivative
  mentioned seventeen times in that portion of
  scripture.

- ✧ God's covenant promises to Moses are strongly
  emphasized in 1 Kings 8:56.

✧ There is a convincing feeling of anticipation in this prayer of dedication that God will totally fulfill His covenant with David (1 Kings 8:26).

✧ Solomon reiterates that God cannot and will not be contained within a building—not even the Temple built to honor His Name (1 Kings 8:27).[74]

One night after the temple dedication, Solomon retired to his chambers and the Lord appeared to him to put His final stamp on the king's efforts. Jehovah assured Solomon, "I have heard your prayer and have chosen this place for myself as a temple for sacrifices" (2 Chronicles 7:12). In one of the most oft-quoted verses of scripture, God encouraged Solomon that should the people sin against Him, there was hope:

"If my people, who are called by my name, will humble themselves and pray and seek my face and turn from their wicked ways, then I will hear from heaven, and I will forgive their sin and will heal their land." (2 Chronicles 7:14)

God had given Solomon the recipe for revival and the results, and that still holds true today.

This, too, is a beautiful picture of what can transpire when God's people are in one accord. The apostle Paul wrote to the Philippians in chapter 2, verses 1–2 (NLT):

Is there any encouragement from belonging to Christ? Any comfort from his love? Any fellow-ship together in the Spirit? Are your hearts tender and compassionate? Then make me truly happy by agreeing wholeheartedly with each other, loving one another, and working together with one mind and purpose.

There is great truth in a sermon preached by Pastor Phil Christensen while worship minister at Stonebridge Church in Cedar Rapids, Iowa:

> If under the old covenant: it was possible for a building of stone, the blood of animals and the singing of David's prayers to usher in the presence of God … if that was possible … Then what might happen when human temples, washed by the Blood of the Son of God, gather in unity?[75]

18

PRIESTS

The duties of the priests in the temple were identical to those of the Levites who served in Moses' tabernacle. Their main duties were to act as liaison between God and man and to protect the holiness of the temple. The principal function of the priests who served in the temple was to oversee sacrifices and offerings. Daily in the temple, the priest on duty was to deliver what has become known as the Aaronic blessing from Numbers 6:22–26, at the close of the morning observance:

> "The LORD bless you and keep you; the LORD make
> his face shine on you and be gracious to you; the LORD
> turn his face toward you and give you peace."

This blessing was prayed daily at the close of the morning observance by the officiating priest. As representatives of Jehovah, the priests were to exhibit compassion, consideration, and care for all the people of Israel. The priests who served in the temple complex were Levites, but not all men of the tribe of Levi were designated as priests—only those who were direct descendants of Aaron:

These are the names of the sons of Aaron: Nadab the firstborn, and Abihu, Eleazar, and Ithamar. These are the names of the sons of Aaron, the anointed priests, whom he ordained to serve as priests. But Nadab and Abihu died before the LORD when they offered unauthorized fire before the LORD in the wilderness of Sinai, and they had no children. So Eleazar and Ithamar served as priests in the lifetime of Aaron their father. (Numbers 3:2–4 ESV)

The Levitical tribe was comprised of three groups based on the descendants of Aaron: Gershonites, Merarites, and Kohathites. The priests were divided into twenty-four clans with various responsibilities ascribed to each. Those who were not of Aaron's line served as helpers, i.e., preparing the offerings, keeping the temple clean, and making necessary repairs. They also served as doorkeepers in the house of the Lord. Biblical History Online defines the role of "doorkeeper":

They guarded the gates of the house of Yahweh [1 Chronicles 9:23], closing and opening them at the proper times [1 Chronicles 9:27] and preventing the unclean from entering the sacred enclosure [2 Chronicles 23:19]; they had charge of the sacred vessels and of the free-will offerings [2 Chronicles 31:14], and dwelt in the chambers about the temple [1 Chronicles 9:27]. They were Levites, and came in from the Levitical villages every seventh day for service in their turn [1 Chronicles 9:25]. Their office was honorable, ranking with the singers, after the priests and Levites [Ezra 2:42; 1 Chronicles 15:18].[76]

It was the psalmist who wrote, "Better is one day in your courts than a thousand elsewhere; I would rather be a doorkeeper in the house of my God than dwell in the tents of the wicked" (Psalm 84:10.) These men were also the *hazzan* or cantors, and musicians. The priests were charged with keeping the wicks trimmed on the lamps and making sure the reservoirs were filled to capacity. Each week the priests ate the bread of the presence in the Holy Place and then laid out fresh bread on Shabbat.

Priests were introduced to tabernacle service at the age of twenty-five (changed to twenty when David became king). A segment of the *Frontline* program on PBS described one High Holy Day—Passover—and the grueling work of the priests:

> Big holidays always draw crowds .... the Temple itself was a focus of ferocious activity. The requirement of Passover was that the Passover lamb be sacrificed. There was a census reported in Jospehus in which tens of thousands of lambs were slaughtered. And it all has to be done in at a particular period just on the cusp of the very beginning of the holiday .... The ultimate responsibility for making sure that things were done correctly ... that the sheep themselves were perfect, ... that the Temple itself was ready and correct, to be a medium for this act of piety and religious enthusiasm, and to make sure that the slaughter of the animals was done correctly [fell to] the Priests .... It would be physically exhausting work. Made exhausting not for the least reason that most Jews had very strong opinions on whether the Priest was doing his business properly or not .... Sometimes reading

ancient sources is like overhearing family quarrels in
a distant room . . . I mean, people who weren't priests
at all would have absolutely firm opinions on how the
Priests should be doing their business. A Priest who
would be a member of a particular group, say a Priest
who had a Pharisaic orientation, might think something should be done one way, and a Priest who didn't
have that orientation would think it would be done
another way. Everybody is . . . on the basis of tradition and improvisation, doing what he thought was
the correct way to do it . . . .[77]

It is easy to understand why the priests were to retire when
they reached fifty, a number later amended to be determined by the
health of the individual.

Levites were charged with a myriad of other duties: teachers,
engravers, judges, and controllers of weights and measures. The
men were also responsible for enforcing the Levitical laws for cleanliness, which were numerous. These laws are not observed by the
general populace today, but could likely have helped prevent some of
the outbreaks of disease in centuries past.

In his book, *None of These Diseases,* Dr. S.I. McMillen wrote of
Viennese physician Dr. Ignaz Semmelweis, a proponent of hand-
washing in the 1840s. The doctor began to study the Mosaic Law for
clues to cleanliness and happened upon Numbers 19:11: "Whoever
touches a human corpse will be unclean for seven days." It was
one of the laws for which the Levites were responsible to enforce.
Why was it important then and conversely, why was it important in
the nineteenth century? Dr. Semmelweis linked the lack of hand-
washing to the skyrocketing deaths of women in labor to what

was called "labor fever." It was the "single most common cause of maternal mortality, accounting for about half of all deaths related to childbirth."[78] Semmelweis began to experiment with the simple act of washing one's hands following the autopsy of a cadaver. He believed that the disease was transmitted from the morgue on the hands of the physicians who were treating the women.

Dr. Semmelweis was castigated by his peers, ridiculed by those who took the oath to "first, do no harm," and banned by the hospitals that most needed his expertise. He chastised the doctors who refused to listen:

> Your teaching ... is based upon the dead bodies of new mothers slaughtered through ignorance. I denounce you before God and the world as a murderer....[79]

Dr. Semmelweis was placed in a sanatorium due to mental illness brought on by his failure to save the lives of countless victims of labor fever. He succumbed to blood poisoning and died in the mental institution. What good might have been done if his fellow physicians had but read the Levitical laws regarding handling of the dead and adhered to them!

The laws of cleanliness handed down from God through Moses had specific purposes. For example, leprosy was highly contagious, thus the necessity for separation from the general populace. It was the duty of the Levites to enforce that division. The punishment was, in fact, so harsh that a leper who wandered into the temple courtyard would be killed outside the camp. The same laws applied both to the worshipers and the priests.

The high priest was to be the earthly mediator between the Israelites and Jehovah. It was a position of the loftiest honor and his duties were sacred. On the Day of Atonement, he was to offer sacrifices for the sins of the people and make intercession before the mercy seat in the Holy of Holies. Routinely, he managed the other priests in their temple duties.

The garments donned by the high priest were very similar to those of Aaron during his lifetime:

- ✧ a tunic of white linen woven in one piece (Note: Could the seamlessly woven robe worn by Jesus at His crucifixion indicate His position as High Priest? Hebrews 4:14, says, "Therefore, since we have a great high priest who has ascended into heaven, Jesus the Son of God, let us hold firmly to the faith we profess.");

- ✧ a robe of dark blue, the hem decorated with purple, scarlet, and blue pomegranates;

- ✧ an apron or ephod woven from threads of gold, blue, purple, and scarlet;

- ✧ a golden girdle tied around the waist;

- ✧ pouches containing twelve onyx stones engraved with the names of the tribes of Israel;

- ✧ a breastplate made of threads of gold, blue, purple, and scarlet linen containing four rows of three jewels. Each jewel in a gold setting was engraved with the name of one of the tribes. It was held in place with rings of gold attached to the shoulder of the ephod. A pocket made

into the breastplate contained the Urim and
Thummim.

✧ the high priest also wore a golden crown on
which was written "Holy to the Lord." Jesus,
our High Priest, had a crown of thorns placed
upon His head—a crown of suffering, a crown of
rejection. Now He sits on the right hand of God
crowned with glory and honor (see Hebrews
2:5–9).

On the Day of Atonement (Yom Kippur), the high priest was
charged predominately with ministering before Jehovah in the Holy
of Holies. It was the most sacred of all his obligations, for the three-
fold cleansing of the children of Israel rested upon his shoulders.
Perhaps he knew that he was the type, the shadow, of the Messiah
who was to come to redeem mankind from the burden of sin. As
Jehovah had prescribed in Leviticus 16:32–33 the offering on Yom
Kippur was made to bring purification, not only for the people, but
for the priest and his own family, as well as the temple in which the
ceremony was held. Moses was instructed that the high priest "is to
put on the sacred linen garments and make atonement for the Most
Holy Place."

Yom Kippur was the day dedicated to the contemplation of one's
sin. The people were to consider from what they had been delivered—the bondage of the Egyptians. On that day, the high priest
was to make the designated sacrifices—two goats and a ram for the
Israelites and a bull and ram for himself and his household. They
were to be without spot or blemish according to the Mosaic Law in
Leviticus 4. As part of the rite of humbling himself, the high priest

would then enter the Holy Place, where he would exchange his priestly robes for the simple linen garments of an ordinary priest.

To me, this is reminiscent of Christ laying aside His garments, donning a towel, and taking on the role of servant to wash the feet of His disciples. It also speaks of Philippians 2:5–8, which reads:

> In your relationships with one another, have the same mindset as Christ Jesus: Who, being in very nature God, did not consider equality with God something to be used to his own advantage; rather, he made himself nothing by taking the very nature of a servant, being made in human likeness. And being found in appearance as a man, he humbled himself by becoming obedient to death—even death on a cross!

The high priest was then required to painstakingly follow the rules laid down by Jehovah—on threat of death. He was to wash himself in the Molten Sea—the brass laver—before slitting the throat of the bullock in preparation to offer its blood in the Holy of Holies. He would then take up incense from the altar in his left hand, while with his right he lifted the censer of live coals. Entering the Holy of Holies, the high priest would set the censer down and take incense from the tray to sprinkle on the hot coals. The rising cloud was symbolic of the glory of God that had filled both the tabernacle and the temple when it was consecrated to Jehovah.

In Isaiah 6:6–7, the prophet was transported to the throne room of heaven, and there realized his inadequacy as a messenger. It is a beautiful picture of the substitutionary work that was to come in the person of Jesus Christ:

> Then one of the seraphim flew to me with a live
> coal in his hand, which he had taken with tongs from
> the altar. With it he touched my mouth and said, "See,
> this has touched your lips; your guilt is taken away
> and your sin atoned for."

Leaving the Holy of Holies, the high priest would take up a basin of blood from the bull and with his finger sprinkle it once eastward toward the mercy seat and the people who waited outside the temple, and seven times on the ark of the covenant. That ceremony was followed by the sacrifice of the goat after which the high priest would return to the Holy of Holies to sprinkle the blood of the goat in the same manner. The difference was the manner in which the goat sacrificed was chosen.

The high priest was responsible not only for choosing the goat that was to be sacrificed but also the one to be sent away into the desert. The two animals were brought, along with an urn containing two gold coins. On one coin was written "for the people" and on the other "azazel" meaning "to go away." The animals were placed at the left and right of the high priest and a coin was laid on the head of each. The one designated azazel had a red thread tied to its horn; the other was slain by the high priest. Once the blood of the first goat had been sprinkled in the Holy of Holies, the priest would exit into the Holy Place and anoint it as well.

David E. Lister of Moriel Ministries said of the two animals:

> Here . . . we see a picture of our Lord. In the bull
> it is the strong dying for the weak; in the goat we see
> the innocent dying for the guilty. While the two goats
> constitute one offering, I see two aspects: first with

the goat that "goes away" I see Barabbas or even me. Jesus took my sin; I got to go free. But I also see the good news: the sins of the people being carried away not to be seen again. "As far as the east is from the west, so far has He removed our transgressions from us." [Psalm 103:12] Oh what a wonderful picture of how Jesus would take our sin away![80]

The last act of the high priest on Yom Kippur was to replace the linen clothing with his robes of office. He would then return to the bronze altar and offer two sacrificial rams—one for himself and one for the people according to the Mosaic laws in Leviticus 4 and 8. The high priest was subject to death if he did not carry out his duties as instructed—an indication of the gravity of his charge. While this was being done, the people stood outside the temple waiting for the azazel to be released to carry their sins into the wilderness, not to be forgiven, but to be postponed for another year. They must have wondered: Had the offering been accepted? Was the high priest counted worthy to represent the people? Had he been slain by Jehovah in the Holy of Holies? Perhaps they listened closely for the tinkle of the bells on his robe that would indicate he had safely returned to the Holy Place.

Randall Price brought his perspective on the sacrifices when he wrote:

> This sacrificial system for Israel was not a permanent institution in God's plan for humanity. God provided a perfect and ultimate sacrifice in his Son, Jesus Christ. Jesus' death on the cross was a voluntary sacrifice to atone for sin.[81]

A look at Hebrews 7:23–28 gives us a picture of the perfect work of Jesus Christ on the cross:

> Now there have been many of those priests, since death prevented them from continuing in office; but because Jesus lives forever, he has a permanent priesthood. Therefore he is able to save completely those who come to God through him, because he always lives to intercede for them. Such a high priest truly meets our need—one who is holy, blameless, pure, set apart from sinners, exalted above the heavens. Unlike the other high priests, he does not need to offer sacrifices day after day, first for his own sins, and then for the sins of the people. He sacrificed for their sins once for all when he offered himself. For the law appoints as high priests men in all their weakness; but the oath, which came after the law, appointed the Son, who has been made perfect forever.

Author Warren Wiersbe offered this insight: "Another proof of Jesus' sinlessness is the fact that our Lord never had to offer sacrifices for His own cleansing, as did the priests." Jesus offered one sacrifice, Himself, and established the plan of forgiveness and reconciliation one time for all time!

> Redeemed, how I love to proclaim it!
> Redeemed by the blood of the Lamb;
> Redeemed through His infinite mercy,
> His child and forever I am.[82]

19

FEASTS:

PASSOVER *and* UNLEAVENED BREAD

Jehovah outlined for Moses several specific feast days that were to be overseen by the priests and faithfully observed by the Israelites. They were: Passover, Unleavened Bread, Firstfruits, Feast of Weeks, Feast of Trumpets, Yom Kippur (Day of Atonement), and the Feast of Tabernacles. Each of these was representative of the Messiah that was to come.

Exodus, the second book of the Pentateuch, is the story of deliverance from bondage and restoration—the establishing of a special relationship between Jehovah and the children of Israel and the first Passover. It is the story of Moses and his birth, life, and sudden departure from Egypt after murdering an Egyptian overseer (see Exodus 2:11–12). Moses fled to the desert of Midian, where God hardened Moses to desert life in the place he would spend another forty years of his life. The adopted son of Pharaoh's daughter learned meekness and humility and, at the same time, grew physically stronger for the task ahead. At the end of forty years on the backside of the desert, Moses was charged by Yahweh with stalking into the throne room of the most powerful man in the region and demanding that he allow the Israelites—his bond slaves—to pack up and leave Goshen. Moses was about to receive enormous preference from the Egyptians because of God's grace and favor.

As he returned to Egypt Moses encountered his blood brother, Aaron, in the desert. The two men made their way to the palace to challenge Pharaoh. With the ruler's refusal to let the Israelites go, God began to visit ten plagues on the land. Rather than persuade the ruler, it did the opposite and the burdens that had been placed on the children of Jacob were intensified. The last plague, the death of all of Egypt's firstborn, was the final straw for the rebellious Pharaoh.

Beginning in Exodus 11:4 (NKJV), Moses and Aaron were sent to warn the Egyptian ruler of the last terrible plague that was to be poured out upon the land and its people:

> "Thus says the LORD: 'About midnight I will go out into the midst of Egypt; and all the firstborn in the land of Egypt shall die, from the firstborn of Pharaoh who sits on his throne, even to the firstborn of the female servant who is behind the handmill, and all the firstborn of the animals. Then there shall be a great cry throughout all the land of Egypt, such as was not like it before, nor shall be like it again. But against none of the children of Israel shall a dog move its tongue, against man or beast, that you may know that the LORD does make a difference between the Egyptians and Israel.' And all these your servants shall come down to me and bow down to me, saying, 'Get out, and all the people who follow you!' After

that I will go out." Then he went out from Pharaoh in great anger.

Moses was vitally aware of what was about to befall the Egyptian people. Remember, as a baby he was saved by Pharaoh's daughter because of an edict that demanded the deaths of all babies born to the children of Israel. The king's disobedience would exact a dire penalty, not only on his household but also on each one in the land of Egypt. Harsh, yes, but Pharaoh had been given numerous opportunities to heed the voice of Jehovah. Because He is a God of love, He made a way for the Israelites to escape the sentence of death that had been pronounced.

In Exodus 12:1–14, we read:

> The LORD said to Moses and Aaron in Egypt, "This month is to be for you the first month, the first month of your year. Tell the whole community of Israel that on the tenth day of this month each man is to take a lamb for his family, one for each household. If any household is too small for a whole lamb, they must share one with their nearest neighbor, having taken into account the number of people there are. You are to determine the amount of lamb needed in accordance with what each person will eat. The animals you choose must be year-old males without defect, and you may take them from the sheep or the goats. Take care of them until the fourteenth day of the month, when all the members of the community of Israel must slaughter them at twilight. Then they are to take some of the blood and put it on the sides and tops of the doorframes of the houses where they eat

the lambs. That same night they are to eat the meat roasted over the fire, along with bitter herbs, and bread made without yeast. Do not eat the meat raw or boiled in water, but roast it over a fire—with the head, legs and internal organs. Do not leave any of it till morning; if some is left till morning, you must burn it. This is how you are to eat it: with your cloak tucked into your belt, your sandals on your feet and your staff in your hand. Eat it in haste; it is the LORD's Passover. On that same night I will pass through Egypt and strike down every firstborn of both people and animals, and I will bring judgment on all the gods of Egypt. I am the LORD. The blood will be a sign for you on the houses where you are, and when I see the blood, I will pass over you. No destructive plague will touch you when I strike Egypt. This is a day you are to commemorate; for the generations to come you shall celebrate it as a festival to the LORD—a lasting ordinance."

With a lamb, God had provided a way of escape for His people— an exchange for the firstborn in each family. Obedience was all that was required for the death angel to pass over Israelite homes. Jehovah then instructed that as a reminder of His graciousness, the Israelites were to observe an annual memorial—Passover. God had stated in precise detail how the event was to be observed:

- ✧ the selection of the lamb and its preparation;

- ✧ it was to be roasted and all eaten (leftovers were to be burned with fire);

✧ its blood was to be brushed on the lintel and doorposts of the home;

✧ the unleavened bread was symbolic of the haste of their departure from Egypt;

✧ the bitter herbs represented the harsh treatment received at the hands of their taskmasters;

✧ the meal was to be eaten fully clothed for the trek that was before them—cloaks donned, sandals fastened, and staff in hand.

God had already promised in Exodus 6:6–8:

> "I am the LORD, and I will bring you out from under the yoke of the Egyptians. I will free you from being slaves to them, and I will redeem you with an outstretched arm and with mighty acts of judgment. I will take you as my own people, and I will be your God. Then you will know that I am the LORD your God, who brought you out from under the yoke of the Egyptians. And I will bring you to the land I swore with uplifted hand to give to Abraham, to Isaac and to Jacob. I will give it to you as a possession. I am the LORD."

Jesus and His disciples gathered for a meal just before His death. The event is referred to by New Testament Believers as the Lord's Supper (or Last Supper), although there is no scriptural basis for that terminology. Jesus, recognizing that the bread and wine were indicative of His death that was to come, broke the bread and directed the disciples to "Take it; this is my body" (Mark 14:22). And, "Then he took a cup, and when he had given thanks, he gave it to them, and they all drank from it. 'This is my blood of the covenant, which is poured out for many'" (Mark 14:23–24). As Jesus distributed the bread and wine, He was informing His disciples that He was the Passover Lamb for whom they had been waiting. In 1 Corinthians 5:7, Paul referred to Christ as "our Passover lamb." And just as none of the bones of the Passover Lamb were to be broken, so were none of Jesus' bones broken as He hung on the cross.

The Passover observance that would take place was a picture of the deliverance and salvation that would come through the Messiah. The prophet Isaiah provided a clear embodiment of what many have called the Suffering Savior (Isaiah 53:3–7):

> He was despised and rejected by mankind, a man of suffering, and familiar with pain. Like one from whom people hide their faces he was despised, and we held him in low esteem. Surely he took up our pain and bore our suffering, yet we considered him punished by God, stricken by him, and afflicted. But he was pierced for our transgressions, he was crushed for our iniquities; the punishment that brought us peace was on him, and by his wounds we are healed. We all, like sheep, have gone astray, each of us has turned to our own way; and the LORD has laid on him the iniquity of us all. He was oppressed and afflicted, yet he did not open his mouth; he was led like a lamb to the slaughter, and as a sheep before its shearers is silent, so he did not open his mouth.

Pastor Randy Moll of Good Shepherd Lutheran Church in Rogers, Arkansas, wrote of this passage in Isaiah:

His form and appearance was nothing unusual so as to draw people to Him or permit them to recognize Him as the Messiah. And, as Jesus carried out His ministry, calling upon all to repent and believe the good news of forgiveness and life in Him, He was despised and rejected.

The religious leaders of Israel hated Him and viewed Him as a threat to their system of worship and sacrifice. The religiously conservative Pharisees hated Him because He pointed out their inner transgressions and failures to keep God's law by loving Him first and foremost and then also loving their neighbor as themselves. The liberal Sadducees hated Him, for He pointed out their unbelief and rejection of the teaching of the Holy Scriptures. Many of the common people recognized His great power and longed to see His miracles; but still, for the most part, they failed to recognize Him as the holy Son of God come into this world a true man to save sinners.[83]

Pastor and teacher Dr. John MacArthur wrote:

As He sat in that secluded room with His disciples, Christ knew what was going to happen. He was preparing Himself and His closest friends for the moment He would be handed over for execution. Over the centuries millions of Passover lambs had been slaughtered—each of them foreshadowing the sacrifice Jesus was about to make to free God's people from the bondage of their sins. The symbols and shadows of the Passover were about to cease—the

true Lamb had arrived. And at exactly the hour of
slaughter on Friday afternoon, He would die, the veil
in the temple would be ripped from top to bottom,
and the system of sacrifice would come to an end. It
was in those final moments with His disciples that
Christ transformed the elements of the Passover celebration, creating a new memorial to God's gracious
deliverance of His people.[84]

Passover and the other feasts celebrated by the Israelites were
conducted to bring the people together as a nation and to remind
them of Jehovah's deliverance from bondage. The observances were
spiritual in that they presented a picture of the truth of iniquity
and immorality, the verdict that accompanied the breaking of God's
laws, the pardon provided by a blood sacrifice, and the inherent need
to praise God for His grace and mercy.

The Israelites were also to celebrate the Feast of Unleavened
Bread beginning the day after Passover. It was to be a memorial of
their hasty departure from Egypt. It truly was "fast food." The bread
was made with only flour and water and without yeast because there
was no time for the dough to rise and loaves to be baked. It is celebrated on the fifteenth day of Nisan, the same month as Passover. It
was a time for purification and spiritual preparation. While Passover
lasted for only one day, the Feast of Unleavened Bread was a seven-
day observance. The first and last days were celebrated with a holy
convocation and offerings. For the entire week, the children of Israel
were to eat only unleavened bread that closely resembled what we
today sometimes call pita or matzo. The dough was pierced to prevent it from ballooning from the heat and to make it cook faster, and
the cooking utensil left a striped pattern on the bread.

Rabbis have subsequently determined that if the bread could be baked within eighteen minutes from preparation to removal from the grill, it was not to be defiled by yeast. The very things that aided in cooking the unleavened bread were, and are, symbols initiated by Jehovah before the beginning of time. Old Testament scriptures predicted the Messiah would be pierced:

> "And I will pour out on the house of David and the inhabitants of Jerusalem a spirit of grace and pleas for mercy, so that, when they look on me, on him whom they have pierced, they shall mourn for him, as one mourns for an only child, and weep bitterly over him, as one weeps over a firstborn." (Zechariah 12:10 (ESV)
>
> For dogs encompass me; a company of evildoers encircles me; they have pierced my hands and feet— (Psalm 22:16 ESV)

In the matzo prepared today, even centuries after the death of and resurrection of Christ, this symbolism—the piercings and stripes—remain as the picture of Jehovah's perfect plan of salvation.

As the Jewish people prepare for the feast, every vestige of yeast is removed from the home. A few pieces of bread are left behind for the children to discover. These are burned outside the home to rid it of the symbol of sin that pervades daily life. What is yeast and why is it compared to sin? The answer:

> Yeast has a decaying affect [sic] on life therefore the Bible uses it as a metaphor for sin. The picture of searching your house for yeast is a great analogy for us to search our lives for any hidden sin. Israel was to take the yeast and rid it from their midst, in the same

way we should rid our lives of sin, removing it from
our life like the yeast.[85]

In 1 Corinthians 5:6–8, the apostle Paul admonished the early
Church on how to deal with "leaven" or sin in their midst:

> Don't you know that a little yeast leavens the whole
> batch of dough? Get rid of the old yeast, so that you
> may be a new unleavened batch—as you really are.
> For Christ, our Passover lamb, has been sacrificed.
> Therefore let us keep the Festival, not with the old
> bread leavened with malice and wickedness, but with
> the unleavened bread of sincerity and truth.

20

FEASTS:
FIRSTFRUITS, WEEKS, TRUMPETS,
YOM KIPPUR, TABERNACLES

The next feast was that of firstfruits, which occurred on the second day of the Feast of Unleavened Bread. It was an offering of appreciation for Jehovah's blessings on the harvest yield. The Israelites were to present a praise offering for God's goodness. The farmer was to gather a sheaf of the first grain cut and carry it to the priest. It would be waved before the Lord of Hosts as an offering on the day following Shabbat. The benefits of the harvest were not to be enjoyed until after the firstfruits had been offered to Jehovah. It was a freewill offering—yet another way to acknowledge God's deliverance of the children of Israel from Egypt and to thank Him for bringing them into a land of plenty—the land He had promised.

Solomon wrote in Proverbs 3:9–10:

> Honor the LORD with your wealth, with the firstfruits of all your crops; then your barns will be filled to overflowing, and your vats will brim over with new wine.

The prophet Jeremiah called Israel "holy to the LORD, the first-fruits of his harvest" (Jeremiah 2:3). It was a pronouncement to all that the Israelites held a special place with Jehovah God. Rev. Ken Overby of JewishAwareness.org wrote of this feast:

> A close look at Leviticus 23 gives a clue as to why this feast had an uphill battle for recognition. To begin with, it lacked visibility due to its proximity to Passover, the most widely observed family oriented feast in Jewish history. Its placement on the next day made it rather anticlimactic. In addition to being placed the day after the Passover Lamb was killed, First Fruits was on the first day of the 7 day Feast of Unleavened Bread. It was sandwiched between two widely observed events in the Mosaic calendar of Judaism. There was also a delayed inauguration of this feast. From the time the instructions about this feast were written until it was observed in the promised land more than 40 years expired. Farm land, planting, sprouting, then harvest are all requirements that couldn't be met in the desert. Once in the land they were to offer to the Lord the first green heads of barley that had sprouted equaling about two quarts. A lamb was to be offered as a whole burnt offering. About two pints of wine were to be poured out before the Lord. Also flour mingled with oil was to be burned as a sweet incense to the Lord, and then, and only then, could they eat new parched grain. This consecrated the entire harvest yet to come to the Lord. It was kind of a faith promise offering, giving Him the first and trusting Him to supply the rest.[86]

In Genesis chapter three, the prophecy was given regarding the seed of woman whose heel would be bruised, but who would in turn crush the head of the serpent—Satan. Jesus perfectly fulfilled that prophecy when He was born of Mary, ministered for thirty-three years, was crucified on the cross and buried on the eve of the observation of Passover. Three days later on the celebration of firstfruits, He triumphantly arose from the dead. Fifty days later, the disciples were filled with the Holy Spirit on the day of Pentecost, and the ministry of Christ's followers began on earth. In a matter of seven weeks (again, the number of completion) three major feasts were fulfilled in the person of Jesus Christ. Saul, the rabbi who became the apostle Paul, wrote in 1 Corinthians 15:20–23 (ESV):

> But in fact Christ has been raised from the dead, the firstfruits of those who have fallen asleep. For as by a man came death, by a man has come also the resurrection of the dead. For as in Adam all die, so also in Christ shall all be made alive. But each in his own order: Christ the firstfruits, then at his coming those who belong to Christ.

Believers have hope that they, too, shall be resurrected when Christ returns for His own.

Fifty days, or seven weeks, following the Feast of Firstfruits, the Feast of Weeks, Shavuot, or Pentecost was to be celebrated signifying the end of the harvest. It was to be a holy convocation. Numbers 28:27–31 (ESV) gives us a much more comprehensive list of the types of offerings that were to be made:

> . . . but offer a burnt offering, with a pleasing aroma to the LORD: two bulls from the herd, one ram, seven

male lambs a year old; also their grain offering of fine
flour mixed with oil, three tenths of an ephah for
each bull, two tenths for one ram, a tenth for each of
the seven lambs; with one male goat, to make atonement for you. Besides the regular burnt offering and
its grain offering, you shall offer them and their drink
offering. See that they are without blemish.

Since about the second century, the practice of reading the book
of Ruth during the celebration of Shavuot or Pentecost has been
adopted. According to Rev. Mark Robinson of Jewish Awareness
Ministries, that custom would play a role in the modern-day church:

For the festival of Shavuot the book of Ruth is read
in the synagogue telling the glorious story of the love
of a Jewish man for a Gentile woman as he followed
the God of Israel's desires. It is no coincidence that
at the festival of Shavuot (Pentecost), a Jewish man,
Jesus, and ultimately, primarily, a Gentile bride, the
church, were brought together, in the birth of the
church. This too is a love story of a Jewish man for
His Bride![87]

For New Testament Believers, the day of Pentecost represents
the day on which the Holy Spirit was poured out on those in the
Upper Room who were awaiting His arrival and empowerment.
Jesus has alerted his disciples of the happening in Acts 1:4–8 (ESV):

And while staying with them he ordered them not
to depart from Jerusalem, but to wait for the promise
of the Father, which, he said, "you heard from me; for
John baptized with water, but you will be baptized

with the Holy Spirit not many days from now." So
when they had come together, they asked him, "Lord,
will you at this time restore the kingdom to Israel?"
He said to them, "It is not for you to know times or
seasons that the Father has fixed by his own authority. But you will receive power when the Holy Spirit
has come upon you, and you will be my witnesses in
Jerusalem and in all Judea and Samaria, and to the
end of the earth."

The prophet Joel had prophesied that the Spirit would come.
Chapter 1 outlined the terrible drought and the plagues that had
beset the Israelites and had decimated the crops. He advised the
people what would happen if they came together to worship and
honor Jehovah:

> "And it shall come to pass afterward, that I will
> pour out my Spirit on all flesh; your sons and your
> daughters shall prophesy, your old men shall dream
> dreams, and your young men shall see visions. Even
> on the male and female servants in those days I will
> pour out my Spirit." (Joel 2:28–29 ESV)

As we read in Acts 2:2–4 (ESV), fifty days following Christ's ascen-
sion, the disciples were gathered together in a room in Jerusalem:

> And suddenly there came from heaven a sound
> like a mighty rushing wind, and it filled the entire
> house where they were sitting. And divided tongues
> as of fire appeared to them and rested on each one
> of them. And they were all filled with the Holy Spirit

and began to speak in other tongues as the Spirit gave them utterance.

The first of the fall feasts was the Feast of Trumpets or *Zikhron Teruah*, and now called Rosh Hashanah. It falls in the seventh month and was introduced to the Israelites in Leviticus 23:23–25:

> The LORD said to Moses, "Say to the Israelites: 'On the first day of the seventh month you are to have a day of sabbath rest, a sacred assembly commemorated with trumpet blasts. Do no regular work, but present a food offering to the LORD.'"

This fifth feast is followed by Yom Kippur or the Day of Atonement, and lastly by the Feast of Tabernacles. The usage of the term *Rosh Hashanah* began in the second century AD after the temple and Jerusalem were razed by the Romans. These final three feasts of the Jewish year parallel events surrounding the coming of the Messiah as foretold in the Bible.

The blowing of the shofar—a musical instrument of ancient origin, made of a horn, traditionally that of a ram, used for Jewish religious purposes[88]—during the Feast of Trumpets is an important ingredient in the Old and New Testaments. It was a public acknowledgment of Jehovah as King of Kings.

There are specific guidelines for the way the shofar is to be blown. The sound of the shofar signals the beginning of Rosh Hashanah and is a sacred appeal for the listener to contemplate his or her transgressions. There is a specific sequence for blasts on the instrument:

✧ The first sound heard is the *Tekiah*, or a long blast on the shofar;

✧ Second is the *Shevarim*, or three short blasts said to mimic the playing of a trumpet. Some have said this sound resembles the cries of a man yearning to reconnect with Jehovah, and believe it is the cry of a "broken spirit; a broken and contrite heart" (Psalm 51:17).

✧ The third sound is the *Teruah*, or nine short blasts. The writers on AISH.com define the call as: The Teruah sound—9 quick blasts in short succession—resembles an alarm clock, arousing us from our spiritual slumber. The shofar brings clarity, alertness, and focus.[89]

Following the Day of Atonement, which we covered in the previous chapter, was the Feast of Tabernacles or Booths. It was a celebration of the fall harvest, which lasted an entire week. The Israelites built temporary dwellings as a reminder of their forty-year trek through the wilderness. Leviticus 23:40 detailed the materials to be used: "On the first day you are to take branches from luxuriant trees—from palms, willows and other leafy trees—and rejoice before the LORD your God for seven days." The branches used to build the booths were symbolic of victory (palm), peace (olive), and willow (blessings).

The Feast of Tabernacles was a feast of expectation; a reminder that one day the children of Israel would be firmly planted in their own land looking forward with anticipation to the arrival of the Messiah. In his book *Thus Shalt Thou Serve: The Feasts and Offerings of Ancient Israel*, author and Bible teacher C. W. Slemming wrote:

Numbers 29 lists the number of animals to be used
in the sacrifices of that week. The young bulls, dimin-
ishing in number from day to day for eight days, were
13, 12, 11, 10, 9, 8, 7, 1. It has been suggested that the
decrease to the one foretells … how the many sacrifices of the law would, in the fullness of time, be
reduced to the One Sacrifice that would be made once
in the end of the age . . . . One the last day of the feast
there were special celebrations and joy.[90]

In John 7:37, we read that Jesus went up to Jerusalem during
this particular feast. While there, He declared, "Let anyone who is
thirsty come to me and drink." Of this declaration, Slemming wrote:

Thus the Lord was turning the thoughts of the
people away from the shadow to the substance, away
from ritual to reality.[91]

The feasts were times when all Jewish males who were physically able were charged with going up to Jerusalem to appear before
the Lord in the place that was symbolic of His presence. There they
called to remembrance what Jehovah had done in bringing them
out of Egypt into the Promised Land. They praised God for His provision and offered up sacrifices that would postpone their sins for
another year.

But when the fullness of time had come, God sent forth his
Son, born of woman, born under the law, to redeem those who were
under the law, so that we might receive adoption as sons. (Galatians
4:4–5 ESV)

21

DEPARTURE,
DEATH, *and* DIVISION

n 1 Kings 3:5–13, God granted Solomon both wisdom and riches. Yet, just eight chapters later, 1 Kings 11:1–3 records the timeline of the downfall of Solomon—his departure from faith in El Elyon, the God Most High:

> King Solomon, however, loved many foreign women besides Pharaoh's daughter—Moabites, Ammonites, Edomites, Sidonians and Hittites. They were from nations about which the LORD had told the Israelites, "You must not intermarry with them, because they will surely turn your hearts after their gods." Nevertheless, Solomon held fast to them in love. He had seven hundred wives of royal birth and three hundred concubines, and his wives led him astray.

Dr. C. F. Keil, German theologian, addresses the differentiation between Pharaoh's daughter and the other wives of Solomon:

> Marriage with an Egyptian princess was not a transgression of the law, as it was only marriages with

Canaanitish women that were expressly forbidden by
Jehovah.... At the same time it was only when foreign
wives renounced idolatry and confessed their faith in
Jehovah, that such marriages were in accordance with
the spirit of the law ... and we cannot find any trace
of Egyptian idolatry in Israel in the time of Solomon,
and, lastly, the daughter of Pharaoh is expressly distin-
guished in ch. Xi.1 from the foreign wives who tempted
Solomon to idolatry in his old age.[92]

When the Law was delivered to Moses, God had given very
precise instructions on what the Israelites were to do when they
entered the Promised Land:

Do not intermarry with them. Do not give your
daughters to their sons or take their daughters for
your sons, for they will turn your children away from
following me to serve other gods, and the LORD's
anger will burn against you and will quickly destroy
you. (Deuteronomy 7:3–4)

David had conquered the nation's enemies by might and bloodshed, so that during Solomon's reign, the nation lived at peace with
its neighbors. Solomon, however, adopted an iniquitous strategy to
placate the kingdoms and city-states that surrounded Israel. His
tactic was to marry the relatives of those leaders in order to institute
political bonds. By the end of his life, Solomon had amassed quite a
harem—300 concubines. Apparently, his wisdom did not extend to
following the law of the Lord.

The king, in order to please his wives, began to worship the
pagan gods the majority had introduced to the nation of Israel—i.e.,

Ashtoreth, Milcom, Chemosh, Molek, and others. Worship of Ashtoreth, goddess of the Sidonians, included "sexual immorality, prostitution, divination, and fortune telling."[93] Molek, god of the Ammonites, "was honoured with human sacrifices. The people would burn their children in fire as a form of sacrifice while others would let their infants pass through the fire as a form of dedication."[94] Chemosh, god of the Moabites, demanded human sacrifice. Second Kings 3:26–27 confirmed the practice:

> When the king of Moab saw that the battle had gone against him, he took with him seven hundred swordsmen to break through to the king of Edom, but they failed. Then he took his firstborn son, who was to succeed him as king, and offered him as a sacrifice on the city wall.

That these are the gods to whom Solomon bowed a knee in place of Jehovah is confirmed in 1 Kings 11:5–8:

> He followed Ashtoreth the goddess of the Sidonians, and Molek the detestable god of the Ammonites. So Solomon did evil in the eyes of the LORD; he did not follow the LORD completely, as David his father had done. On a hill east of Jerusalem, Solomon built a high place for Chemosh the detestable god of Moab, and for Molek the detestable god of the Ammonites. He did the same for all his foreign wives, who burned incense and offered sacrifices to their gods.

The apostle Paul wrote in 1 Corinthians 8:4 (NKJV), "We know that an idol *is* nothing in the world, and that *there is* no other God but one." Solomon, upon whom God showered wisdom, was not wise enough to follow in the footsteps of his father, David. Though Solomon's sin would eventually rend the kingdom asunder, Jehovah's judgment would not fall until after the king's death.

As Solomon neared the end of his days on earth, he called to his bedside Jeroboam, an Ephraimite superintendent working in Jerusalem, and assigned him the task of overseeing his kinsmen who labored in Jerusalem. Far from being a wise choice, Jeroboam secretly plotted a revolt against the king because of the burdensome labors and heavy taxes that had been levied against his people. Following his appointment, Jeroboam set out on a journey to Ephraim only to be met along the way by Ahijah, a prophet. In 1 Kings 11:2–40, he prophesied that the kingdom of Israel would be divided, ten of the twelve tribes would be given to Jeroboam and the remainder would fall to Solomon's son Rehoboam. Judah, the tribe of David, and Jerusalem, the City of God, were to remain under the rule of David's descendants. (The preponderance of Levites, who were not counted as one of the twelve tribes of Israel, resided predominately in Judah because of their service in the temple.)

Rather than trust God to bring to pass His prophecy, Jeroboam rebelled against Solomon and found himself on the run—all the way to Egypt and its ruler, Shishak. He remained there until word of the death of Solomon reached him.

After Solomon's death, the kingdom was split. Samaria became the kingdom of the northern tribes of Israel. All that was left to Jerusalem was the tribe of Judah. By then, Jerusalem with its temple had become fixed in the hearts and minds of all true worshipers of Yahweh as the place to bring one's sacrifices, fulfill one's vows, and offer loud songs of praise.

This posed a problem for the northern rulers who didn't want their subjects to make pilgrimages to Jerusalem—capital of a rival kingdom. They sought to offer the people substitute places of worship with manmade gods. The worship of Yahweh barely survived in the north. That it did so is due to prophets like Elijah and Elisha, who never let the fires go out. It was essentially a time of decline. In the south where the worship of Yahweh was still the official religion, decline happened more slowly. It was occasionally interrupted by revival, but most kings who ruled in Jerusalem were little better than the kings who sat in Samaria. The worship of Yahweh was fading, almost irretrievably.

In the south, Rehoboam was anointed king over the nation. Rather than go up to Jerusalem, the members of the ten northern tribes gathered at Shechem. Having sent to Egypt for Jeroboam, the plan was to proclaim him king in Shechem. Once there, Jeroboam led a delegation of men to petition Rehoboam:

> "Your father put a heavy yoke on us, but now
> lighten the harsh labor and the heavy yoke he put on
> us, and we will serve you." (1 Kings 12:4)

Rehoboam sent the delegation away for three days while he consulted the wise men of the kingdom. Rejecting the advice of Solomon's counsel to lighten the tax load, the king turned to the young men with whom he had spent his childhood. Their advice drove an irreparable wedge in relations between Judah and the ten northern tribes. They advised Rehoboam to answer thusly:

> "These people have said to you, 'Your father put
> a heavy yoke on us, but make our yoke lighter.' Now
> tell them, 'My little finger is thicker than my father's

waist. My father laid on you a heavy yoke; I will make
it even heavier. My father scourged you with whips; I
will scourge you with scorpions.'" (1 Kings 12:10–11)

After three days, the delegation from the north returned to
Rehoboam, and much to the chagrin and disappointment of the
petitioners, the new king responded to their appeal by saying, "My
father made your yoke heavy; I will make it even heavier. My father
scourged you with whips; I will scourge you with scorpions" (1
Kings 12:14).

The heaviness that sprang from the king's answer quickly
turned to rebellion, and the Ephraimites crowned Jeroboam king of
Israel. The division was a direct result of Solomon's rebellion and his
failure to follow the laws and precepts of Jehovah.

Soon after Rehoboam ascended to the throne of Solomon, he
completely forsook the laws of God and reaped the divine punishment that came with rebellion. Shishak, king of Egypt, launched an
offensive against Jerusalem, capturing Judean fortified towns along
the way. It was his intent to reestablish authority over the region
that had fallen to the Israelites. Judah became a vassal state, paying
homage to the Pharaoh who had sacked the temple and carried
away its treasure, as well as that amassed by Rehoboam, to Egypt.
Author Leon Wood, in his treatise *A Survey of Israel's History*, said
of Shishak:

> His country at home, however, apparently was
> too weak for him to maintain a permanent hold [on
> Judah]. His design of establishing Egyptian authority
> in Palestine was not realized.[95]

✧   ✧   ✧

Meanwhile, Jeroboam in the northern territory had his own problems, the greater being keeping the Israelites from returning to Jerusalem to worship Yahweh. With that in mind, he had walls built around Shechem, his capital, and around Penuel on the east side of the Jordan River.

To turn the eyes of the people from the temple, Jeroboam committed a great sin lifted straight from the history of the Israelites as they fled Goshen. He had golden calves erected in Dan and in Bethel and instituted worship of the graven images. In direct rebellion to God's edicts, he then selected priests from every tribe and class and established a feast day to worship the idols. The result of his iniquity was quick in coming in the form of an unnamed prophet sent from Judah. He delivered a message to Jeroboam:

> "Altar, altar! This is what the LORD says: 'A son named Josiah will be born to the house of David [three centuries later]. On you he will sacrifice the priests of the high places who make offerings here, and human bones will be burned on you.'" That same day the man of God gave a sign: "This is the sign the LORD has declared: The altar will be split apart and the ashes on it will be poured out." When King Jeroboam heard what the man of God cried out against the altar at Bethel, he stretched out his hand from the altar and said, "Seize him!" But the hand he stretched out toward the man shriveled up, so that he could not pull it back. Also, the altar was split apart and its ashes poured out according to the sign given by the man of God by the word of the LORD. (1 Kings 13:2–5)

Jeroboam was horrified when he looked down at his withered hand and began to plead with the prophet for his hand to be restored. The prophet from Judah interceded for Jereboam, and his hand was restored. In gratitude, the king offered sustenance to the man who refused to accompany Jeroboam back to his home:

> "Even if you were to give me half your possessions, I would not go with you, nor would I eat bread or drink water here. For I was commanded by the word of the LORD: 'You must not eat bread or drink water or return by the way you came.'" So he took another road and did not return by the way he had come to Bethel. (1 Kings 13:8–10)

22

THE GOOD,

THE BAD, *and the* PROPHETIC

srael and Judah were bitter enemies as recorded in the books of Kings and Chronicles. A good king blessed by God would be succeeded by a depraved king, i.e., Ahab, and retribution would fall (see Appendix A). A series of prophets ordained by Jehovah would bring messages designed to elicit repentance that would last for a time, but eventually human nature and rebellion would win out. Finally, under the leadership of Jehoshaphat, the north and south were reunited when his son Jehoram was betrothed to Athaliah, daughter of Ahab. She reintroduced Baal worship in Judah, a move that eventually led to it having become the foremost religion in the land within a generation. Minister and author Herbert Lockyer wrote of the scion of Ahab:

> Of this union Ahaziah was born who, with such a revolting figure as a mother, licentious and the personification of despicable arrogance, never had a chance to develop finer qualities of character. With such a mother as his wicked counselor what else could he do but walk in the ways of godless Ahab (2 Chronicles 22:3).

After reigning for eight years Jehoram died, unmourned, of a predicted incurable disease. While he reigned, he was dominated by Athaliah who had the stronger character of the two, and who, having inherited from her evil mother strength of will and fanatical devotion to the worship of Baal, made Judah idolatrous. Ahaziah only reigned for a year. Wounded in battle by Jehu, he fled to Megiddo, where he died, and his wicked mother (2 Chronicles 24:7) became envious of the throne. But the sons of Ahaziah stood in her way, and with fanatical ambition she seized the opportunity and massacred all the legal heirs—so she thought. This wholesale, merciless, cruel-hearted murderess sought to exterminate the last vestiges of the House of David through which the promised Messiah was to come. Behind her dastardly crime to destroy "The Seed Royal" we can detect the evil machinations of the devil—a murderer from the beginning—to annihilate the promised seed of the woman predestined to bruise the satanic head. A bad woman bent on destruction is doubly dangerous.[96]

Second Chronicles 23:12–15 relates that Athaliah died trying to foil the investiture of Joash, a true descendant of King David, and who had been saved as a young child from the murderous intent of the queen consort:

When Athaliah heard the noise of the people running and cheering the king, she went to them at the temple of the LORD. She looked, and there was the king, standing by his pillar at the entrance. The officers and the trumpeters were beside the king, and all the people of the land were rejoicing and blowing trumpets, and musicians with their instruments were leading the praises. Then Athaliah tore her robes and shouted, "Treason! Treason!" Jehoiada the priest sent out the commanders of units of a hundred, who were in charge of the troops, and said to them: "Bring her out between the ranks and put to the sword anyone who follows her." For the priest had said, "Do not put her to death at the temple of the LORD." So they seized her as she reached the entrance of the Horse Gate on the palace grounds, and there they put her to death.

✧　✧　✧

Under the reign of apostate kings and at least one queen, the temple had fallen into great disrepair. Not only had it been allowed to become dilapidated, but Athaliah had ordered the sacred vessels to be used in the worship of Baal. Joash called together the priests and Levites who had neglected their duties in the temple and instructed them to go throughout Judah to collect funds to repair the house of God. When they dragged their feet in response to his order, Joash had a chest built and placed outside the temple entrance. He then issued an order that the tax required by Moses should be placed in the chest to be used for temple repairs. Second Chronicles 24:10–12 provides the response of the people:

> All the officials and all the people brought their contributions gladly, dropping them into the chest until it was full. Whenever the chest was brought in by the Levites to the king's officials and they saw that

there was a large amount of money, the royal secretary and the officer of the chief priest would come
and empty the chest and carry it back to its place.
They did this regularly and collected a great amount
of money. The king and Jehoiada gave it to those who
carried out the work required for the temple of the
LORD. They hired masons and carpenters to restore
the LORD's temple, and also workers in iron and
bronze to repair the temple.

When sufficient funds had been amassed, repairs were made
to the temple. Such was the response of the people that there was
enough to replace the altars and the objects of gold and silver used
in the worship of Yahweh. Verse 14 tells us that "As long as Jehoiada
[the high priest] lived, burnt offerings were presented continually
in the temple of the LORD." So great was Jehoida's contribution to
the restoration of the worship of Jehovah that when he died, he was
buried "with the kings in the City of David."

Teddy Kollek and Moshe Pearlman give a glimpse of the dete-
rioration of Jerusalem:

The buildings of David and Solomon remained, but
the transactions conducted therein were no longer
the affairs of a large and prosperous country . . . . The
steady stream of people from all over the land to visit
the Temple now ceased. Most of the men of Israel did
not enter Judah.

But some did. These were 'the priests and Levites'
(the priestly tribe); for Jerusalem retained the one
great symbol which sanctified the city as the spiritual centre of the nation—Solomon's Temple. And

this may well have been the principal element which sustained Jerusalem through its misfortunes, eventually led to the Israel-Judah rapprochement, and ultimately brought about the restoration of the city's status, power and influence over the Hebrew nation.[97]

The rulers over the ten tribes of Israel were wicked men and women given to idolatry. None returned to the worship of Jehovah from the time that Jeroboam became king. Second Kings 17:6–8 relates the reasons surrounding the Israelites being carried away captive:

> In the ninth year of Hoshea, the king of Assyria captured Samaria and deported the Israelites to Assyria. He settled them in Halah, in Gozan on the Habor River and in the towns of the Medes. All this took place because the Israelites had sinned against the LORD their God, who had brought them up out of Egypt from under the power of Pharaoh king of Egypt. They worshiped other gods and followed the practices of the nations the LORD had driven out before them, as well as the practices that the kings of Israel had introduced.

It is a sad commentary on the lives of those who chose to follow after the gods of the world rather than surrender to Jehovah, the one true God. It was as if Isaiah's prophecy in chapter 9, verses 8 through 17 had suddenly come to pass:

> The Lord has sent a message against Jacob; it will fall on Israel . . . . So the LORD will cut off from Israel both head and tail, both palm branch and reed in a

single day; the elders and dignitaries are the head, the prophets who teach lies are the tail. Those who guide this people mislead them, and those who are guided are led astray. Therefore the Lord will take no pleasure in the young men, nor will he pity the fatherless and widows, for everyone is ungodly and wicked, every mouth speaks folly.

It was the Assyrians under Tiglath-Pileser and his successors, Shalmaneser V and Sargon II that Israel was finally totally conquered and its residents exiled to Mesopotamia and Media.

In 722 BC, Samaria fell to the Assyrians, and in 568 BC Jerusalem succumbed to the Babylonians—just as Jeremiah had warned (see Jeremiah 3). On each occasion inhabitants of the cities were carried into exile by their captors. The sharp rebuke of exile had a cleansing effect on those who suffered it. In losing Jerusalem, they began to value it as never before. Perhaps they sang:

Beside the rivers of Babylon, we sat and wept as we thought of Jerusalem. We put away our harps, hanging them on the branches of poplar trees. For our captors demanded a song from us. Our tormentors insisted on a joyful hymn: "Sing us one of those songs of Jerusalem!" But how can we sing the songs of the LORD while in a pagan land? If I forget you, O Jerusalem, let my right hand forget how to play the harp. May my tongue stick to the roof of my mouth if I fail to remember you, if I don't make Jerusalem my greatest joy. (Psalm 137:1–6 NLT)

Jerusalem had become much more than David's capital. Because of the temple Solomon had built there, it had become God's special dwelling place on earth. It was not that He was contained there, but in that building and its environs He had covenanted to receive the worship of His people and to hear their prayers. It was there that Yahweh met His people in a very special way. Although He could, and can, be praised anywhere in all the earth, Jerusalem became the only place appointed for the sacrifice of burnt offerings for the sins of the people.

Babylon fell to the Persians in 539 BC, and a year later the Persian emperor Cyrus issued a decree authorizing the rebuilding of Yahweh's temple in Jerusalem.

A remnant of God's people returned to the hills of the Holy City, but their arrival was not greeted with rejoicing by those who had made the area their home during the previous fifty years. Questions of ownership and authority gave an immediate reason for conflict.

It didn't help the cause when locals—some of them cross-breed Samaritans who had adopted the worship of Yahweh—were offended when offers of help to rebuild the temple were rebuffed. They actively opposed the work of the Jews by trying to frighten or discourage them. They sometimes bribed the Persian officials to do whatever could be done to hinder progress.

The Jews did manage to quickly erect an altar on the temple site and secure the other items needed for sacrifices and offerings that were at the heart of Yahweh's worship. Rebuilding the temple—a more modest structure than the one erected by Solomon—took much longer, for poverty and shortages persisted in and around Jerusalem.

DIVISION *and* DISPERSAL

With the Ten Tribes scattered and the country destroyed, Jerusalem again became the singular capital of the Jews. The City of David was once more the solitary trustee of the faith as evidenced by the symbol of God's eternal presence, the temple. Worship was again centered in Jerusalem. Yet overshadowing the lives of the two remaining tribes of Judah and Benjamin was the threat of the Assyrians camped along their border. The land of Judah under the rule of King Ahaz was at the mercy of the Assyrians. As Tiglath-Pileser moved against Jerusalem, the prophet Isaiah appeared with a message for the king: "Take heed, and be quiet; do not fear or be fainthearted" (Isaiah 7:4 NKJV).

The prophet's greatest sphere of influence would be in the life of Ahaz's successor, Hezekiah. Kollek and Pearlman give us more insight into the relationship between the king and Isaiah as the nation was threatened with invasion by the marauding Assyrians:

> Isaiah, through his burning words, rouses the king
> and people to meet it not only by making the fortifica-
> tions more secure, but above all by a strengthening of

the spirit. He emphasizes the moral and religious significance of Jerusalem, the spiritual fountain it was and must again become, 'the faithful city ... full of judgment [and] righteousness'. It has been debased, but the Lord has not forsaken it. Later, when the battle is joined, his words take on a crucial urgency—and, at the critical moment, decide the issue.

Meanwhile, Hezekiah got to work on the physical strengthening of Jerusalem. The new Assyrian ruler, Sennacherib, was smashing his way even further southwards, and although Hezekiah could and did put off the confrontation by various alliances with kingdoms equally threatened by the Assyrians, he knew that eventually Jerusalem would be attacked .... he [Hezekiah] introduced radical religious reforms, repairing the Temple, purifying it, breaking up the idols that had made their appearance in the previous reign, and outlawing pagan worship and the barbaric forms this sometimes took.[98]

The Assyrians, under the leadership of Sennacherib, finally marched against David's capital in 701 BC. In the flurry of activity surrounding the siege, the Assyrian leader made a grave mistake: He denigrated the power of Jehovah-Gador Milchamah—the Lord Mighty in Battle. The message he delivered to Hezekiah and the people who had taken refuge inside the city of Jerusalem ended with:

> "'Now therefore, do not let Hezekiah deceive you or persuade you like this, and do not believe him; for no god of any nation or kingdom was able to deliver

his people from my hand or the hand of my fathers. How much less will your God deliver you from my hand?'" (2 Chronicles 32:15 NKJV)

Isaiah then delivered a message from God to Hezekiah designed to strengthen the king's resolve:

> Thus says the LORD: "Do not be afraid of the words which you have heard, with which the servants of the king of Assyria have blasphemed Me. Surely I will send a spirit upon him, and he shall hear a rumor and return to his own land; and I will cause him to fall by the sword in his own land." (Isaiah 37:6–7 NKJV)

Lo and behold, even as Sennacherib's troops prepared to take Jerusalem, something very strange happened in the midst of the Assyrian camp:

> Then the LORD sent an angel who cut down every mighty man of valor, leader, and captain in the camp of the king of Assyria. So he returned shamefaced to his own land. And when he had gone into the temple of his god, some of his own offspring struck him down with the sword there. Thus the LORD saved Hezekiah and the inhabitants of Jerusalem from the hand of Sennacherib the king of Assyria, and from the hand of all others, and guided them on every side. (2 Chronicles 32:21–22 NKJV)

All the good that was done during Hezekiah's reign was negated almost instantaneously when Manasseh ascended the throne of David. Second Chronicles 33:2 gives a nine-word synopsis of his life:

"He did evil in the eyes of the LORD." The declaration is even more devastating because Manasseh—and evil—reigned over Judah for fifty-five years. In verses 3–6, we see the ruin he visited on the land:

> He rebuilt the high places his father Hezekiah had demolished; he also erected altars to the Baals and made Asherah poles. He bowed down to all the starry hosts and worshiped them. He built altars in the temple of the LORD, of which the LORD had said, "My Name will remain in Jerusalem forever." In both courts of the temple of the LORD, he built altars to all the starry hosts. He sacrificed his children in the fire in the Valley of Ben Hinnom, practiced divination and witchcraft, sought omens, and consulted mediums and spiritists. He did much evil in the eyes of the LORD, arousing his anger.

God sent prophets with calls for repentance, but Manasseh ignored them all. Writer Jon W. Quinn says, "In fact, according to oral rabbinical tradition, Manasseh executed the prophet Isaiah by having him sawn asunder."[99] Jehovah was patient and longsuffering, but the day came when Manasseh's wickedness was called to a halt:

> So the LORD brought against them the army commanders of the king of Assyria, who took Manasseh prisoner, put a hook in his nose, bound him with bronze shackles and took him to Babylon. (2 Chronicles 33:11)

In his suffering, Manasseh turned to Jehovah, humbling himself and seeking God's deliverance. Rather than turning His back and washing His hands of the king, God heard Manasseh's plea and allowed him to return to Jerusalem. With the realization that

Jehovah was the one true God, Manasseh began at once to attempt to undo all the evil he had initiated in Judah. His task was great, for he had led the nation down the slippery slope of rebellion against God. The people had long been deprived of hearing the Word of God and their ignorance was acute, but Manasseh was determined to try to right the wrong he had caused.

The king began at once to make provisions for the safety of his people by rebuilding the fortifications of cities in Judah. He broke down altars that had been erected to false gods and had repairs made to the temple altar. He did his best to reacquaint an entire generation with the Law of God.

Upon his death, Manasseh's son, Amon, became king. He was a graphic illustration, but not in a good way, of the proverb to "train up a child . . . and when he is old, he will not depart from it" (Proverbs 22:6 KJV). Amon's life had been spent watching his father defy Jehovah and worship false gods. His training was that of rebellion against El Elyon—the Lord Most High. When elevated to the role of king, "He did evil in the eyes of the LORD, as his father Manasseh had done" (2 Chronicles 33:22). Unlike Manasseh, Amon chose not to repent and was assassinated in his palace.

Amon's son, Josiah, succeeded him and is known for restoring the traditional worship of Jehovah. The highlight of his reign was the restoration of the temple, during which the discovery of the forgotten book of the law was made in a storeroom in the temple. After reading the manuscript, Josiah was greatly disturbed for fear that the wrath of God would be poured out on the land because of disobedience. In 2 Chronicles 34:29–31:

> Then the king called together all the elders of
> Judah and Jerusalem. He went up to the temple of

the LORD with the people of Judah, the inhabitants of Jerusalem, the priests and the Levites—all the people from the least to the greatest. He read in their hearing all the words of the Book of the Covenant, which had been found in the temple of the LORD. The king stood by his pillar and renewed the covenant in the presence of the LORD—to follow the LORD and keep his commands, statutes and decrees with all his heart and all his soul, and to obey the words of the covenant written in this book.

For all the days of his reign, Josiah led the remnant of Israelites in the worship of Jehovah God. The failure of the kings who followed him led to the ultimate downfall of Judah and the onslaught of the Babylonians under Nebuchadnezzar.

✧ ✧ ✧

The Lord is "slow to anger," says Psalm 103:8. What an understatement! Decade after decade—century after century—God's heart has been broken because of the idolatry of the children of Israel. As He had promised Abraham, the Israelites were led out of slavery in Egypt and into the Promised Land. God had established them in the land promised unconditionally to Abraham, Isaac, Jacob, and their descendants, in the royal land grant.

Time after time the people left the worship of the one true God and followed after pagan gods in the nations surrounding them. A righteous king of the line of David would bring reform and revival, and the groves and high places where Baal, Asherah (Ishtar), and other idols worshiped were torn down. The next king would then prove to be as wicked as the previous one, and pagan beliefs would again be practiced by God's chosen people—even that of child sacrifice.

Prophet after prophet warned the people to return to God or face the consequences. Yet this "stiff-necked" people refused to obey God's commands. The Bible reveals in Jeremiah 27 that He *allowed* Nebuchadnezzar, the Babylonian king, to conquer Israel and expand his empire. He was but a tool in God's hand because His children refused to repent of continued idolatry.

The people failed to heed Jeremiah's warning. Why? His message was one of gloom and doom; they much preferred teachers who assured that all would be peaceful. Perhaps they were much like those the apostle Paul referred to when he wrote:

> For the time will come when people will not put up with sound doctrine. Instead, to suit their own desires, they will gather around them a great number of teachers to say what their itching ears want to hear. (2 Timothy 4:3)

Those in Jeremiah's day simply could not imagine that God's punishment would fall and the temple, the sanctuary where He placed His name, would be destroyed. The Israelites continued to worship, but their hearts were far from Yahweh. Jeremiah 7:12, 14 warned that the temple would face destruction just as the tabernacle at Shiloh had earlier:

> "Go now to the place in Shiloh where I first made a dwelling for my Name, and see what I did to it because of the wickedness of my people Israel .... Therefore, what I did to Shiloh I will now do to the house that

bears my Name, the temple you trust in, the place I
gave to you and your ancestors."

For forty years Jeremiah faithfully delivered God's Word to the
people without any sign of repentance. From reading the historical
account, one may assume that Nebuchadnezzar, the well-known
Babylonian conqueror of the sixth century BC, simply decided one
day that Israel would be a nice little piece of real estate to add to his
collection. In 697 BC, he captured the city, plundered the temple, and
according to historical sources carried away the king, Jehoiakim,
along with between 10,000 and 12,000 men. In that day, as in many
Asian and Islamic cultures today, only the men were counted; therefore, the totals could have been as high as 48,000 Hebrew men,
women, and children wrenched from their homeland and forced
into slavery.[100]

Rather than returning Jehoiakim to Jerusalem as ruler, in 596
BC Nebuchadnezzar elevated the king's uncle, Zedekiah, to the
throne. He rebelled against the Babylonian king, and in Jeremiah
34:2–3 (ESV), the prophet delivered a warning that any attempt to
defy their captors would be met with destruction:

> "Thus says the LORD, the God of Israel: Go and
> speak to Zedekiah king of Judah and say to him,
> 'Thus says the LORD: Behold, I am giving this city into
> the hand of the king of Babylon, and he shall burn it
> with fire. You shall not escape from his hand but shall
> surely be captured and delivered into his hand. You
> shall see the king of Babylon eye to eye and speak
> with him face to face. And you shall go to Babylon.'"

The prophecy proved to be accurate. In 586 BC the Babylonians launched another army to put down Zedekiah's rebellion. They overran Judah and for eighteen long months, the marauders stripped the region bare and then built siege walls outside the city before attacking. A horrific famine beset the inhabitants of Jerusalem. The Lamentations of Jeremiah chapter 4, verses 9 and 10 describe the gruesomeness of the times:

> Those killed by the sword are better off than those who die of famine; racked with hunger, they waste away for lack of food from the field. With their own hands compassionate women have cooked their own children, who became their food when my people were destroyed.

The ramparts of Jerusalem were breached and then toppled; the city was pillaged, and Solomon's temple desecrated and burned. Its treasures were carried to Nebuchadnezzar's storehouses in Babylon.

Zedekiah, the king of Jerusalem, and his sons attempted to escape the wrath of the invading army but were caught trying to flee Jerusalem. They were chained and dragged away to Babylon. Being the despot that he was, Nebuchadnezzar had the sons of the Hebrew king put to death while their father was forced to watch. As the last son met his demise, Zedekiah's eyes were gouged out and he was led away to a dungeon.

The writer of 2 Chronicles in chapter 36, verses 14–16 gives us insight into why murder and exile were visited on the inhabitants of Judah:

> Furthermore, all the leaders of the priests and the people became more and more unfaithful, following all the detestable practices of the nations and defiling

the temple of the LORD, which he had consecrated in Jerusalem. The LORD, the God of their ancestors, sent word to them through his messengers again and again, because he had pity on his people and on his dwelling place. But they mocked God's messengers, despised his words and scoffed at his prophets until the wrath of the LORD was aroused against his people and there was no remedy.

Yet God did not altogether abandon the Israelites. The prophecy of judgment delivered by Jeremiah also gave a promise of restoration. Just as God had brought them out of Egypt, there would be a second exodus: God would bring His people out of Babylon after they had endured seventy years of captivity. Jeremiah prophesied that, in time, even legal documents would be sealed with the phrase:

> "As surely as the LORD lives, who brought the descendants of Israel up out of the land of the north and out of all the countries where he had banished them." (Jeremiah 23:8)

As God had promised, the exiles returned home, rebuilt the temple, and reconstructed the walls of their beloved city.

24

DESTRUCTION

The death of Josiah was the beginning of the end for Solomon's temple, the national symbol of the presence of God in the City of David. Discord reigned as first one and then the other of his three sons assumed the role of king. Regardless of which of the brothers sat on the throne, idolatry was again openly embraced in Judah.

During the chaotic rule of the last kings of Judah, the prophet Jeremiah was directed by Jehovah to deliver a message to the people from the court of the temple. He warned:

> "Raise a signal flag as a warning for Jerusalem: 'Flee now! Do not delay!' For I am bringing terrible destruction upon you from the north." (Jeremiah 4:6 NLT)

Jewish history gives us some insight into the life of Jeremiah:

> After the death of Josiah, there were four kings before the destruction: Jehoahaz, Jehoiakim, Jehoiachin and Zedekiah, covering a period of 23 years. Jeremiah was the main prophet during each of their reigns. Even those kings who were well-meaning were unwilling to accept the burden that Jeremiah placed upon them. When he got too much for them they mocked him or

were physically violent toward him .... Sadly, their disregard for the prophet's words did not forestall disaster. Everything came completely true as Jeremiah predicted them.[101]

In Jeremiah 36, the prophet is instructed by Jehovah to write down all the counsel that God had given Israel and Judah. When the scroll had been completed, Jeremiah's servant took it to the temple court and read it first to the people, and then to all the princes of Judah. Upon hearing the news, King Jehoiakim (one of the sons of Josiah) demanded that the scroll be brought to him. He defiantly cut the scroll to shreds and burned the remnants. His actions did not forestall the judgment of God upon the land.

The next three years set the stage for the "destruction from the north" prophesied by Jeremiah. The Assyrians, once dominant in the region, had been besieged by a coalition of Babylonians, Scythians, and Medes, and their cities laid waste. The void left by the Assyrian destruction was quickly filled by the Egyptians and Babylonians, who warred for control of the region. Judah stood directly in the path of the two enemies contending for supremacy. Ultimately, the Babylonians under the brilliant young king, Nebuchadnezzar, won the prize.

Judah was quickly reduced to that of a slave state from which homage and allegiance was demanded. King Jehoiachin and his entire family, all who served him, the upper classes—including Daniel, Shadrach, Meshach, and Abednego—as well as the majority of the inhabitants of Judah were deported to Babylon. The king's uncle, Zedekiah, was elevated to little more than a puppet-king as a subdued Judah served the Babylonians for nine years before the rebellion roiling beneath the surface exploded. Jeremiah thought the rebellion hopeless, as the captivity was in direct response to God's judgment against the apostasy of the Jews.

In 588 BC, Nebuchadnezzar returned and his troops moved to crush the rebellion. They camped outside Jerusalem and established a blockade around the city. While the people within the walls faced starvation, the Babylonians simply waited. The summer of 587 saw the city walls breached and its starving inhabitants subdued. Second Kings 25:5–7 (NLT) reveals the fate of Zedekiah:

> But the Babylonian troops chased the king and overtook him in the plains of Jericho, for his men had all deserted him and scattered. They captured the king and took him to the king of Babylon at Riblah, where they pronounced judgment upon Zedekiah. They made Zedekiah watch as they slaughtered his sons. Then they gouged out Zedekiah's eyes, bound him in bronze chains, and led him away to Babylon.

This was in fulfillment of Ezekiel's prophecy in chapter 12, verse 13, which reads:

> Then I will throw my net over him and capture him in my snare. I will bring him to Babylon, the land of the Babylonians, though he will never see it, and he will die there. (NLT)

About a month following the entrance into Jerusalem by his troops, Nebuchadnezzar dispatched Nebuzaradan, captain of the Babylonian guard, with strict instructions: He was to completely destroy the temple of the Lord in Jerusalem, as well as the royal palace. All municipal buildings were to be torn down, as were the walls of the city of Jerusalem. Its residents were to be taken by force to Babylon, except for the poorest of them, who were to be left behind to care for the vineyards and fields.

Before being burned to the ground, the temple was stripped of every gold, silver, and bronze article left—pillars, basins, altars, shovels, ladles, and anything else used for sacrificial offerings. Second Kings 25:18–19 (NLT) relates that the weight of the bronze from Solomon's temple was too great to be measured.

The priests did not escape the reach of Nebuzaradan. In his sweep of the city, he detained:

> Seraiah the high priest, Zephaniah the priest of the second rank, and the three chief gatekeepers. And from among the people still hiding in the city, he took an officer who had been in charge of the Judean army; five of the king's personal advisers; the army commander's chief secretary, who was in charge of recruitment; and sixty other citizens.

They were marched to Nebuchadnezzar's campaign headquarters at Riblah, where they were executed.

With its inhabitants scattered, its walls in shambles, its temple smashed and burned, Jerusalem was desolate. It was worthy of the lament written by the psalmist in chapter 137:1–4:

> By the rivers of Babylon we sat and wept when we remembered Zion. There on the poplars we hung our harps, for there our captors asked us for songs, our tormentors demanded songs of joy; they said, "Sing us one of the songs of Zion!" How can we sing the songs of the LORD while in a foreign land?

The Jews would have to wait fifty years before a glimmer of hope would break through the clouds of captivity when, under Cyrus the Great, the Babylonian Empire would be subjugated and the new Persian Empire would arise.

Unlike other conquerors, Cyrus did something that was completely uncommon: Seventy years after they were taken captive by Nebuchadnezzar, Cyrus allowed the Jewish people to return home to Israel. (This is what Daniel had prayed for in Daniel 9:17–19.) Enter Zerubbabel, who led the first wave of exiles back to Jerusalem during the reign of Darius II. Zerubbabel was a prince of the lineage of Zedekiah, the last king of Judah. He had no idea how great was his task to rebuild the temple, nor that it would take over twenty years to accomplish.

Zerubbabel immediately began the work assigned him. The altar was rededicated even as artisans were engaged to rebuild the temple. After two years of construction on the foundation alone, labor ceased. Stringent opposition came from the Samaritans, who were offended because they were not asked to help with the restoration. Questions of ownership and authority gave immediate cause for conflict, as did the call for repentance and a return, not only to worshiping Yahweh in Jerusalem but also to the tenets of the law of Moses.

The undertaking of rebuilding the temple in the ravaged city of Jerusalem was daunting. Poverty and the very struggle to survive the less-than-ideal conditions were confounding, and while aid did come via Persian coffers, it was not adequate for the task. Yet after more than fifteen long and difficult years, the temple stood once again on Mount Moriah in Jerusalem, "the sole great edifice in a city whose walls were still in ruins."[102]

The people gathered together for the dedication—the younger inhabitants filled with joy, the older with sadness:

When the builders laid the foundation of the temple of the LORD, the priests in their vestments and with trumpets, and the Levites (the sons of Asaph) with cymbals, took their places to praise the LORD, as prescribed by David king of Israel. With praise and thanksgiving they sang to the LORD: "He is good; his love toward Israel endures forever." And all the people gave a great shout of praise to the LORD, because the foundation of the house of the LORD was laid. But many of the older priests and Levites and family heads, who had seen the former temple, wept aloud when they saw the foundation of this temple being laid, while many others shouted for joy. No one could distinguish the sound of the shouts of joy from the sound of weeping, because the people made so much noise. And the sound was heard far away. (Ezra 3:10–13)

The new temple was dedicated around 515 BC under the direction of Zerubbabel the prince and Joshua the priest. Later Ezra, a priest thoroughly versed in God's law, arrived with authorization from the Persian emperor, Artaxerxes. Ezra was chosen to take the funds to Jerusalem and do everything he could to strengthen temple worship and devotion to Yahweh there, for the temple is referred to in rabbinical literature as *Beit HaMikdash*, or "The Sanctified House." Only the temple in Jerusalem is referred to by this name.

Then God sent Nehemiah to rebuild the walls of Jerusalem. Approximately fifty years later in Babylon, Nehemiah, a cupbearer to Artaxerxes I, met a group of men who had recently returned from the Holy City. What he heard, as recorded in Nehemiah 1:3, was heart rending:

> They said to me, "Those who survived the exile and are back in the province are in great trouble and disgrace. The wall of Jerusalem is broken down, and its gates have been burned with fire."

What was his reaction to this news? Did he just shake his head and walk away? No; Nehemiah wrote in verses 4–7:

> When I heard these things, I sat down and wept. For some days I mourned and fasted and prayed before the God of heaven. Then I said: "LORD, the God of heaven, the great and awesome God, who keeps his covenant of love with those who love him and keep his commandments, let your ear be attentive and your eyes open to hear the prayer your servant is praying before you day and night for your servants, the people of Israel. I confess the sins we Israelites, including myself and my father's family, have committed against you. We have acted very wickedly toward you. We have not obeyed the commands, decrees and laws you gave your servant Moses."

Nehemiah's first thought was not to rush into the throne room and throw himself down before a worldly king; rather, he approached Yahweh—the King of kings. He wept, mourned, fasted, prayed, and repented. For four months—from Chisleu to Nisan, Nehemiah sought God's direction. The answer came in a way totally unexpected. One day while in the king's presence, and though he had worked diligently to keep his grief hidden, the monarch noticed the sadness of Nehemiah's countenance:

> So the king asked me, "Why does your face look so sad when you are not ill? This can be nothing but sadness of heart." I was very much afraid, but I said to the king, "May the king live forever! Why should my face not look sad when the city where my ancestors are buried lies in ruins, and its gates have been destroyed by fire?" The king said to me, "What is it you want?" Then I prayed to the God of heaven, and I answered the king, "If it pleases the king and if your servant has found favor in his sight, let him send me to the city in Judah where my ancestors are buried so that I can rebuild it." (Nehemiah 2:2–5)

Once the king had given his permission to return to Jerusalem, Nehemiah asked for letters of safe conduct through the territories that lay between him and Judah. He then requested materials necessary to repair the breeches in the walls of the city and for his own residence. Verse 8 of chapter 2 says, "And because the gracious hand of my God was on me, the king granted my requests."

With each entreaty granted, Nehemiah set out for Jerusalem. After the long and taxing trip, he allowed three days for rest and recuperation before he began to survey the city—and even then he went under cover of darkness. He inspected the walls and counted the cost of rebuilding.

Alan Redpath, Christian author and speaker, wrote:

> Imagine his grief of heart as he stumbled among those ruins of what was once a great and mighty

fortress! Whenever a real work of God is to be done . . .
some faithful, burdened servant has to take a journey
such as Nehemiah took, to weep in the night over the
ruins, to wrestle in some dark Gethsemane in prayer
. . . . Are our hearts ever stirred like that?[103]

Following his midnight ride around the circumference of the
city, Nehemiah called upon the people to restore the walls. It would
not be an easy task. The Samaritans, led by two troublemakers,
Sanballat and Tobiah, accused the Hebrews of rebelling against the
very king who had approved the venture. Having had their fingers in
the till for so long, these men were not about to have their very lucra-
tive money-making schemes revealed and destroyed. Nehemiah
sternly responded to the complaints and charges (2:20):

> "The God of heaven will give us success. We his
> servants will start rebuilding, but as for you, you have
> no share in Jerusalem or any claim or historic right
> to it."

The work was hard, the task challenging and dangerous, but
Nehemiah was certain their success lay in God's divine provision:

> Therefore I stationed some of the people behind
> the lowest points of the wall at the exposed places,
> posting them by families, with their swords, spears
> and bows. After I looked things over, I stood up and
> said to the nobles, the officials and the rest of the
> people, "Don't be afraid of them. Remember the Lord,
> who is great and awesome, and fight for your fami-
> lies, your sons and your daughters, your wives and
> your homes." When our enemies heard that we were

aware of their plot and that God had frustrated it, we
all returned to the wall, each to our own work. From
that day on, half of my men did the work, while the
other half were equipped with spears, shields, bows
and armor. The officers posted themselves behind
all the people of Judah who were building the wall.
Those who carried materials did their work with one
hand and held a weapon in the other, and each of the
builders wore his sword at his side as he worked. But
the man who sounded the trumpet stayed with me.
Then I said to the nobles, the officials and the rest of
the people, "The work is extensive and spread out, and
we are widely separated from each other along the
wall. Wherever you hear the sound of the trumpet,
join us there. Our God will fight for us!" (Nehemiah
4:13–20)

Finally the task was completed. Nehemiah refused to take any
credit for the achievement:

When all our enemies heard about this, all the
surrounding nations were afraid and lost their self-
confidence, because they realized that this work had
been done with the help of our God. (Nehemiah 6:16)

Once the last stone was placed in the wall, Nehemiah called
Ezra to read the law of Moses to those assembled in its shadow. As
the men and women gathered together in obedience and in prayer,
they and the temple priests covenanted to obey the law and keep
themselves separate from all other nationalities.

Nehemiah had worked diligently and courageously in the face

of violent resistance. He arranged for more people to live inside the city walls, recognizing that its puny population was insufficient to defend it.

Between Ezra and Nehemiah, the worship of Yahweh and the life of His people underwent change. Some could even argue that it was in this time of revival that the essential groundwork for modern Judaism was laid. These men loved and endeavored to serve the God of David. They cared greatly about His laws and sought to observe them strictly. Intermarriage with Gentiles was banned, the weekly Sabbath was honored, land reforms limited the extent to which the rich could exploit the poor, tithing was observed, and priests and Levites were properly certified and ordained for service in the temple.

The fire was still burning—perhaps less intensely than in the days of David—but still burning after it had been nearly extinguished by waves of adversity and judgment. Jerusalem was and remains the symbol of the persistence and perseverance of the Jews—led by David—to inhabit his city with the praise and worship of Yahweh. David is known for his worship of the Lord, and so is his city, Jerusalem.

Under Ezra and Nehemiah, the worship of Yahweh and the life of His people underwent change. Some would even posit that it was during this time of revival that the essential groundwork for modern Judaism was laid. These men loved and endeavored to serve the God of David. They cared greatly about His laws and sought to observe them strictly.

Ezra had arrived in the sadly neglected Holy City only to learn that Jewish men had taken Gentile women as their wives—despite God's law forbidding mixed marriages. He fell on his face and repented for the sins of Israel, and then challenged those men who had taken heathen wives to dissolve the forbidden marriages and purify themselves before God.

Cyrus was unique, not only because he allowed the Jews to return to Israel but also because his birth and his name were foretold by the prophet Isaiah almost 150 years before. God also revealed Cyrus's mission to the prophet Isaiah, who recorded that Cyrus would accomplish specific tasks under God's direction during his lifetime. King Cyrus was destined to carry out God's plan as it related to His chosen people. It was through Cyrus that the Babylonian Empire and seventy years of Jewish captivity came to an end.

Isaiah 44:28, reveals:

> Who says of Cyrus, "He is my shepherd and will accomplish all that I please; he will say of Jerusalem, 'Let it be rebuilt,' and of the temple, 'Let its foundations be laid.'"

It may surprise you to discover that God doesn't predict the future; He reveals what He has already created. God foretells events to His prophets, who in turn prophesy to the people those things that God has disclosed. God disclosed His future plans to the prophets of old—Isaiah, Jeremiah, Daniel, Ezekiel, and others. Then in His perfect timing, the prophesied events became reality. He used ancient kings and kingdoms to chastise and direct His errant children, and He used those same kings and kingdoms to return them to their rightful place.

In the first year of King Cyrus, the king issued a decree concerning the temple of God in Jerusalem:

> Let the temple be rebuilt as a place to present sacrifices, and let its foundations be laid. It is to be sixty

cubits [ninety feet] high and sixty cubits [ninety feet] wide, with three courses of large stones and one of timbers. The costs are to be paid by the royal treasury. Also, the gold and silver articles of the house of God, which Nebuchadnezzar took from the temple in Jerusalem and brought to Babylon, are to be returned to their places in the temple in Jerusalem; they are to be deposited in the house of God. (Ezra 6:3–5)

Sadly, some of the furnishings so lovingly fashioned for the wilderness tabernacle and Solomon's temple had been looted from the edifice. These included the ark of the covenant, the Urim and Thummim, and the holy anointing oil. Another difference was that in the second temple, the Holy of Holies was separated from the Holy Place by curtains rather than a wall. Still, the Jews had regained the symbol of the presence of Jehovah in their midst.

While Cyrus's invasion of Babylon set the stage for the Israelites to return to Jerusalem and rebuild the temple, Nebuchadnezzar's capture of the people of Judah had one profound effect on those who eventually returned to their land: Never again would they be led astray by the idols of their enemies. Ezra and Nehemiah completed the task of rebuilding the temple, and the Jews repented and returned to the worship of the one true God—the One who had delivered them from the clutches of their adversaries.

25

HEROD, *the* ARCHITECT

For three hundred fifty years following the rebuilding of the temple and the walls of Jerusalem by Zerubbabel, Ezra, and Nehemiah, Israel suffered neither invasion nor desecration of the temple. That came to an end during the second century BC when the Seleucid ruler Antiochus marched into the city, slaughtered many of its inhabitants and defiled the temple. History relates that on December 6, 167 BC, the Gentile ruler polluted the altar in the temple courtyard by slaying a pig—an animal considered unclean by the Jews. He then erected a statue of Zeus Olympias in the temple. His antics and violation of the temple were the glue that united the people of Israel under the leadership of Mattathias, and later one of his five sons, Judah Maccabee (Hebrew for "hammer").

Antiochus gave little credence to the uprising, a fatal underestimation on his part. After being galvanized into action, the Jews bested the first troops sent by the Seleucids to halt the rebellion. When that small company was soundly routed, the king sent another, larger band. It, too, was decisively defeated, with Jerusalem retaken by the Maccabees and their supporters in 164 BC. The first order of business was to purify the temple and reestablish proper sacrifices.

It was from this rededication of the temple that the celebration of Hanukkah began. After the temple was cleansed, only one small cruse of oil for use in the holy lamps was found. The decision was made to light the temple Menorah, the seven-branched candelabra. To the total amazement of everyone, the Menorah burned brightly for eight days . . . until new oil was available.

The rededication of the altar is still observed with eight days of joy and gladness during the same season each year, beginning on the twenty-fifth of the Jewish month Kislev. The light of the Menorah is the symbol of the light of Yahweh. At the heart of the celebration is not only the recounting of the revolt and renewal, but the miracle of the oil.

Although it took twenty long years for the Jews to retake the whole of the land of Israel, it had been accomplished by 142 BC. Sadly, interfamily squabbles led to a civil war that weakened the nation and led to an open door for the Roman general Pompey to invade the city. With little regard for Jewish monotheistic worship, he was determined to see for himself what lay beyond the curtain in the sacred Holy of Holies. Montefiore relates the general's entrance into the sacred structure:

> Pompey and his entourage entered the Holy of Holies, an unspeakable sacrilege given that even the high priest visited it only once a year. The Roman was probably only the second gentile (after Antiochus IV) ever to penetrate the Sanctuary. Yet he respectfully examined the golden table and the holy candelabra—and realized that there was nothing else

there, no godhead, just an intense sanctity. He stole nothing.[104]

The historian Josephus expounded on Pompey's visit:

> Of the Jews there fell twelve thousand, but of the Romans very few .... and no small enormities were committed about the temple itself, which, in former ages, had been inaccessible, and seen by none; for Pompey went into it, and not a few of those that were with him also, and saw all that which it was unlawful for any other men to see but only for the high priests. There were in that temple the golden table, the holy candlestick, and the pouring vessels, and a great quantity of spices; and besides these there were among the treasures two thousand talents of sacred money: yet did Pompey touch nothing of all this, on account of his regard to religion; and in this point also he acted in a manner that was worthy of his virtue. The next day he gave order[s] to those that had the charge of the temple to cleanse it, and to bring what offerings the law required to God; and restored the high priesthood to Hyrcanus, both because he had been useful to him in other respects, and because he hindered the Jews in the country from giving Aristobulus [the Jewish ruler] any assistance in his war against him.[105]

Following twenty-five years of rebellion by various Jewish factions against invaders, Jerusalem ultimately fell to the armies of Herod as they broke down both the outer and inner walls and

marched into the city. During the ensuing battle many were butch-
ered—including priests and temple defenders. Herod had been the
recipient of many adjectives—none of which were *kind, gentle, gracious,* or *forbearing.* Instead, attached to him were words such as
brutal, shrewd, ruthless, hotheaded, and more. Once ensconced in
Jerusalem, the cruel crowned head over the Jews ordered the mass
slaying of more than 50 percent of the Sanhedrin, the highest religious and civil council of Jewish law. Herod showed no mercy to his
own family, having executed his mother-in-law, wife, Mariamne I,
her grandfather, and High Priest Hyrcanus, as well as three of his
own sons. He was an ogre who kept control of the region through
fear and rabid repression. The *Dictionary of the Bible,* edited by
James Hastings, says of Herod:

> His temperament was one of headlong passion; and
> when, in the later period of his life, the power and sus-
> piciousness of the tyrant had sapped the real magna-
> nimity of his nature, it converted him into a butcher,
> exercising his trade upon his own household as well
> as his opponents .... He made life and property in
> Palestine safe from every foe but his own tyranny.[106]

Montefiore wrote of Herod's kinfolks, "His brothers were piti-
less intriguers; his sister Salome ranks as a peerless monstress and
his own harem of women were all apparently as ambitious and as
paranoid as the king himself."[107]

Herod boasted a number of wives and appeared to be pursuing
Solomon's record for the most concubines with a harem 500 strong.
Despite all the intrigue in his court, a constant struggle to bal-
ance the loathing and distrust of his various wives and offspring,

and attempts to keep his enemies at bay, Herod was determined to leave his architectural mark on the region. He was so occupied with building projects it is difficult to imagine that he had the time necessary to deal with all the familial intrigues that surrounded him.

In the first century BC Herod was responsible for the building of his palace, the reconstruction of the temple, the Antonia Fortress, the Jerusalem water channel, Masada, three winter palaces, the Herodium (supposedly Herod's burial site), the large enclosure over the caves of the patriarchs in Hebron, and a multitude of additional projects. (The covering over the cave of the patriarchs is the only Herodian structure to fully survive the ravages of time.)

Perhaps Herod's most memorable undertaking was the temple. The king was determined to follow the biblical design standards for the structure as well as the Mosaic law that determined the legal aspects. In the midst of all those requirements was Herod's underlying wish to remain in the good graces of the Roman government. With that in mind, he had the temple rebuilt to Jewish specifications, but filled the remainder of the Temple Mount with Hellenistic designs.

Josephus wrote of Herod's reasons for undertaking the reconstruction of the temple:

> Our fathers, indeed, when they were returned from Babylon, built this temple to God Almighty, yet does it want sixty cubits of its largeness in altitude; for so much did that first temple which Solomon built exceed this temple; nor let any one condemn our fathers for their negligence or want of piety herein, for it was not their fault that the temple was no higher; for they were Cyrus, and Darius the son of Hystaspes, who

determined the measures for its rebuilding; and it
hath been by reason of the subjection of those fathers
of ours to them and to their posterity, and after them
to the Macedonians, that they had not the opportunity to follow the original model of this pious edifice,
nor could raise it to its ancient altitude; but since I
am now, by God's will, your governor, and I have had
peace a long time, and have gained great riches and
large revenues, and, what is the principal filing of all,
I am at amity with and well regarded by the Romans,
who, if I may so say, are the rulers of the whole world,
I will do my endeavor to correct that imperfection,
which hath arisen from the necessity of our affairs,
and the slavery we have been under formerly, and to
make a thankful return, after the most pious manner,
to God, for what blessings I have received from him,
by giving me this kingdom, and that by rendering his
temple as complete as I am able.[108]

And according to Randall Price, author of *Rose Guide to the
Temple*, "Even though Herod's rebuilding of the temple may have
appeared to be an act of devotion to God, at this same time he also
built a temple to the goddess Roma at Caesarea."[109]

Nor were his appointments of the men designated as high
priests of a particularly religious nature. They were, rather, a means
to achieve his political goals:

In 36 BC he named his 17-year-old son-in-law
Aristobulus III as high priest (although murdering
him the very next year), and in 23 BC he married the

high priest Simon's daughter (his third wife, whom
he also murdered).[110]

The massive undertaking to extend and rebuild Zerubbabel's
temple was to be on a par with that erected by Solomon, which
was done in record time—one and a half years. The outer court was
reconstructed in eight years. The speed with which the temple was
completed was achieved as a means to assuage the doubts of the
Jewish leaders that the existing temple would be demolished and
not replaced.

To achieve his goal, Herod had 1,000 priests schooled as builders
and stonemasons to fashion the edifice. He again went to Lebanon
for the cedar needed for beams. The quarries around Jerusalem dis-
gorged the massive stones needed for construction. As had Solomon,
Herod directed that everything be prepared off-site so that no sound
of hammer on stone was heard on the Temple Mount. Slowly and
silently, the gargantuan stones were slipped into place, the edges
aligned. According to Montefiore:

> The Roman engineer Vitruvius had created enor-
> mous devices—wheels, sledges and cranes—to trans-
> port such stones. Large wheels over 13 feet in diam-
> eter served as axles pulled by teams of oxen. Then
> there were winches—horizontal rotating beams with
> attached poles and cranks which enabled teams of
> ten men or fewer to use them. This way, eight men
> could lift 1-1/2 tons.[111]

Herod instructed his builders to find the bedrock beneath the
mount to provide the same firm foundation that both Solomon
and Zerubbabel had employed for earlier buildings. While the

dimensions for the temple changed with the addition of a second
floor above the sacred inner chambers, the dimensions of the Holy
of Holies as prescribed by Solomon likely remained the same. This
was due to the foundation stone that jutted into the temple—the site
where Abraham offered Isaac and where David built his altar to halt
the death angel (see 2 Samuel 24). The workers were so well organized that sacrifices continued to be offered in the courtyard during
the reconstruction.

Mount Moriah, on which resided what has come to be known
as Herod's temple, was positioned on the edge of the Kidron Valley;
Gethsemane sat just to the west. It was bordered on the northwest
corner by the Antonia Fortress, which housed a garrison of Roman
soldiers whose duty was to quell any disturbances that might erupt
near the temple.

Around the perimeter of the imposing walls were covered walk-
ways skirted on the inside by ranks of high marble pillars. There
were entrances on each of the four sides: two on the south, four on
the west, an underground passage on the north, and on the east the
legendary Golden Gate (or Eastern Gate), which provided access to
the temple from the Kidron Valley:

> The Bible indicates that Jesus passed through this
> gate many times while he was in Jerusalem. Jewish
> religious tradition teaches that the coming Messiah
> will enter Jerusalem through this gate. To prevent
> this, the Muslims sealed the gate during the rule of
> Suleiman. Visitors to the Mount of Olives stand on
> holy ground. Nearly 2,000 years ago, Jesus Christ
> stood on this hillside overlooking the Old City making
> prophesies that would change the world. According

to Jewish tradition, the Messiah will come through the Golden Gate (or Gate of Mercy) of the Old City and bring about the resurrection of the dead in the cemetery on the Mount. Unlike the lush expanses of grass associated with many cemeteries, the Mount of Olives is a mountainside of stones. Ironically, Jesus ascended up into Heaven from the Mount of Olives, which overlooks the Eastern Gate to the west. Ironically, from that stony mountain top Jesus ascended as the chief cornerstone for the up-building of Mount Zion. It is to the Mount of Olives that Jesus will return in the last days.[112]

The prophet Ezekiel prophesied that the gate would be walled up:

Then the man brought me back to the outer gate of the sanctuary, the one facing east, and it was shut. The LORD said to me, "This gate is to remain shut. It must not be opened; no one may enter through it. It is to remain shut because the LORD, the God of Israel, has entered through it. The prince himself is the only one who may sit inside the gateway to eat in the presence of the LORD. He is to enter by way of the portico of the gateway and go out the same way." (Ezekiel 44:1–3)

In AD 1530, the Ottoman Turks, apparently fearing the return of the Jewish Messiah, used huge stones to close the opening that was the Eastern Gate. A cemetery was then established at the foot of what had been the gate to the Temple Mount. Muslim reasoning was that no Jew would dare walk through the cemetery to reach the gate, thus forestalling the return of the Messiah. What they missed was that they were simply fulfilling a prophecy that had been made centuries before. Solomon reminds us in Proverbs 21:1 (NKJV), "The king's heart is in the hand of the LORD, like the rivers of water; He turns it wherever He wishes."

Certainly, God turned the heart of Suleiman to achieve His purpose.

The portico that flanked the east wall was called Solomon's Porch, and it was there that at the age of twelve, Jesus astounded the Jewish scholars with His knowledge (see Luke 2:46–47). It is thought that the southeast corner of the wall surrounding the Temple Mount was the pinnacle as described in Luke 4, the chapter outlining the temptation of Christ:

> Then he [Satan] brought Him to Jerusalem, set Him on the pinnacle of the temple, and said to Him, "If You are the Son of God, throw Yourself down from here. For it is written: 'He shall give His angels charge over you, To keep you,' and, 'In their hands they shall bear you up, Lest you dash your foot against a stone.'" And Jesus answered and said to him, "It has been said, 'You shall not tempt the LORD your God.'" (Luke 4:9–12 NKJV)

As with both the tabernacle and Solomon's temple, the courtyard was reserved for the altar upon which sacrifices were made. Unlike the bronze altars of the first two structures, the altar in Herod's temple was constructed of uncarved stones. This could have been because of God's command to Moses in Exodus 20:25, "If you make an altar of stones for me, do not build it with dressed stones, for you will defile it if you use a tool on it." Located behind the stone altar was a laver that sat atop twelve bronze bulls. There, as in the other two temples, the priests washed their hands and feet before presenting daily sacrificial offerings to Jehovah or before entering into the Holy Place. On the north side of the courtyard were six rows of four rings each where the animals to be offered were tied before being slaughtered in as humane a way as possible.

Within the temple proper, the Holy Place held the same articles as had Solomon's temple—the altar of incense, the seven-branched lampstand, and the table of shewbread. Sadly, the Holy of Holies was bare; the ark of the covenant had long since been lost to the Jewish people. Still, once each year on the Day of Atonement the high priest made his way into the room where the symbol of God's presence was to have rested. There atop the foundation stone, or the *Even Ha-Shetiyah*, the high priest sprinkled the blood where the mercy seat had once rested.

Although the temple was constructed during Jesus' lifetime, work on the Temple Mount continued for more than sixty years after His death. It would stand during His life and ministry and would fall in AD 70, just as He had proclaimed:

> As Jesus was leaving the temple, one of his disciples said to him, "Look, Teacher! What massive stones! What magnificent buildings!"
>
> "Do you see all these great buildings?" replied Jesus. "Not one stone here will be left on another; every one will be thrown down." (Mark 13:1–2)

26

JESUS *and the* TEMPLE

The birth of Christ is recounted in Luke and the story of the wise men from the east in Matthew. It is a story that has captured the imagination of multitudes since that fateful night in Bethlehem so many centuries ago. Legend has endowed the wise men with names: Melchior, Caspar, and Balthazar. There are, however, two people whose names we find in the biblical account of the birth of Jesus that have great significance: Simeon and Anna. Their role in the birth and then in Mary's purification is unquestionably vital in God's plan for His Son, Jesus Christ.

It is unlikely that you have ever heard the names of Anna and Simeon in a Christmas pageant, as that story is seldom told. We hear of shepherds and angels and "Glory to God in the highest, and on earth peace, good will toward men" (Luke 2:14 KJV). It is the information we find in verses 25–38 that is charged with excitement. Why? This man and woman, these two witnesses, confirm the identity of the Child being presented in the temple. This is crucial because in both Numbers 35:30 and Deuteronomy 17:6 we read that two or three witnesses are required as confirmation. Paul reaffirmed this in 2 Corinthians 13:1.

Pastor and teacher Dr. John MacArthur wrote:

> That testimony needs to be confirmed. And so Luke
> in this section brings in the testimony of witnesses.
> First, there is the testimony of Joseph and Mary, the
> parents' testimony. Secondly, there is the testimony
> of a man named Simeon. And thirdly, there is the tes-
> timony of a woman named Anna. And finally, there is
> the testimony of God Himself. Four testimonies are
> given . . . the testimony of His parents, the testimony
> of Simeon, the testimony of Anna, and the affirma-
> tion and testimony of God Himself as to the identity
> of this child. And so the passage confirms the cred-
> ibility of Luke's account that this child is indeed the
> Messiah, the Son of God, the anointed Christ and the
> Savior of the world.[113]

Anna and Simeon were not the only two people who testified
that Jesus was the Messiah. The lives of his earthly parents, Mary
and Joseph, were constant reminders that this firstborn Son was
special. Jehovah God led them every step of the way in preserving
the life of His Son—the trip to Bethlehem, the visit to the temple
for the rite of purification, the encounter with the prophet Simeon
and prophetess Anna, and shortly thereafter, the flight to Egypt to
escape Herod's deadly edict. Even before His birth, Mary visited
her aunt Elizabeth, who was pregnant with the one who came to be
known as John the Baptist:

> When Elizabeth heard Mary's greeting, the baby
> leaped in her womb, and Elizabeth was filled with the
> Holy Spirit. In a loud voice she exclaimed: "Blessed

are you among women, and blessed is the child you will bear! But why am I so favored, that the mother of my Lord should come to me? As soon as the sound of your greeting reached my ears, the baby in my womb leaped for joy. Blessed is she who has believed that the Lord would fulfill his promises to her!" (Luke 1:41–45)

Jesus' first trip as an infant was to the temple, according to Leviticus 12. He would have been circumcised on the eighth day after His birth, and on the fortieth day Mary and Joseph would have followed verses 6–9:

> "When the days of her purification for a son or daughter are over, she is to bring to the priest at the entrance to the tent of meeting a year-old lamb for a burnt offering and a young pigeon or a dove for a sin offering. He shall offer them before the Lord to make atonement for her, and then she will be ceremonially clean from her flow of blood. These are the regulations for the woman who gives birth to a boy or a girl. But if she cannot afford a lamb, she is to bring two doves or two young pigeons, one for a burnt offering and the other for a sin offering. In this way the priest will make atonement for her, and she will be clean."

The mother of the Messiah followed the Mosaic law of circumcision even though the Child she held in her arms was the sinless Son of God. A month later, while the young family was in the temple, they encountered a stranger—Simeon—just as they were presenting the baby to the Lord. The old man walked up and took the baby right from Mary's arms. Neither Mary nor Joseph were alarmed; after all, they had very recently entertained angels and shepherds in a stable. It was a fitting introduction for the child who would turn the world upside down.

The old man cradled the child gently in his arms, and with tears in his eyes, turned his face heavenward. Quietly he prayed:

> "Lord, now You are letting Your servant depart in peace, according to Your word; for my eyes have seen Your salvation which You have prepared before the face of all peoples, a light to bring revelation to the Gentiles, and the glory of Your people Israel." (Luke 2:29–32 NKJV)

Perhaps Simeon explained to the awed mother that God had promised him he would see the Messiah before he died. As the years passed and he grew old, maybe he had begun to wonder if God would keep His promise—the promise he now held in his arms. However, there was more to Simeon's message. Along with the good news of the arrival of the Messiah, he gave Mary an admonition:

> Then Simeon blessed them, and he said to Mary, the baby's mother, "This child is destined to cause many in Israel to fall, but he will be a joy to many others. He has been sent as a sign from God, but many will oppose him. As a result, the deepest thoughts of many hearts will be revealed. And a sword will pierce your very soul." (Luke 2:34–35 NLT)

As Simeon paused, an old woman hurried up to the group and gave thanks to Jehovah for sending the One who would be the redemption of Israel.

From His birth, Jesus was recognized as the promised Messiah by many in Jerusalem. In Matthew 2:1–6 (NLT), readers are introduced to Herod, who out of fear for his throne would try to have the Christ child murdered:

> Jesus was born in Bethlehem in Judea, during the reign of King Herod. About that time some wise men from eastern lands arrived in Jerusalem, asking, "Where is the newborn king of the Jews? We saw his star as it rose, and we have come to worship him." King Herod was deeply disturbed when he heard this, as was everyone in Jerusalem. He called a meeting of the leading priests and teachers of religious law and asked, "Where is the Messiah supposed to be born?" "In Bethlehem in Judea," they said, "for this is what the prophet wrote: 'And you, O Bethlehem in the land of Judah, are not least among the ruling cities of Judah, for a ruler will come from you who will be the shepherd for my people Israel.'"

Matthew 2:7 (NLT) gives us a picture of Herod's predicament when faced with the "king-hunters":

> Then Herod called for a private meeting with the wise men, and he learned from them the time when the star first appeared. Then he told them, "Go to Bethlehem and search carefully for the child. And when you find him, come back and tell me so that I can go and worship him, too!"

As you read that last verse, are you tempted to end it with "Yeah, right!" It seems a very transparent ploy. Thankfully, the wise men were prevented by a God-given dream from returning to Jerusalem for a tête-à-tête with Herod. They returned home by another way. That same night, an angel of the Lord appeared to Joseph in a dream:

> "Get up! Flee to Egypt with the child and his mother [Mary]," the angel said. "Stay there until I tell you to return, because Herod is going to search for the child to kill him." (Matthew 2:13 NLT)

As the light of the holy messenger faded from the room, Joseph packed up his little family, harnessed the donkey, and they set out for Egypt as instructed. Even as they fled the country, Herod, enraged that the wise men had defied his instructions, ordered that every child under the age of two years was to be slaughtered. His demand elicits from the writer of Matthew a quote from the book of Jeremiah—I think one of the most poignant and heartrending verses in the Bible:

> "A voice is heard in Ramah, weeping and great mourning, Rachel weeping for her children and refusing to be comforted, because they are no more." (Matthew 2:18)

Mary, Joseph, and Jesus remained in Egypt until another heavenly visitor revealed to Joseph that Herod had died; it was safe to return to Nazareth.

The next time we read of Jesus and the temple in Scripture is His trip to Jerusalem with Joseph and Mary to celebrate Passover. His intervening years would have been spent in Nazareth in the carpenter shop with Joseph and in the synagogue school studying the law and the prophets. When He reached the age of twelve, the time had come for Jesus to take His place among the men of the village and participate in the various Jewish observances.

As Mary and Joseph prepared for the trek to Jerusalem to observe Passover, Jesus likely joined with friends near His age. While it was necessary for all men who had reached the age of twelve, Jewish women were not required to make the trip. Mary, however, accompanied Joseph and Jesus to the City of David—about sixty-four miles to the south of Nazareth. The young family enjoyed their stay in Jerusalem, not for the required two days, but for seven days.

At the conclusion of the feast, the family gathered its belongings and joined the crowd returning to Nazareth. After having traveled a full day, the parents suddenly realized Jesus was not in the company of His friends. Apparently He was a trustworthy boy old enough to celebrate His first *bar mitzvah* and therefore His absence had not raised an alarm. Perhaps it was time for dinner when He was missed, and a frantic Mary and Joseph turned their donkey around and began the long journey back to Jerusalem. After three days of fear and anguish, of searching and longing, the parents found Jesus in the temple court.

It is likely that Jesus stayed behind, not to cause pain to His parents, but from an insatiable desire for knowledge, and maybe for another reason altogether. It could be that the reason is found in Luke 2:48–50 (NKJV):

> So when they saw Him, they were amazed; and His mother said to Him, "Son, why have You done this to us? Look, Your father and I have sought You anxiously." And He said to them, "Why did you seek Me? Did you not know that I must be about My Father's

business?" But they did not understand the statement which He spoke to them.

Rev. John Piper, Minneapolis teacher and seminarian, said of this event:

> They were searching and searching and finally they turn him up at the temple. Where did they search? In the playground, the local swimming hole, in the shops, at the bakery? Jesus answers: You shouldn't have had to seek at all. For you know, don't you, that there is laid on me an inner necessity to be in my Father's house (or about his business—either translation is possible)?[114]

British evangelist and theologian G. Campbell Morgan said of this encounter with the temple scholars:

> The picture of Christ here is very full of beauty, although too often the natural fact is obscured by false ideas concerning the attitude of Jesus towards the teachers. A very popular conception of His action here is that of a boy delighting to ask questions that will show His own wisdom and puzzle the doctors. This would seem to be utterly contrary to the facts. Jesus, a pure, beautiful boy, physically strong, mentally alert, spiritually full of grace, moving into new and larger experiences of His life, answered the questions of the doctors with a lucidity that astonished them and submitted problems to them which showed how remarkable was the calibre of His mind and how intense the fact of His spiritual nature. So great an

opportunity was this to Him that He tarried behind,
still talking with these men.[115]

Could there be yet another explanation? Perhaps the young
child was driving home a point that Mary had missed in her earlier temple encounter with Simeon? The old man had warned the
mother of Jesus that "yes, a sword will pierce through your own soul
also" (Luke 2:35). The pages of Scripture are filled with types and
shadows. Might not this be another example of a time that would
come at the conclusion of Christ's ministry on the earth—when the
Son of Man would be suspended on a cross between heaven and
earth? When an anguished Mary would again stand vigil, but this
time beneath the cross that held her son?

27

The TEMPTATION of CHRIST

The Bible is silent about the years of Jesus' life between the ages of twelve and thirty. Where was He? What was He doing? The only glimmer we have is a verse tucked away in Luke 2:52, "And Jesus grew in wisdom and stature, and in favor with God and man." He became grounded in education, physical health, moral teachings, and social interaction. At the age of twelve, rather than proclaiming to Joseph and Mary the importance of His mission and insisting that He be allowed to begin His earthly ministry, Jesus humbled himself and went home to Nazareth. There He worked alongside Joseph in the carpenter shop, sat beside him in the synagogue, and learned obedience.

It was early Christian theologian St. Augustine who said:

> He was created of a mother whom He created. He was carried by hands that He formed. He cried in the manger in wordless infancy, He the Word, without whom all human eloquence is mute.[116]

His entire life was one of obedience, to His earthly parents and to His heavenly Father. In his letter to the Philippian church, Paul wrote:

> And being found in appearance as a man, He humbled Himself and became obedient to the point of death, even the death of the cross. (Philippians 2:8 NKJV)

After eighteen years of apparent obscurity, Jesus burst on the scene. He was now thirty years old. Some Bible theologians believe there was a reason for this period of virtual obscurity. *The Pulpit Commentary* postulates:

> This was the age at which the Levites entered upon their work; the age, too, at which it was lawful for scribes to teach. Generally speaking, thirty among the Jews was looked upon as the time of life when manhood had reached its full development.[117]

When Jesus reappeared in the public eye, it was on the banks of the Jordan River near Bethabara. The incident is relayed in Matthew 3:13–17:

> Then Jesus came from Galilee to the Jordan to be baptized by John. But John tried to deter him, saying, "I need to be baptized by you, and do you come to me?" Jesus replied, "Let it be so now; it is proper for us to do this to fulfill all righteousness." Then John consented. As soon as Jesus was baptized, he went up out of the water. At that moment heaven was opened, and he saw the Spirit of God descending like a dove and alighting on him. And a voice from heaven said,

"This is my Son, whom I love; with him I am well pleased."

As the Son of God, Jesus was to be the perfect example for all men. His baptism was not one of repentance, as John was calling those around him to do; it was rather an act of public consecration. Today, the rite of baptism is an outward sign of the inward work of salvation. It identifies the Believer as having died to sin and then being resurrected to newness in Christ. It is a powerful witness of God's work in an individual's life.

As the Son of Man emerged from the waters of the Jordan, Matthew tells us that the heavens were opened; a dove descended and alighted on Jesus. Could this have been a signal of how God would accomplish His will and purpose through His Son? The Jews were awaiting a Messiah who would rescue them from the oppression of the Romans and establish His kingdom on earth—a warrior King. They were seeking the Lion of the tribe of Judah (see Revelation 5:5); instead, the Messiah was to be the gentle Jesus, the loving Savior, Light of the World, Bread of Life, and Living Water. As Elijah had discovered at Horeb:

> Then a great and powerful wind tore the mountains apart and shattered the rocks before the LORD, but the LORD was not in the wind. After the wind there was an earthquake, but the LORD was not in the earthquake. After the earthquake came a fire, but the LORD was not in the fire. And after the fire came a gentle whisper. (1 Kings 19:11–12)

Jesus would be rejected, in a sense, because He did not appear with tornadic might or the shaking of an earthquake or the

destruction of a fire; He came as a still, small voice. Jesus came not
to create chaos in the known world, but to work in the hearts of men
who would be sent forth to turn the world upside down (see Acts 17:6).

✧   ✧   ✧

Matthew 4 tells us that immediately after His baptism Jesus
was "led" into the wilderness. Mark 1:12 (NKJV) says that "the Spirit
drove Him into the wilderness," so that, once He had distanced
himself from the crowds that were sure to gather after His baptism,
Jesus, the Son of Man, fasted and prayed through forty days and
nights of temptation. According to G. Campbell Morgan:

> Jesus was led by the Spirit into the wilderness to
> be tempted of the devil. He was tempted of the devil
> during forty days, during the whole of which period
> He was still led by the Spirit. The Spirit took Him to
> the place of temptation, and was with Him through
> the process of temptation. Not in His Deity did He
> resist, but in His perfect Manhood. Manhood is how-
> ever never able to successfully resist temptations of
> the devil save when fulfilling a first Divine intention,
> that, namely, of depending upon God, and thus being
> guided by the Spirit of God. Thus the Man Jesus was
> led by the Spirit into the wilderness, and was led by
> the Spirit through all the process of temptation.[118]

During this solitary experience, Jesus was tempted in three
different measures: body, soul, and spirit. It is important to understand the difference between *temptation* and *testing.* Satan was not
tempting Jesus in an attempt to discover who He was; Satan knew

without a doubt that he was addressing the Son of God. He knew how that One would react; but would the Son of Man be more inclined to fall for the lies of the consummate Liar?

Paul Lee Tan included the following in his book *Encyclopedia of 7700 Illustrations*:

> Temptation often comes not at our strongest, but our weakest moments. When we are at the limit of our patience, love, etc. we are tempted to be unChristian, beware. Jesus' temptation began *after* 40 days of fasting.[119]

When God tests His child, it brings victory, strength, and goodness into that one's life. Obstacles overcome bring joy and reward to the overcomer:

> God blesses those who patiently endure testing and temptation. Afterward they will receive the crown of life that God has promised to those who love him. (James 1:12 NLT)

The first Adam was tempted by the serpent and failed miserably; the second Adam also faced seduction by the same one who wanted to be equal with God. The first temptation leveled at Jesus targeted the body—the lust of the flesh, the desire for food. Satan said to Him (paraphrased), "Since you are the Son of God, turn these hot desert stones into crusty bread and satisfy your hunger." Jesus answered with the Word from Deuteronomy 8:3 (NKJV):

> So He humbled you, allowed you to hunger, and fed you with manna which you did not know nor did your fathers know, that He might make you know

that man shall not live by bread alone; but man lives by every word that proceeds from the mouth of the LORD.

Charles Spurgeon translated Satan's challenge this way:

> This was, in effect, saying, "Leave off trusting in Your Heavenly Father. He has evidently deserted You— He has left You in the wilderness among the wild beasts and though He feeds *them*, He has not fed You! He has left You to starve—therefore, help Yourself—exercise Your own power! Though You have put it under God's keeping and, being here on earth, You have become Your Father's Servant, yet steal a little of Your service from Your Father and use it on Your own behalf. Take some of that power which You have devoted to His great work and employ it for Your own comfort. Leave off trusting in Your Father—command these stones to be made bread."[120]

Spurgeon went on to say of Jesus' response to Satan's challenge, "This answer of our Lord to the tempter teaches us that the sustenance of our life, although naturally and according to the ordinary appearance of things depends upon bread, yet really depends upon God!"[121]

The second temptation had Satan taking Jesus to the temple compound, a place to which He would return again and again during His ministry. In Matthew 4:5–7, we read:

> Then the devil took him to the holy city and had him stand on the highest point of the temple. "If you are the Son of God," he said, "throw yourself down. For it is written: 'He will command his angels concerning you, and they will lift you up in their hands, so that you will

not strike your foot against a stone.'" Jesus answered him, "It is also written: 'Do not put the Lord your God to the test.'"

There are many Bible scholars who believe that location would have been the intersection of the Royal Portico and Solomon's Porch. From that vantage point one could look down a dizzying 450 feet into the Kidron Valley. A jump from that height would have meant certain death for the Son of Man and a vast departure from His Father's plan for the Son of God. Satan, the Deceiver, was willing to go to any lengths—or heights—to stop God's redemptive design.

A second possibility of the location of the pinnacle would have brought Jesus to the ground right in the midst of the crowds that gathered in the temple courtyard during the day. Knowing that Jesus fully trusted His Father, Satan tried the "dear old Dad won't allow you to be injured" card. Perhaps he painted a picture of immediate gratification: Jesus jumps; God guards Him, instant adoration. There would be no trips through the agonizingly hot desert, no dealing with skeptics, no arrest, no trial, no scourging, and no unspeakable pain. Jesus would be spared an ignominious death on the cross—but the souls of men would be forever lost.

The Father of Lies then tried to seal the offer with a smattering of scripture, carefully selected and adroitly applied:

> For He shall give His angels charge over you, to keep you in all your ways. In their hands they shall bear you up, lest you dash your foot against a stone. (Psalm 91:11–12 NKJV)

Faced with such a diabolical lie, Jesus retaliated as one who had been in the presence of the Father. I can imagine His terse reply taken directly from Deuteronomy 6:16 (NKJV), "You shall not tempt the LORD your God." The late pastor and biblical expositor Ray Stedman wrote of this temptation:

> The greatest display of faith is not in some spectacular demonstration, but in the quiet trust of the heart that rests upon what God has said. Not just what is said in one place, but balanced truth. Perhaps the most important word in the whole of scriptures in many respects, is this one word that he adds, "It is written *again*." Truth does not come to us in capsule form. It is a complete account, and one truth needs to be balanced against another. We never have arrived at the whole until the complete account is laid out and we see it in its total revelation.[122]

With the third temptation, Satan offered Jesus "all the kingdoms of the world." He appealed to the pride of life. Having come to earth to free it from Satan's grip, this move would have offered no hope of freedom from the evil grip of the destroyer. The only thing the tempter asked in return was that Jesus bow down and worship at his cloven-hooved feet. Jesus again took up the "sword of the Spirit, which is the word of God" (see Ephesians 6:17 KJV) and vanquished the Enemy with the words:

> "Away with you, Satan! For it is written, 'You shall worship the LORD your God, and Him only you shall serve.'" (Matthew 4:10 NKJV; Deuteronomy 6:13)

I am reminded of the old hymn "Stand Up, Stand Up for Jesus," which states, "This day the noise of battle, the next the victor's song."[123]

The devil departed, and immediately the Father sent ministering angels to meet Jesus' earthly needs. Was this the end of Satan's attempts to foil the Father's plan? Not by any stretch of the imagination; Calvary is the confirmation of his continuing efforts to halt the work of grace. But each time the Enemy came against the Son, Jesus raised the banner of truth to defeat Satan's attacks—in Gethsemane and at Calvary. The reply from the lips of our Savior was, "Not my will, but Thy will be done."

28

THE LAST WEEK:
Sunday, Monday, *and* Tuesday

The time had finally come for Jesus to make His way to Jerusalem. Luke 9:51 (NKJV) tells us that He "steadfastly set His face to go to Jerusalem." Luke could have just as readily echoed the verse found in Isaiah 50:7 (NLT): "Therefore, I have set my face like a stone, determined to do his will."

Three of the holy days so significant to the Jews—the feasts of Passover, Firstfruits, and Unleavened Bread—fell within an eight-day period whose dates were contingent on the lunar calendar. Luke 22:7 refers to this time as "the day of Unleavened Bread," while John simply calls it the week of "the Passover." The feasts were all dictated by Mosaic law as set forth in Exodus, Leviticus, and Numbers. What is now often referred to as Passion Week began on Sunday, the tenth of Nisan. In John 12:1 (NLT), the disciple started the countdown to the most horrific event in the life of Christ, yet the most gratifying for Believers:

> Six days before the Passover celebration began, Jesus arrived in Bethany, the home of Lazarus—the man he had raised from the dead.

The following morning Jesus and His disciples set out for Jerusalem. It was on that particular day that the lambs were culled from the flocks in the fields near Bethlehem. They were then driven to Jerusalem, through the Sheep Gate, and readied for Passover selection. The lambs were chosen on the ninth day of Nisan so that they could be in the family home by sundown, which began the tenth day of Nisan. Passover would be celebrated on the fourteenth day.

On that morning, Jesus dispatched two of His disciples to Bethphage on a very specific mission:

> "Go to the village ahead of you, and at once you will find a donkey tied there, with her colt by her. Untie them and bring them to me. If anyone says anything to you, say that the Lord needs them, and he will send them right away." This took place to fulfill what was spoken through the prophet: "Say to Daughter Zion, 'See, your king comes to you, gentle and riding on a donkey, and on a colt, the foal of a donkey.'" (Matthew 21:2–5)

Jerusalem was overrun with people who had amassed to celebrate the Feast of Passover. Women were busy preparing for the Seder—the meal that, true to this day, symbolizes the deliverance of the Jews from slavery in Egypt. Yearly, they prayed that God would send the Messiah to rescue His people from Roman tyranny. So Jesus' instructions were fulfilled and the donkey was brought to Him. The disciples had removed their cloaks to pad the bony back of the donkey, creating a makeshift saddle by layering their coats on the colt. Jesus climbed astride and began His ride into Jerusalem—a city whose ranks had swelled by several thousand celebrants.

Biblical scholar Alfred Edersheim wrote of Jesus' entry into Jerusalem:

> Immediately before was the Valley of the Kedron, here seen in its greatest depth as it joins the Valley of Hinnom, and thus giving full effect to the great peculiarity of Jerusalem, seen only on its eastern side—its situation as of a City rising out of a deep abyss. It is hardly possible to doubt that this rise and turn of the road—this rocky ledge—was the exact point where the multitude paused again, and "He, when He beheld the City, wept over it." Not with still weeping (edakrusen), as at the grave of Lazarus, but with loud and deep lamentation (eklausen). The contrast was, indeed, terrible between the Jerusalem that rose before Him in all its beauty, glory, and security, and the Jerusalem which He saw in vision dimly rising on the sky, with the camp of the enemy around about it on every side, hugging it closer and closer in deadly embrace, and the very 'stockade' which the Roman Legions raised around it; then, another scene in the shifting panorama, and the city laid with the ground, and the gory bodies of her children among her ruins; and yet another scene: the silence and desolateness of death by the Hand of God—not one stone left upon another![124]

The gates of Jerusalem had seen the entry of a number of kings: massive entourages, heralds with trumpets, numerous guards and soldiers armed with swords and marching in step. This was customary and was designed to intimidate those about to be taken into captivity. Jesus was a different kind of king. He came not to dominate with power, but to serve in humility. He entered the city, not on a magnificent white stallion signifying war, but on a donkey— a mark of humility, of meekness.

Jesus was welcomed with the sound of waving palm branches, the swish muffled by the shouts of "Hosanna to the Son of David!" "Blessed is he who comes in the name of the Lord!" "Hosanna in the highest heaven!" (Matthew 21:9)

Of course, the Pharisees chided Jesus and His followers and called for Him to "rebuke your disciples." Jesus replied that if the people were silenced, the very stones would cry out. (See Luke 19.)

Chuck Warnock, pastor of Chatham Baptist Church, wrote of the triumphal entry:

> They have been looking for a hero, and Jesus is the flavor of the day. And, of course, there were strange reports that he could heal people, feed people, and that when he prayed evil spirits fled from those they possessed. All the more reason to admire Jesus—he was both a revolutionary and a mystic. A great combination for the nation.
>
> But the problem with admirers is that they see what they want to see in their hero of the day. What the crowds saw in Jesus was the son of Joseph, not the Son of God. They saw him as a revolutionary, not as Redeemer. They wanted another Maccabee, not a new Messiah. In short, they admired Jesus because they thought he was the answer to all their problems.[125]

The reception Jesus received was not a precursor to a hero being crowned king of Israel; it was instead preparation for Jesus' death on the cross. He didn't need the adulation of the crowd to determine who He was. He knew without question that He was the Son of God, the Messiah, the red thread of salvation that runs through the pages of scripture from Genesis to Revelation. Jesus was a different kind of monarch. He knew that at the end of His mission, He would mount not a throne but a cross. Now He must make a statement bold enough to force the hand of the high priest and the Sanhedrin—the time had come.

Teddy Kollek and Moshe Pearlman wrote of Jesus' decision to go to Jerusalem for Passover:

> By the time he [Jesus] came to Jerusalem on what was to be his last Passover, he was already well known—and marked as a dangerous rebel. He was aware of the threat to his life if he forsook the comparative safety of Galilee and made this pilgrimage, when Jerusalem would be thronged with visitors and the Romans would be on the alert for revolt.[126]

What better way to provoke both the Romans and the Jewish leaders than for the people to proclaim Him "King of the Jews." Heretofore, He had stayed in the background, trying as much as possible to avoid large gatherings and the accompanying publicity. This day was different; this day was a declaration of His purpose—to fulfill the Old Testament prophecies regarding the Messiah that was to come.

In John 10:18 (NLT), Jesus said:

> "No one can take my life from me. I sacrifice it voluntarily. For I have the authority to lay it down when

I want to and also to take it up again. For this is what
my Father has commanded."

With that knowledge, He chose the day of revelation. Jesus
chose the method by which He would make himself known. He
chose the day His fate would be sealed and humbly offered His life.
He was well aware of the outcome of His choice—death!

✧   ✧   ✧

Monday morning, Jesus and the disciples walked to the temple.
Matthew 21:12–13 (NKJV) relates what happened when they arrived:

> Then Jesus went into the temple of God and drove
> out all those who bought and sold in the temple, and
> overturned the tables of the money changers and the
> seats of those who sold doves. And He said to them,
> "It is written, 'My house shall be called a house of
> prayer,' but you have made it a 'den of thieves.'"

What prompted Jesus to make such an uncompromising move?
He was in Jerusalem for Passover, the most sacred of all Jewish
feasts. It was the time in the celebration, just before the Seder, that
all women cleansed their homes from any trace of leaven, a symbol of
sin. Jesus looked about with what must have been great dismay; His
Father's house was rife with the greediness of the money changers
and merchants who had taken up residence in the temple court.

No longer was Jehovah at the center of temple worship; greed
reigned. As the Jews from Roman and Greek regions filed into
Jerusalem to celebrate Passover, a temple tax was collected. The only
currency acceptable to the priests was the shekel, which was coined

in Israel. It was open season for money changers who would take the foreign currency and, for a fee, exchange it for the customary shekel.

Then there were the animal vendors who were there, ostensibly to ensure that the people had the proper, flawless animal to offer to Jehovah. That practice, too, had become tainted by materialism and deception. The Mosaic law stated that only the best of the flocks were to be offered (see Exodus 12). The Levites in charge of examining the worthiness of the offerings would often reject the sacrifice. The animal would then have to be exchanged for one that was deemed suitable; this was nothing more than a scam. The vendor would take the tainted animal and, again for a fee, exchange it for one that had passed inspection—one that just moments before had likely been rejected as flawed.

In the days leading up to the Passover, many of the merchants had set up shop outside Jerusalem on the roads leading into the city. Once the majority of the pilgrims had arrived, the hawkers moved into the temple court to ply their trade. Among the sellers were those who supplied pigeons to the poor, the lowliest of all sacrifices allowed by the Law. The problem was that the price for a common bird was so exorbitant the poor could not afford them as an offering.

Into the center of this maelstrom of greed taking place in His Father's house walked the Son of God, filled with righteous indignation. Author and teacher Charles Swindoll wrote of Jesus' response:

> Very often, people portray Jesus as the meek and mild teacher who taught His followers to love others as themselves, to avoid retaliation by turning the other cheek, to pursue peace, and to avoid judging others. While Jesus did indeed possess these qualities and teach these values, the picture is incomplete.

These passages reveal that Jesus was more than the pale, languid figure often portrayed in art, on television, and in movies.[127]

John (2:17) concludes this event with, "Then His disciples remembered that it was written, 'Zeal for Your house has eaten Me up.'" (See Psalm 69:9.) Such zeal had brought Him, early in His ministry, on a collision course with evil and those who practiced it. (See the first account in John 2.) Not having learned the lesson Jesus had taught early in His ministry, the money changers and vendors returned to the temple during the Passover celebration.

The remainder of Jesus' day was spent in ministry in the temple court. Matthew 21:14–17 (NKJV) tells us:

> Then the blind and the lame came to Him in the temple, and He healed them. But when the chief priests and scribes saw the wonderful things that He did, and the children crying out in the temple and saying, "Hosanna to the Son of David!" they were indignant and said to Him, "Do You hear what these are saying?" And Jesus said to them, "Yes. Have you never read, 'Out of the mouth of babes and nursing infants You have perfected praise'?" Then He left them and went out of the city to Bethany, and He lodged there.

Even with the horrors that were about to come upon Him, Jesus had great compassion on the lame and blind who had remained in the temple. He reached out in love and took time to meet their needs.

Danish sculptor Bertel Thorvaldsen is said to have set about creating a statue of Jesus:

He wished to see if the statue would cause the right reaction of heart in those who saw it. He brought a little child and bade him look at the statue, and asked him: "Who do you think that is?" The child looked, and then answered: "It is a great man." And Thorvaldsen knew that he had failed. So he scrapped his first statue and began again . . . when he had finished, he brought the little child . . . and again asked the same question: "Who do you think that is?" And the child smiled and answered: "that is Jesus who said: 'Let the children come to me.'" And Thorvaldsen knew that this time he had succeeded. He submitted the statue to the test of the eyes of a child. When all is said and done that is no bad test . . . . The goodness which can meet the clear gaze of a child, and which can stand the test of a child's simplicity, is goodness indeed.[128]

✧   ✧   ✧

Scribes and Pharisees are mentioned some sixty times in Matthew, Mark, and Luke but only once in John as he retells the story of the woman taken in adultery. It was the duty of the scribes, scholarly men, to study the law of Moses, reproduce it, and pen interpretations of it. They were very serious and exacting as they went about their duties. It was those men who so correctly preserved the Old Testament for posterity. Scribes belonged predominantly to the sect of the Pharisees and were held in high regard by the people. This despite the man-made traditions that were added to the law; burdens that made it almost impossible for anyone to fulfill God's Word.

Outwardly, the men appeared to be precise and faithful keepers of the law, but Jesus took them to task severely in the entire chapter of Matthew 23 with warning after warning. In verses 27–28 (NKJV), Jesus counsels them with:

> "Woe to you, scribes and Pharisees, hypocrites! For you are like whitewashed tombs which indeed appear beautiful outwardly, but inside are full of dead men's bones and all uncleanness. Even so you also outwardly appear righteous to men, but inside you are full of hypocrisy and lawlessness."

Dr. John F. Walvoord, long-time president of Dallas Theological Seminary, wrote of this condemnation:

> Only Matthew records this scathing denunciation of these religious leaders of the Jews. These woes, in contrast to the Beatitudes, denounce false religion as utterly abhorrent to God and worthy of severe condemnation. No passage in the Bible is more biting, more pointed, or more severe than this pronouncement of Christ upon the Pharisees. It is significant that He singled them out, as opposed to the Sadducees, who were more liberal, and the Herodians, who were the politicians. The Pharisees, while attempting to honor the Word of God and manifesting an extreme form of religious observance, were actually the farthest from God.[129]

The scribes should have realized as they studied that God alone was to be the recipient of the praise of men, but in fact, the majority of the recorders were enamored by the adulation they received from the people. Wearing his white linen robe, with an identical mantel fringed on the bottom, the scribe would parade his occupation and thus his knowledge through the streets of Jerusalem. Surrounded by those clad in homespun garments, the scholarly man would stand out among the throngs who daily trod the highways and byways of the city.

As the scribe made his way around the city, men would rise when he walked by as a sign of respect for his office, and referred to him as rabbi and master. A scribe commanded the highest place of honor at a banquet and enjoyed a reserved seat in the local synagogue.

In Luke 20, Jesus was teaching in the temple when challenged by the chief priests and scribes; He responded with parables. As He neared the end of His discourse, Luke 21:1–4 (NKJV) gives us this picture:

> And He looked up and saw the rich putting their gifts into the treasury, and He saw also a certain poor widow putting in two mites. So He said, "Truly I say to you that this poor widow has put in more than all; for all these out of their abundance have put in offerings for God, but she out of her poverty put in all the livelihood that she had."

In Luke 21, Jesus tried to get the scribes and Pharisees to focus on what was important as He pointed out the poor widow making her way to one of the trumpet-shaped containers that stood along a wall in the Court of the Women. Made of metal rather than stone, the cylinders were receptacles for offerings—ones that would resound with the noise of coins being dropped inside. As all eyes turned toward the humble woman making her way toward the offering container, it was apparent that she had only two tiny copper coins (lepton) to drop inside—worth about one-eighth of a cent in US currency. *Forum Ancient Coins* has this to say about the offering:

> The lepton is the very smallest denomination and is probably the true "widow's mite." In fact, the lepton is probably the lowest denomination coin ever struck by any nation in all of history! Lepton and prutah were carelessly and crudely struck, usually off center ....Because they circulated for a long period, they are usually very worn. Legends are almost always unreadable. The actual size of a prutah is less than 1/2 inch in diameter. A lepton is usually about the same diameter as a pencil eraser.[130]

Were the scribes and Pharisees impressed? Unlikely! But Jesus was blessed by her offering. Not only did she offer all the coins she possessed, she offered her next purchase of food, raising the possibility that she might not meet her own survival needs. The scribes thought all they needed was for someone to take care of them—to provide food, clothing, shelter—and they labored diligently to add to their list of patrons. The poor widow was the perfect example of generosity, faith, and commitment.

For their work in the temple, the scribes lived on contributions and subsidies, and were not paid a salary. Often scribes were supported by a specific family that was held in high regard for underwriting the scholarly copyist. Because families sometimes placed their wealth at the disposal of one of the scribes, there was ample room for abuse associated with the practice. Although those men were to use the Word to point men to Jehovah, all too often they pointed only to themselves and their wants and needs. The scribes totally missed the golden opportunity to become spiritually rich and were instead poor in the real blessings of God.

Tuesday of Passion Week ended with Jesus and His disciples walking to the Mount of Olives on the east side of Jerusalem. As they were leaving the city, some of the disciples who perhaps had not visited Jerusalem often—or had never been in the Holy City—turned to view its walls. According to Barclay, this is what they would have seen:

> . . .marble plated with gold, and it shone and glinted in the sun so that a man could scarcely bear to look at it . . . . The Temple area was surrounded by great porches . . . upheld by pillars cut out of solid blocks of marble in one piece . . . . At the corners of the Temple angle stones have been found which measure from 20 to 40 feet in length, and which weigh more than 100 tons . . . . Little wonder that the Galilaean fishermen looked with awe on these vast stones, and these amazing buildings, and called Jesus' attention to them.[131]

The disciples were awed by the sight of the temple glimmering in the afternoon sun, but Jesus saw a different sight as He turned to look:

> And Jesus said to them, "Do you not see all these things? Assuredly, I say to you, not one stone shall be left here upon another, that shall not be thrown down." (Matthew 24:2 NKJV)

Instead of reliving the day's events, the triumphal entry into the city, the people clamoring for Him to be declared King, Jesus remembered how He had wept over the city that lay before Him, wept over its inglorious future. In AD 70, Jesus' prophecy was fulfilled. The Romans, exasperated with repeated rebellions in Judea, marched into Jerusalem and demolished the temple—stone by stone. Is there any wonder Jesus cried? William Barclay penned a truth that would be well remembered today:

> Jesus knew that the way of power politics can only end in doom. The man and the nation which will not take the way of God are heading for disaster.[132]

The whole of Matthew 24 has come to be known as the "Olivet Discourse." In that chapter, as well as Mark 13 and Luke 21, Jesus gave the disciples an overview of what the future held, first for Jerusalem, and second at the end of the age. Fuller Theological Seminary professor George Eldon Ladd wrote:

> There can be little doubt but that the disciples thought of the destruction of the temple as one of the events accompanying the end of the age and the coming of the eschatological Kingdom of God.[133]

Jesus had spent the days before teaching His followers through parables; now He was to deliver His most important discourse. Instead of giving a rousing "Crown Me King" speech, He spared nothing with His warning of what was to come to their beloved city:

> "For days will come upon you when your enemies will build an embankment around you, surround you and close you in on every side, and level you, and your children within you, to the ground; and they will not leave in you one stone upon another, because you did

not know the time of your visitation." (Luke 19:43–44 NKJV)

One of Satan's most effective tools is the word *tomorrow*. No man knows the day or the hour when Jesus will return and set His feet once again on the Temple Mount. On this day, He was preparing to lay down His life so that those who would believe on Him in the ages to come would have no fear of tomorrow. We have the promise that "whoever believes in Him should not perish but have everlasting life." (John 3:16 NKJV)

29

THE LAST WEEK:
WEDNESDAY *and* THURSDAY

Wednesday would likely have been a day of rest and preparation for Jesus, as there is no mention of any activities surrounding Him in the Gospels. It was, however, a pivotal day for Judas, the betrayer. Throughout the New Testament and beyond, that is how he was known—the Betrayer of Jesus.

Only God knows how long Judas had been fantasizing about forcing Jesus to declare His kingship. How had Satan tempted this disciple into treachery? Did Judas believe if Christ was, indeed, crowned King of Judah, the disciples would have elevated roles in the kingdom? Or was it just simple avarice that prompted Judas? If it was, it is perhaps the singular best example in 1 Timothy 6:10 (KJV): "For the love of money is the root of all evil: which while some coveted after, they have erred from the faith, and pierced themselves through with many sorrows." Jesus knew from the very beginning which of His trusted companions would be the one to betray Him. With this knowledge, why did Jesus entrust this particular disciple with the money bag? Why did He not just leave Judas behind and take another more trustworthy disciple? Could it have had to do with a parable Jesus told His followers—the one in Matthew 13? The enemy had crept into the wheat field and surreptitiously scattered tares in with the wheat. Tares as they began to grow looked very much like the young shoots of wheat that burst forth from the ground. It was almost impossible to distinguish one from the other. The farmer was asked if the tares should be pulled up, and declined:

> "No . . . you'll uproot the wheat if you do. Let both grow together until the harvest. Then I will tell the harvesters to sort out the weeds, tie them into bundles, and burn them, and to put the wheat in the barn." (Matthew 13:29–30 NLT)

Perhaps Jesus was thinking of how many of His disciples would be deeply wounded by Judas' treachery, and would turn back in disappointment. They were likely not aware of the disciple's past history. In John 12:1–6, after Jesus had set His face toward Jerusalem, we see a picture of Judas and his deceit:

> Six days before the Passover, Jesus came to Bethany, where Lazarus lived, whom Jesus had raised from the dead. Here a dinner was given in Jesus' honor. Martha served, while Lazarus was among those reclining at the table with him. Then Mary [Martha's sister] took about a pint of pure nard, an expensive perfume; she poured it on Jesus' feet and wiped his feet with her hair. And the house was filled with the fragrance of the perfume. But one of his disciples, Judas Iscariot, who was later to betray him, objected, "Why wasn't this perfume sold and the money given to the poor? It was worth a year's wages." He did not

say this because he cared about the poor but because he was a thief; as keeper of the money bag, he used to help himself to what was put into it.

After all the teaching, all the miracles, all the prayers, all the fellowship, still Judas was willing to hand Jesus over to the authorities. On that particular Wednesday, Judas stealthily made his way to the high priest and members of the Sanhedrin. Almost since He burst on the scene, the Jewish authorities had set out to trap Jesus, and now He was being handed to them on a platter made of thirty pieces of silver—the legal price of a slave. In Zechariah 11:12–13 (NKJV), we read:

> Then I said to them, "If it is agreeable to you, give me my wages; and if not, refrain." So they weighed out for my wages thirty pieces of silver. And the LORD said to me, "Throw it to the potter"—that princely price they set on me. So I took the thirty pieces of silver and threw them into the house of the LORD for the potter.

Judas would never know what might have been had he remained faithful to Jesus, the Messiah. Rather, he would have to eventually face the consequences of his choices. And make a proactive choice, he did: he chose death rather than life! It was a moment in time that would echo throughout eternity. It was fulfillment of a prophecy pronounced by Caiaphas in John 11:47–52 (ESV):

> So the chief priests and the Pharisees gathered the council and said, "What are we to do? For this man performs many signs. If we let him go on like this, everyone will believe in him, and the Romans will

come and take away both our place and our nation."
But one of them, Caiaphas, who was high priest that
year, said to them, "You know nothing at all. Nor do
you understand that it is better for you that one man
should die for the people, not that the whole nation
should perish." He did not say this of his own accord,
but being high priest that year he prophesied that
Jesus would die for the nation, and not for the nation
only, but also to gather into one the children of God
who are scattered abroad.

It was the duty of the high priest to select the lamb that would be
slain during the Passover. Caiaphas, with his machinations against
Jesus, had no understanding that he had just chosen Jesus to die for
the sins, not just of the Jewish people, but "the children of God who
are scattered abroad."

Unknowingly, Judas had become a pawn in the hands of those
who wished to be rid of Jesus. But soon the weight of his actions would
come crashing down on him as Wednesday morphed into Thursday
and the Passover meal began to take precedence.

✦ ✦ ✦

The sun rose in the eastern sky on the morning of the Passover
celebration. A lamb had been selected—a male without spot or defect
of any kind (see Exodus 12:5). The high priest was unaware that he had
chosen the Lamb when bartering with Judas for the cost of disloyalty.
When baptized by John in the river Jordan, Jesus was referred to as
the Lamb of God (see John 1:29). Born to be the Passover Lamb, Jesus
was now fulfilling those requirements. He was a male with no birth

defects and had been in Jerusalem for four days prior to Passover. Some of the disciples had questioned Jesus about where the observance of Passover would take place. In Matthew 26:17–19 we read:

> On the first day of the Festival of Unleavened Bread, the disciples came to Jesus and asked, "Where do you want us to make preparations for you to eat the Passover?" He replied, "Go into the city to a certain man and tell him, 'The Teacher says: My appointed time is near. I am going to celebrate the Passover with my disciples at your house.'" So the disciples did as Jesus had directed them and prepared the Passover.

The life of Jesus had been offered for the price of a lamb. So Judas took the sum offered by the Jewish authorities, pocketed it, and went on his way to eat the Passover Seder with Jesus and his fellow disciples. As practicing Jews, Jesus and the Twelve would have chosen a Passover lamb to be roasted and eaten at the traditional four-course meal. Unlike today's often too-quickly remembered Lord's Supper, the Seder could take several hours. The table would likely have been set with at least four cups, the meaning of which we find in Exodus 6:6–7:

- ✧ The Cup of Blessing—"I am the Lord."

- ✧ The Cup of Judgment—"I will bring you out from under the yoke."

- ✧ The Cup of Redemption—"I will redeem you with an outstretched arm."

- ✧ The Cup of Praise—"I will take you as my own people, and I will be your God."

Biblical scholars are unsure if each disciple had four cups at his place setting, or if those were allotted only to Jesus. We do know that at least the third cup—the Cup of Redemption—was shared with all at the table.

It was, however, after the first cup that Jesus removed His robe and took on the role of servant to wash the feet of His disciples. This was a role that generally fell to the individual of the lowest rank at the table. If that were Peter, it might explain his horror that Jesus was about to bow and wash his feet. It had been in Capernaum in Mark 9:35, that Jesus said, "Anyone who wants to be first must be the very last, and the servant of all."

With the Cup of Judgment, the bitter herbs (*maror*) were served—a representation of the terrible bitterness of sin. Perhaps it is at this juncture that Jesus revealed His betrayal and betrayer.

And here we find one of the saddest exchanges in the Gospels— one of Love reaching out to save. *The Message* gives us a very contemporary yet graphic translation of the exchange between Jesus and Judas:

> After sunset, he and the Twelve were sitting around the table. During the meal, he said, "I have something hard but important to say to you: One of you is going to hand me over to the conspirators." They were stunned, and then began to ask, one after another, "It isn't me, is it, Master?" Jesus answered, "The one who hands me over is someone I eat with daily, one who passes me food at the table. In one sense the Son of Man is entering into a way of treachery well-marked by the Scriptures—no surprises here. In another sense that man who turns him in, turns

traitor to the Son of Man—better never to have been born than do this!" Then Judas, already turned traitor, said, "It isn't me, is it, Rabbi?" Jesus said, "Don't play games with me, Judas." (Matthew 26:20–25)

The next cup was to be the Cup of Redemption. A talented blogger with "Fishing from the Abyss," wrote of Judas's departure:

> Notice that, since Judas leaves immediately after eating the bitter herbs (the only item dipped from a dish as part of the meal), he does not share in the Cup of Redemption, and he is left with the symbolic taste of sin in his mouth, which is never washed away before his death, the following day.

The Cup of Redemption is the same cup shared by Believers. Jesus said, "This do in remembrance of me" (Luke 22:19 KJV). Observance of the Lord's Supper is symbolic of the relationship between Jesus and His followers; and it is also a promise of an event to come. Jesus said, "Truly I tell you, I will not drink again from the fruit of the vine until that day when I drink it new in the kingdom of God" (Mark 14:25).

After partaking of the Cup of Praise and singing the *hallel* (Psalm 113–118), Jesus and His disciples—minus Judas, of course—went out to the Mount of Olives to the garden of Gethsemane. The requirement to stay within the walls of Jerusalem until after midnight—the hour the death angel visited Egypt—had been fulfilled, and it was now permissible to leave the upper room. As they made their way from the city, the little band would have had to cross a rivulet known as Kidron. For much of the year, the brook was but a trickle, but at Passover the blood of the sacrifices was channeled from the Temple

Mount into the stream, now overflowing with it. I wonder: Did Jesus compare that to the stream that would soon flow from His hands, feet, and side? Poet William Cowper wrote:

> There is a fountain filled with blood drawn from
> Emmanuel's veins;
> And sinners plunged beneath that flood lose all their
> guilty stains.
> Lose all their guilty stains, lose all their guilty stains;
> And sinners plunged beneath that flood
> lose all their guilty stains . . . .
>
> Dear dying Lamb, Thy precious blood shall never
> lose its power
> Till all the ransomed church of God be saved, to sin
> no more.
> Be saved, to sin no more, be saved, to sin no more;
> Till all the ransomed church of God
> be saved, to sin no more.[134]

Jesus and His followers entered the garden. Mark described the scene in 14:32–36 (NKJV):

> Then they came to a place which was named Gethsemane; and He said to His disciples, "Sit here while I pray." And He took Peter, James, and John with Him, and He began to be troubled and deeply distressed. Then He said to them, "My soul is exceedingly sorrowful, even to death. Stay here and watch." He went a little farther, and fell on the ground, and prayed that if it were possible, the hour might pass

from Him. And He said, "Abba, Father, all things are possible for You. Take this cup away from Me; nevertheless, not what I will, but what You will."

Gethsemane is translated as "oil press." John MacArthur says of the garden:

> It probably belonged to a friend of the Lord. While it is famous in our day, and still exists just outside the city of Jerusalem, in the Lord's day it was probably a small garden enclosed by a wall and guarded by a gate . . . . It was a place Jesus often visited with His men, Luke 22:39. Gethsemane seems to have been a refuge for the Lord. It was a place where He could find solitude from the crowds and ministry that occupied His life. It was a place where He could go to find a private moment to commune with His Father. It was a sanctuary from the attacks of His enemies. It was a place of refreshment from the long days of ministry. It was a special place for the Lord and His men. The name *Gethsemane* is Aramaic in origin . . . and [was] a place where olive trees grew and produced their fruit. The olives were collected, placed in a press and the precious olive oil was extracted from the olives under intense pressure. . . . On this night, our Lord would enter the *"Olive Press"* and the sweet oil of grace and submission to the Father would be extracted from the Lord's life. For Jesus, the garden of Gethsemane would be a place of intense pressures. Our text tells us about some of the pressures He faced that night.[135]

Perhaps it was there in the garden that Jesus really understood the severity of the task ahead of Him. He would have read the words of Isaiah the prophet in chapter 53, verses 4–10. Again, *The Message* gives these verses such a graphic quality:

> But the fact is, it was *our* pains he carried—*our* disfigurements, all the things wrong with *us*. We thought he brought it on himself, that God was punishing him for his own failures. But it was our sins that did that to him, that ripped and tore and crushed him—*our sins!* He took the punishment, and that made us whole. Through his bruises we get healed. We're all like sheep who've wandered off and gotten lost. We've all done our own thing, gone our own way. And GOD has piled all our sins, everything we've done wrong, on him, on him. He was beaten, he was tortured, but he didn't say a word. Like a lamb taken to be slaughtered and like a sheep being sheared, he took it all in silence. Justice miscarried, and he was led off—and did anyone really know what was happening? He died without a thought for his own welfare, beaten bloody for the sins of my people. They buried him with the wicked, threw him in a grave with a rich man, even though he'd never hurt a soul or said one word that wasn't true. Still, it's what GOD had in mind all along, to crush him with pain. The plan was that he give himself as an offering for sin so that he'd see life come from it—life, life, and more life. And GOD's plan will deeply prosper through him.

There in the garden of Gethsemane, it all came flooding in—what

He must endure, how He must die, the degradation and pain of crucifixion—and it was overwhelming. Luke paints the picture of Jesus'
travail as He prayed the prayer that never fails:

> And He was withdrawn from them about a stone's
> throw, and He knelt down and prayed, saying, "Father,
> if it is Your will, take this cup away from Me; **never-
> theless not My will, but Yours, be done.**" Then an
> angel appeared to Him from heaven, strengthening
> Him. And being in agony, He prayed more earnestly.
> Then His sweat became like great drops of blood fall-
> ing down to the ground. (Luke 22:41–44 NKJV, empha-
> sis mine.)

It is at this point, I believe, the knowledge that He was to be the
sacrifice hit like the force of a huge boulder rolling downhill and slam-
ming into the valley below. He, Jesus of Nazareth, was the "Lamb
slain from the foundation of the world" (Revelation 13:8 KJV). Perhaps
it was then that His "sweat was as it were great drops of blood falling
down to the ground" (Luke 22:44 KJV). Was it here that He began to
feel the burden of the sins of all mankind descending on His sinless
shoulders—lust, greed, anger, murder, debauchery, hatred? He who
was about to be betrayed into the hands of His accusers was served a
foretaste of what was to happen the following day.

The Son of Man was so overcome by the magnitude of what He
was about to face that He prayed in desperation. Jesus was staggered
at the bitterness of the cup He had been asked to drink, at the cross
He had been asked to shoulder, and yet He just as desperately wanted
to do the Father's will. He desired that more than He valued His own
life. Jesus was about to be crushed by the weight of sin just as the
olives were crushed by the stone press. Pressed from our Savior was

not oil, but rather a plan for our salvation fueled by a love that will not let us go.

While Jesus was in a garden permeated with agony, Judas was in a room filled with jubilation. Jesus of Nazareth, the One who had foiled the Pharisees again and again, was about to be seized and sacrificed. Judas must have been rife with self-importance. He would be the one to force the hand of the Messiah; he would be the one to receive the accolades of the other disciples when they took their rightful places in the kingdom Judas thought was to come. He was ready to march with the troops that were to be dispatched to arrest Jesus:

> So Judas came to the garden, guiding a detachment of soldiers [KJV reads "band of men"] and some officials from the chief priests and the Pharisees. They were carrying torches, lanterns and weapons. (John 18:3)

Rising from the rocky ground, Jesus turned to His sleeping disciples and roused them. As they stretched and rubbed the sleep from their eyes, the sounds of the approaching crowd captured their attention.

Author and Bible teacher Rick Renner says of the soldiers sent to the garden:

> The Greek word for "a band of men" is *spira*. This is the word that describes a military cohort—the group of 300 to 600 soldiers mentioned above. These extremely well-trained soldiers were equipped with the finest weaponry of the day.[136]

We also read that the soldiers were accompanied by "officers from the chief priests and Pharisees." Renner says:

Once a judgment was given from the religious court of law, it was the responsibility of the temple police to execute these judgments. This fearsome armed force worked daily with the cohort stationed at the Tower of Antonia and reported to the chief priests, the Pharisees, and the Sanhedrin. These were the "officers" who accompanied the Roman soldiers to the Garden of Gethsemane. We can therefore conclude that when the Roman soldiers and temple police arrived to arrest Jesus, the hillside where the Garden was located was literally covered with Roman soldiers and highly trained militia from the Temple Mount.[137]

Apparently the hillside was crawling with soldiers who had been sent to arrest one man—One Man. The ebullient Judas walked up to Jesus and greeted Him with a kiss. Then when asked to identify himself, Jesus did so without hesitation, cautioning His disciples not to retaliate on His behalf. Jesus was then bound and marched back into Jerusalem, while Judas, the man who would be hero, followed along behind. Perhaps all dreams of glory evaporated as he trudged back across the foul Brook of Kidron awash in the blood of lambs and goats.

How soon after Jesus' arrest did Judas realize what a horrendous mistake he had made? Was it immediately following the capture? Was it when Jesus was being scourged? Was it when the soldiers ridiculed Him? We don't know the timing, but we do know that his remorse was crushing. Judas should not have been taken unawares at the consequences of his actions, but he was. Suddenly he realized that he had made the biggest blunder of his life: he had betrayed the Son of God into the hands of those who wanted only to kill Him. Beset with guilt he raced to the temple court, money bag in hand. "Stop!" he screamed. "This man is innocent!" But it was too late. The chief priests only laughed at him. They no longer had any use either for him or the thirty pieces of silver. It was now blood money; it could not be returned to the temple coffers. Besides, what they had wanted they now had: Jesus in their clutches.

Too late Judas realized that he had been a pawn in the hands of Satan; he had betrayed the One whose love was unconditional. Possessed of that knowledge, Judas did the only thing he could think of to do at that moment; he threw the silver coins at the feet of the chief priests and raced out into the night. Matthew 27:5–8 gives us a glimpse of the sad end to Judas' life:

> Then he went away and hanged himself. The chief priests picked up the coins and said, "It is against the law to put this into the treasury, since it is blood money." So they decided to use the money to buy the potter's field as a burial place for foreigners. That is why it has been called the Field of Blood to this day.

Author and speaker Ray Pritchard wrote of Judas's desertion:

> In terms of experience, whatever you can say about James, Peter and John, you can say also about Judas. Everywhere they went, he also went. He was right there, always by the side of Jesus. He heard it all, saw it all, experienced it all. However you explain his defection, you cannot say he was less experienced than the other apostles.[138]

A line in the poem "Maud Muller" by John Greenleaf Whittier may well be applicable to Judas:

> For of all sad words of tongue or pen,
> The saddest are these: "It might have been!"[139]

30

THE LAST WEEK:

FRIDAY

T he Roman soldiers and temple guard had arrested the Man whom Judas kissed. He was the perpetrator, the rebel, the one whose crimes had made Him a target of the chief priests. They knew not what He had done to raise the ire of that august body, but they had done their job. Of course, they had heard rumors of His antics—healings, the dead raised to life, water turned to wine, and the way the people praised Him as He rode into Jerusalem. Silly stories! Now they were ready for a night of high jinx at the expense of their captive. What they did not know as He was marched off to the palace of Annas, the former high priest, was that the Man bound in the garden and led away as a criminal was the Lamb of God.

While awaiting a decision from High Priest Caiaphas and the Sanhedrin, the guards laid a fire in the courtyard to take away the chill of the night. It was there that Peter was challenged and denied knowing his Lord, not once, but three times, just as Jesus had prophesied. After having been found guilty of blasphemy, Jesus spent the night being mocked and goaded. At dawn, the taunting ceased; Jesus was dressed in His own clothing and taken to Pilate. The prelate

swiftly determined that Jesus should be transferred to the juris-
diction of Herod Antipas, who, in turn, sent Him back to Pilate for
sentencing.

After being condemned to death, Jesus was scourged:

> The Roman scourge, also called the "flagrum" or
> "flagellum" was a short whip made of two or three
> leather (ox-hide) thongs or ropes connected to a
> handle . . . The leather thongs were knotted with a
> number of small pieces of metal, usually zinc and
> iron, attached at various intervals. Scourging would
> quickly remove the skin. According to history the
> punishment of a slave was particularly dreadful. The
> leather was knotted with bones, or heavy indented
> pieces of bronze.[140]

Jesus had been dragged before Pontius Pilate, convicted, and
stripped of His outer garments. Roman soldiers had placed a wicked
crown made of thorns on His head and proclaimed Him "King of the
Jews." Mocking laughter reverberated through the palace halls as
Jesus, the Galilean, was ridiculed. His aching body bore the stripes
that had been laid upon His back, and blood oozed from the cuts
inflicted by the cat-o'-nine-tails applied during the lashing.

And then He was led away to Golgotha—the place of the skull,
and there "the Darling of Heaven"[141] was crucified. Jesus' words of
forgiveness directed at those who crucified Him constitute the most
powerful message ever spoken. It was nine o'clock in the morning
on an ordinary day in Jerusalem. The sun was shining; the streets
were filled with people going about their daily business. There was
an underlying element of excitement. Word had spread that the

Teacher had been arrested the night before and tried for blasphemy. Mobs had gathered to shout, "Crucify Him! Crucify Him!"

As shopkeepers opened their doors and raised their curtains, the sounds of marching feet and the noise of something heavy being dragged through the streets could be heard in the distance. Closer and closer they came until the curious could at last see the soldiers who were driving a bloody and exhausted man toward the Damascus Gate. Across the road from the gate near the plot where Jeremiah, the prophet, was buried, is a flat ledge atop a hill that resembles a skull. Golgotha, they call it—the Hill of the Skull. This was the Roman killing ground. Here criminals died, and the time had come. Three men were to be crucified that day. Two of them were thieves; the third was the Son of God.

The soldiers waiting on the hillside had likely been chosen at random. It was just another day's work for them. They were on the crucifixion squad; it was not a pleasant task, but someone had to do it. The executioners were ready for the task at hand. Guilty—they didn't know or care. Innocent—maybe, maybe not. It was only a job.

Soon the mob exited the gate and crossed the road. Dragging the cross was a brawny man—a Cyrene, by the looks of him. A man could be seen following him, trudging a few steps forward and then falling, only to be hauled upright and shoved another few steps along. He was totally unrecognizable. Isaiah the prophet had written, "He has no form or comeliness; and when we see Him, there is no beauty that we should desire Him." (Isaiah 53:2 NKJV)

That was certainly true of the man struggling to make His way to the place where the soldiers awaited. His back looked like shredded meat; His swollen face a series of bleeding holes where the crown of thorns had pierced His flesh; His beard had been torn out by its roots. He appeared to be more dead than alive. Accustomed to criminals fighting their destiny, the executioners rejoiced, as it meant the man now lying on the ground would be more easily subdued for the task at hand.

With a thud, Simon, the Cyrene, dropped the cross to the ground. Shuddering, he covered his face, turned away, and stumbled to the sidelines. As he turned, he was horrified to see that the body of Jesus had been laid on the cross. His arms were stretched to their limits and ropes were wrapped around to secure them to the crossbeam. Deftly, one of the executioners placed a spike on Jesus' wrist, and then the hammer rang out, each stroke securing the arm to the cross. The process was repeated on the opposite arm, and then one through the feet that rested on a small platform.

With the spikes and ropes in place, the cross was raised against the sky, and then, with a thud, it hurtled unimpeded into the hole that would hold it upright. As the cross dropped into the hole, the jarring collision of wood with earth ripped flesh secured by the spikes. Some in the crowd looked upon Jesus—naked before the world, beaten to within an inch of His life, bruised and bloody—with satisfaction. Their purpose had been accomplished. I can easily imagine that Satan and all the demons in hell were dancing with glee. The Son of God was near death. The Enemy was certain he had won!

Mary, His mother, and other bystanders bowed their heads in a mixture of love, shame, and compassion. Their beloved friend and companion hung exposed to the world. Tears rolled down those faces, and sobs could be heard echoing from the hillside. As they watched in agony, the indifferent soldiers gathered in a circle at the foot of the cross. "Got any dice?" one called. "Let's cast them for His clothes."

As they began to gamble, a whisper loud enough to ring through eternity issued from the mouth of Jesus, His first words spoken from the cross:

> "Father, forgive them, for they do not know what
> they are doing." (Luke 23:34)

Astonished, the soldiers halted their grisly game and looked heavenward. They were accustomed to hearing screams and curses, pleas of innocence, entreaties for mercy, appeals for water, but a prayer for forgiveness—unimaginable! The Man on the cross had prayed for them, pleading for God's forgiveness for their actions.

The Son knew the Father in all of His mercy and His richly abounding love. He knew the words penned in Exodus:

> "The LORD, the LORD, the compassionate and gra-
> cious God, slow to anger, abounding in love and faith-
> fulness, maintaining love to thousands, and forgiving
> wickedness, rebellion and sin." (Exodus 34:6–7)

Did those men even know the name of the Man they had nailed to the cross—whose side they would pierce? Did they know His name was Jesus and that He was the Lamb of God, the One God had loved before the foundations of the world were even laid? It is likely none knew just how much they would need the forgiveness offered by the One hanging above them. They simply heard, "Father, forgive them, for they do not know what they are doing."

None understood that Jesus had taken on the role of advocate, defending the actions of those who had wronged Him. His teachings of "Love your enemies, bless those who curse you, do good to those who hate you, and pray for those who spitefully use you and persecute you" (Matthew 5:44 NKJV) were more than mere utterances; they were a lifestyle. It was an act of the will. He was teaching a world about true forgiveness.

Jesus taught that there was a relationship between forgiving and receiving God's forgiveness:

> "And whenever you stand praying, if you have anything against anyone, forgive him, that your Father in heaven may also forgive you your trespasses. But if you do not forgive, neither will your Father in heaven forgive your trespasses." (Mark 11:25–26 NKJV)

The prayer for forgiveness on the cross was not meant to be the last act of a dying man; it was an example for His followers. As they had been forgiven, so were they to forgive those who sinned against them (see Matthew 6:9–13, the Lord's Prayer). But God had a lesson, not only for Israel, but for all mankind: He loved them with an everlasting love. It was a mirror of God's constant love that reaches far beyond our sinfulness all the way to the Cross, where Love hung between heaven and earth.

And it was the third hour of the day. In the temple courtyard, the first of two daily sacrifices, the *Tamid*, or perpetual sacrifice, was prepared. In Exodus 29:38–39, 41–42 we read:

> "This is what you are to offer on the altar regularly each day: two lambs a year old. Offer one in the morning and the other at twilight. Sacrifice the other lamb at twilight with the same grain offering and its drink offering as in the morning—a pleasing aroma, a food offering presented to the LORD. For the generations to

come this burnt offering is to be made regularly at the entrance to the tent of meeting, before the LORD."

These sin offerings were to be made as the first ceremony in the morning and the last at night. It was to be a constant reminder of sin and that the people could only be redeemed by a blood sacrifice. According to the Temple Institute, two lambs had been chosen:

> Although the lamb which had been selected for the tamid sacrifice had already been ascertained as being free of any disqualifying blemish, nonetheless as an added precaution—since the Bible strongly prohibits the offering of blemished animals—it is checked again now by torchlight, after its removal from the chamber. This is to preclude the unlikely event that perhaps something has befallen it since it was last examined, which would render it unfit.
>
> After it has been selected, the lamb is given water to drink before it is slaughtered, for this makes its skin easier to remove. It is watered from a golden vessel; everything done in the Temple was always conducted with as much honor as possible.[142]

One of Jesus' utterances from the cross was, "I am thirsty." (See John 19:28.) Just as the sacrificial lamb was given water to drink, so was the Lamb of God offered liquid. Alfred Edersheim wrote of the daily sacrifices:

> The sacrifice was held together by its feet, the fore and hind feet of each side being tied together; its head was laid towards the south and fastened through a ring, and its face turned to the west, while the sacrificing

priest stood on the east side. The elders who carried the keys now gave the order for opening the Temple gates. As the last great gate slowly moved on its hinges, the priests, on a signal given, blew three blasts on their silver trumpets, summoning the Levites and the 'representatives' of the people (the so-called 'stationary men') to their duties, and announcing to the city that the morning sacrifice was about to be offered. Immediately upon this the great gates which led into the Holy Place itself were opened to admit the priests who were to cleanse the candlestick and the altar of incense.[143]

From noon until the sixth hour, or about 3:00 in the afternoon, "darkness came over all the land." (See Matthew 27:45.) Rev. Lonnie Branam, pastor of San Fernando Church of Christ, wrote of this phenomenon:

> I would suggest that God darkened the earth in broad daylight because the last dying moments of Christ's life was too sacred for human eyes to see. Normally, we don't want a crowd around a loved one who is struggling for breath and about to die. This is a private moment in every person's life. The presence of loved ones and dearest friends is fitting, but around Christ that day was an irreverent crowd of revelers, skeptics, scoffers and unbelievers who couldn't wait for Him to draw His last breath. They had stripped Him nearly naked and gambled for the very clothes that were on His back. That darkness was a sacred concealment of the wounded body of Jesus, wounded even for all those around Him who hated Him and wanted Him

dead. Thus it was most fitting that God should cover Him, hide Him away from brutal eyes that they might not see all that He suffered when He was made sin for us. Suffice it to say that the last three hours of the Lord's sufferings was far too sacred for human eyes to see. None of us who believe in Him will ever know just how sacred this scene was.[144]

It was about the sixth hour that the second daily sacrifice was brought into the temple courtyard and tied to the altar in readiness for the evening rite that was to occur at the ninth hour, the time that Jesus "gave up his spirit." (See Matthew 27:50.) It was also at that moment that "the curtain of the temple was torn in two from top to bottom. The earth shook, the rocks split and the tombs broke open" (Matthew 27:51–52).

The ninth hour has significance through the Old and New Testaments, for it was then that Elijah stood on Mount Carmel before the prophets of Baal and petitioned God to send fire from heaven (see 1 Kings 18). Daniel was praying at the ninth hour when God sent Gabriel to answer his request (see Daniel 9:21). The first miracle by the apostles was wrought by Peter and John when they went to the temple to pray at the ninth hour (see Acts 3:1). And it was about the ninth hour that Cornelius prayed and an angel of the Lord told him to send for Peter (see Acts 10:3). It is a difficult note to include, for when Jesus prayed at the ninth hour, "My God, my God, why have you forsaken me?" the Father turned away from the sight of my sins and your sins hanging on the cross. He had to forsake His only begotten Son.

When Jesus breathed His last breath and gave up the ghost, Matthew tells us that "the veil of the temple was rent in twain from the top to the bottom" (Matthew 27:51 KJV). The high priest must have been terribly frightened! His work was finished. The Lamb of God had been offered sacrificially for the sins of all. As the high priest made his way into the Holy of Holies to sprinkle the blood of the evening sacrifice on the horns of the altar, the veil that separated man from God was ripped from top to bottom. It was a symbol that we no longer have to wait to be represented by the high priest yearly:

> Seeing then that we have a great high priest, that is passed into the heavens, Jesus the Son of God, let us hold fast our profession. For we have not an high priest which cannot be touched with the feeling of our infirmities; but was in all points tempted like as we are, yet without sin. Let us therefore come boldly unto the throne of grace, that we may obtain mercy, and find grace to help in time of need. (Hebrews 4:14–16 KJV)

Believers now have free access into the presence of God so that, "by prayer and supplication with thanksgiving let [our] requests be made known unto God" (Philippians 4:6 KJV).

The beautiful David Phelps song "End of the Beginning" says it all:

> And though He never ever did a single thing wrong
> The angry crowd chose Him.
> And then He walked down the road and died on the cross
> And that was the end of the beginning . . .
> Three days later, He rose![145]

The work that Christ had been sent to do had been finished.

$$31$$

THE TEMPLE:
PROPHECY FULFILLED

Before His crucifixion and resurrection, Jesus made one astonishing prophecy recorded in Mark 13:1–4 (NKJV):

> Then as He went out of the temple, one of His disciples said to Him, "Teacher, see what manner of stones and what buildings are here!" And Jesus answered and said to him, "Do you see these great buildings? Not one stone shall be left upon another, that shall not be thrown down." Now as He sat on the Mount of Olives opposite the temple, Peter, James, John, and Andrew asked Him privately, "Tell us, when will these things be? And what will be the sign when all these things will be fulfilled?"

The Jews, under Roman rule, lived very ordered but relatively stable lives. Those placed in authority over Jerusalem were often greedy and bereft of the Mosaic law. Because of their lack of knowledge, the Romans were prone to confer insult rather than honor. Civil war raged from time to time, launched by Zealots attempting to overthrow Roman rule. The uprisings were often suppressed with massacres that left legions dead.

The last king to rule Judah was Herod Agrippa, the son—or grandson—of Herod. Herod had been well-known for his incestuous habits, so it is within reason to believe that Agrippa could have been a son. Although appointed by the Romans to rule the region, Agrippa was known as a righteous king and frequently received favorable comments. Under his kingship, it appeared that the relationship between the government in Rome and the religionists in Judea had turned a corner and were, at least, harmonious if not overtly friendly.

According to the Jewish Virtual Library:

> The three years of Agrippa's reign were a period of relief and benefit for the Jewish people of Judea. The residents of Jerusalem were exempted from the impost on houses .... He omitted the patronymic [surname] "Herod" from coins minted for him and followed a markedly pro-Jewish policy when he was required to arbitrate disputes between Jews and non-Jews ... Agrippa made frequent changes in the appointment of the high priest. He was highly sympathetic to the Pharisees and was careful to observe Jewish precepts. He married his daughters to Jewish notables, and withdrew his consent to the wedding of one daughter to Antiochus, king of Commagene, when the latter refused to be circumcised.[146]

Sent to Rome as a child, Agrippa became acquainted with a nephew of Augustus Caesar, Gaius Julius Caesar Augustus Germanicus, or, as he was known, Caligula ("little boots," a moniker he despised). The connection between Agrippa and Caligula would later avert a donnybrook in Judea after the death of Emperor Tiberius. Caligula was known by numerous epithets: mad, insane, unstable, and unhinged. He declared himself to be a living god. He had his nephews who stood between him and the throne of Tiberius murdered, thereby paving the way to emperor with the blood of his relatives. Caligula was the personification of insanity and his bloody reign one of utter horror. According to author Michael Farquhar, "Caligula had the heads removed from various statues of gods and replaced with his own in some temples."[147]

During his rush to be seen as a living god, Caligula dictated that his statue be placed in the temple in Jerusalem where the Jews would be required to worship the man. Such a move was guaranteed to spark rebellion in the region:

> Accordingly he sent Petronius with an army to Jerusalem to place his statues in the temple, and commanded him that, in case the Jews would not admit of them, he should slay those that opposed it, and carry all the rest into captivity.[148]

Into that quagmire stepped Agrippa, and likely laying his own head on the block, he petitioned Caligula not to move forward with desecrating the Jewish temple. The emperor acquiesced and the order was rescinded, making Jerusalem the only city in the Roman Empire without a statue of Caligula. After approximately four years on the throne in Rome, the emperor's own Praetorian Guard grew tired of his antics and assassinated Caligula.

The Romans were brutal, however, toward anyone attempting to foment rebellion in Jewish ranks. After the demise of Agrippa, graft and corruption rekindled the fires of Jewish revolt, and finally the Pharisees joined forces with the Zealots. War broke out in the summer of AD 66. Caught off guard, Roman forces in Judea quickly lost control of the Masada and Antonia fortresses and were slaughtered by the rebels. At Masada rebels discovered a vast quantity of arms and dried food supplies. Herod the Great had stockpiled the matériels more than one hundred years earlier in preparation for a possible war with Cleopatra. The storehouse proved fortuitous, and Jerusalem was soon in Jewish hands.

In Jerusalem the leaders of the rebellion coined money, collected taxes, and organized defenses for the entire country. From Rome, Nero dispatched Roman Consul Vespasian with several legions to crush the uprising, the most stubborn and desperate revolt Rome had ever faced. Bloody fighting for the next three years resulted in the isolation of the rebels in Jerusalem and Masada.

Vespasian was crowned emperor in AD 70 and returned to Rome, leaving his son Titus in charge of the Judean campaign. Titus laid siege to Jerusalem with eight thousand veteran troops. Fewer than a third as many Jews defended the city. In the face of incredible shortages and starvation, they clung tenaciously to their city. By late July, Titus had captured the Antonia Fortress. The defenders who were hollow-eyed with hunger regrouped. From the roof of the portico around the edge of the temple platform they rained down stones, arrows, and fiery brands against the legionnaires. The Romans then burned the roofs from under the Jewish defenders. The attackers gained access to the platform itself, and the defenders retreated behind the wall of the temple proper into the Court of the Women and the Court of Israel. More flaming projectiles set the sanctuary ablaze, and a bloody slaughter ensued. Biblical scholar Ray Stedman wrote of that desperate time:

During the long siege a terrible famine raged in the city and the bodies of the inhabitants were literally stacked like cordwood in the streets. Mothers ate their children to preserve their own strength. The toll of Jewish suffering was horrible but they would not surrender the city. Again and again they attempted to trick the Romans through guile and perfidy. When at last the walls were breached Titus tried to preserve the Temple by giving orders to his soldiers not to destroy or burn it. But the anger of the soldiers against the Jews was so intense that, maddened by the resistance they encountered, they disobeyed the order of their general and set fire to the Temple. There were great quantities of gold and silver there which had been placed in the Temple for safekeeping. This melted and ran down between the rocks and into the cracks of the stones. When the soldiers captured the Temple area, in their greed to obtain this gold and silver they took long bars and pried apart the massive stones. Thus, quite literally, [and as had been foretold by Jesus] not one stone was left standing upon another. The Temple itself was totally destroyed, though the wall supporting the area upon which the Temple was built was left partially intact and a portion of it remains to this day, called the Western Wall.[149]

The Jewish historian Josephus, who had defected to the Romans earlier in the rebellion, was an eyewitness to the event. He claimed that the streams of blood pouring from the corpses of the defenders were more copious than the fire that engulfed everything flammable in the vicinity. Before the Roman legions had finished, the city lay in ruins with the exception of Herod's palace, where the Tenth Legion was stationed as a permanent force of occupation. It would be three more years before the imperial armies recaptured Masada, the last stand of the Jewish revolt. Nearly one thousand men, women, and children had been hiding in this isolated mountaintop fortress. When the Roman armies finally scaled the awesome heights and reached the fortress, they were met with an eerie silence. All the Jews at Masada had committed suicide, preferring to die at their own hands than be slaughtered by the armies of Rome.

The destruction of the temple began the second exile. The Diaspora scattered the Jews around the globe for the next eighteen centuries, but there was always a remnant in Jerusalem. Others, although separated from their beloved land, never forgot the Holy City or the destruction of the temple. The cry first went forth, "Next year, Jerusalem."

Judea, prostrate from the war, was slow to recover. Early in the second century, Hadrian, a new emperor, came to the throne. A great administrator, he organized Roman law under a uniform code, sought ways to improve government efficiency, instituted an empire-wide communications system not unlike the Pony Express, and fortified the frontiers. Seeking to unify and strengthen the empire, Hadrian invoked laws to eliminate regional peculiarities. One of these, which prohibited "mutilations," was aimed at the Jewish practice of circumcision.

During his reign, Hadrian's Wall was built to mark the northern limit of Roman Britain. A substantial portion of the wall still stands. Hadrian also drew up a plan to rebuild Jerusalem as a center of pagan worship in honor of the gods Jupiter, Juno, Venus, and, of course, himself. The city's name would be changed to Aelia Capitolina in honor of the Aelian clan, Hadrian's family.

The new plan saw little progress before it drew a response from Simon Bar-Kokhba, a charismatic Jewish leader. He united the Jews and enticed recruits from throughout the Diaspora, including Samaritans and Gentiles. His troops totaled nearly four hundred thousand when rebellion exploded in AD 132. It took three years and five legions of battle-hardened Roman troops to retake Jerusalem. Bar-Kokhba remained elusive but was eventually captured and executed in AD 136.

After its victory, the Roman army took a terrible revenge. Some of the rebel leaders were skinned alive prior to their executions. Massacres during the fighting had been common; now the survivors were either sold into slavery or simply allowed to starve. Burial was not permitted, so heaps of corpses lay decomposing in the streets and fields. The Temple Mount was literally plowed under and an entirely new city was constructed north of the old. It contained two buildings, together with pagan temples. The temple platform was used as a public square on the south side of the city. It was decked with statues of Hadrian and other Roman notables. An offense punishable by death was established to prevent Jews from entering Jerusalem; neither were they allowed to observe the Sabbath, read or teach the Law, circumcise, or otherwise follow God's law.

Hadrian changed the name of Judea to Syria Palaestina and made its capital Caesarea. Jerusalem, no longer a capital city, was renamed Aelia. Syria Palaestina is the origin of the name Palestine and in modern times applies to the area that would eventually become the national homeland of the returning Diaspora Jews. It was said that Hadrian renamed Judea after the ancient enemy of the

Jews, the Philistines. Romans in general, and Hadrian in particular, despised Jews.

Of all the nations Romans conquered, the Jewish people were the only group that would never quite submit to the Roman yoke. For that reason, Hadrian was determined to erase the memory of Judea and its people from the pages of history. For the next five hundred years, Jews would only be allowed in the city of Jerusalem on the anniversary of the burning of the temple.

With the Jewish population thoroughly subdued, Rome turned its attention to another foe that threatened its cultural survival: Christianity. Christians, who refused to sacrifice to the emperor and believed in none of the pantheon of Roman gods, were said to be atheists. Persecution against the early church continued off and on for over two centuries.

Although Jews were forbidden in Jerusalem, Gentile Christians were not. Consequently, members of the church who had all but disappeared from the city after AD 70, began to reappear there. Sometime in the second century, the first church building was erected on Mount Zion. Early in the fourth century, the emperor Constantine underwent a conversion to Christianity. He moved the capital of the empire from Rome to Byzantium, which he renamed Constantinople, partly as a consequence of the conversion.

Jerusalem suddenly began to regain prestige. Constantine sent funds to Jerusalem to be used to excavate and preserve Christian relics and sites. Later, his mother, Helena, an elderly pious woman, went to Jerusalem to supervise and pay for the erection of a number of churches, among them the Church of the Holy Sepulchre. In addition, she also saw to the demolition of the temple of Aphrodite. It was on the site of this pagan temple that, as tradition holds, Jesus had been buried after the crucifixion; thus the origin of the Church of the Holy Sepulchre, which was built in AD 335.

A plan to rebuild the temple emerged in AD 363 during the reign of Flavius Claudius Julianus, or Julian. He imported Jews who wanted to be part of the project from every nation. Julian laid out the necessary funds and work began on the third temple, but soon tragedy struck. Ammianus Marcellinus, a friend of Julian, wrote of this building project:

> Julian thought to rebuild at an extravagant expense the proud Temple once at Jerusalem, and committed this task to Alypius of Antioch. Alypius set vigorously to work, and was seconded by the governor of the province; when fearful balls of fire, breaking out near the foundations, continued their attacks, till the workmen, after repeated scorchings, could approach no more: and he gave up the attempt.
>
> The failure to rebuild the Temple has been ascribed to the Galilee earthquake of 363 CE, and to the Jews' ambivalence about the project. Sabotage is a possibility, as is an accidental fire. Divine intervention was the common view among Christian historians of the time.[150]

✧ ✧ ✧

In AD 636 Islam arrived on Jerusalem's doorstep when the army of Caliph Omar began a two-year siege of the city. When Patriarch Sophronius decided it was time to surrender, he remembered the bloodshed that had accompanied the Persian conquest twenty-four years earlier, and sent out a request that the caliph come to Jerusalem to receive the surrender in person.

Omar and Sophronius met at the Muslim encampment on the Mount of Olives. Omar was disposed to be generous, and permitted the Christians complete freedom to practice their religion and retain their holy sites. The main change would be that taxes would be paid to Muslims instead of the Byzantines. Omar's tolerance was also extended to the Jews who would, for the first time in five hundred years, be allowed to live in Jerusalem.

As conqueror, Omar wanted to visit the Temple Mount and the sacred rock from which Muhammad purportedly had ascended to heaven. When they arrived at the site, he and his men discovered that the area had been turned into a garbage dump, likely a gesture of disdain toward the Jewish inhabitants.

Appalled, Omar started work on the spot to clean the area. The thousand men with him were enlisted in the project so that the job was completed in reasonably short order. As they knelt at the southern end of the platform to face Mecca and pray, surely Sophronius looked on in abject horror. The Temple Mount had been defiled by Muslim infidels. It was dedicated as a Muslim place of worship and renamed *Haram esh-Sharif,* or "Noble Sanctuary."

Omar and his followers opted not to establish their district capital in Jerusalem, but governed from various other locations. Abd al-Malik, 5th Umayyad Caliph, however, did have a particular stake in Jerusalem as a rival caliph controlled both Mecca and Medina.

In an attempt to attract pilgrims to Jerusalem and to erect a structure that would rival all other churches in the city, Omar approved the construction of the Dome of the Rock. Begun in AD 687, the edifice required four years for completion. Al-Malik succeeded in erecting a building that to this day dominates Jerusalem's skyline and outshines all the city's churches. However, his attempt failed to draw Muslims away from their principal devotion to Mecca and Medina.

32

THE WESTERN WALL

ollowing the Roman subjugation of Judea were the Byzantines, Muslims (twice), Crusaders, Ottoman Turks, and the British. In October 1943, in the midst of World War II, three men—Winston Churchill, Chaim Weizmann, and Clement Atlee—sat down in London to discuss the latest partitioning plan, which called for Jerusalem to be a separate territory under a British high commissioner. The plan would have to be kept secret until after the war, Churchill explained, but he wanted the other two men to know that Israel had a friend in him. He explained that when Hitler had been crushed, the Jews would have to be reestablished in the land where they belonged. Churchill added, "I have an inheritance left to me by Balfour, and I am not going to change. But there are dark forces working against us."[151]

The prime minister probably didn't know how dark and powerful were those forces. No matter how firm his commitment to Zionism, the British Foreign Office and the authorities in Jerusalem who had charge of the mandate hindered him from stating his position. The all-too-familiar story of the bitter struggle and disappointment for the Jewish people continued—Palestine would not be opened to the hapless survivors of the concentration camps.

In the months between November 29, 1947, when the UN General Assembly voted for partition, and May 14, 1948, when the last British troops left and the state of Israel was reborn, Jerusalem was the scene of interminable conflict. The Israeli Ministry of Foreign Affairs offers a concise summation of events following the declaration of independence:

> Less than 24 hours later, the regular armies of Egypt, Jordan, Syria, Lebanon, and Iraq invaded the country, forcing Israel to defend the sovereignty it had regained in its ancestral homeland. In what became known as Israel's War of Independence, the newly formed, poorly equipped Israel Defense Forces (IDF) repulsed the invaders in fierce intermittent fighting, which lasted some 15 months and claimed over 6,000 Israeli lives (nearly one percent of the country's Jewish population at the time).
>
> During the first months of 1949, direct negotiations were conducted under UN auspices between Israel and each of the invading countries (except Iraq, which refused to negotiate with Israel), resulting in armistice agreements which reflected the situation at the end of the fighting.
>
> Accordingly, the Coastal Plain, Galilee and the entire Negev were within Israel's sovereignty, Judea and Samaria (the West Bank) came under Jordanian rule, the Gaza Strip came under Egyptian administration, and the city of Jerusalem was divided, with Jordan controlling the eastern part, including the Old City, and Israel the western sector.[152]

Once again, the Jews were denied access to any part of the Temple Mount.

✧   ✧   ✧

In 1965 Teddy Kollek was elected mayor of West Jerusalem. Two years later, following the reunification of Jerusalem, he became the first mayor of a united city. During his tenure in office, the atmosphere between Jordanian East Jerusalem and the western part of the city was, while not cordial, relatively quiet. There were isolated incidents, but the real boiling cauldron was in Egypt and Syria, where the Soviets were pulling out all stops to court the two countries. Israel had been on the receiving end of the Soviets' courtship following World War II, but little came of it.

Both Egyptian president Gamal Nasser and Syrian president Amin al-Hafez were recipients of an enormous amount of military and economic aid from Russia. In 1967 Soviet rhetoric reached a crescendo when the Israelis were accused of fostering an ominous arms buildup along the Syrian border and the Golan Heights. It was a patent falsehood.

In mid-April 1967 Soviet ambassador to Israel Leonid Chuvakhin complained to Prime Minister Levi Eshkol about the purported buildup. Apparently, Ambassador Chuvakhin had no need to learn the truth; the abounding rumors were enough for him. Eshkol offered to drive him to the Syrian border to show him that the accusations were untrue. It was a useful diplomatic tool. If the rumors of Israeli aggression failed to materialize, the Soviets could brag that it was their support of the Syrian Ba'athist regime that had saved the day.

The Soviets, however, stoked the fire just a tad too long and it would soon boil over, scalding them. Nasser amassed an army on

the Sinai Peninsula, opposite Israel's border. He closed the Strait at
Sharm El-Sheikh at the mouth of the Gulf of Aqaba. It was the classic
provocation. Israel had already notified the UN Security Council
that if measures warranted, it would act in its own self-defense. UN
Secretary General U Thant failed to act forcefully to execute conditions of the truce that had existed since 1956. The UN peacekeeping
forces standing between Nasser's army and the Israelis timidly
packed up their tents and left town. On May 19, 1967, nothing stood
between the Egyptians and the border of Israel.

Israel launched a lightning attack against the Arab states
at ten minutes after seven on the morning of the fifth of June.
Well before noon nearly the entire Egyptian aircraft fleet lay in
flaming wreckage. Their air force was destroyed on the ground
by Israeli fighter jets as God blinded the eyes of the Egyptians.
In similar attacks, Israel destroyed Syrian jets and Jordanian
planes.

Simultaneously, Israeli ground forces struck the Egyptian army
amassed in the Sinai with a fist that virtually demolished Egypt's
capacity to respond. As an important part of Israeli strategy for victory, the defense minister, Lt. General Moshe Dayan, had ordered
a complete blackout of news. None of the stunning victories of
June 5 were acknowledged for a twenty-four-hour period. This
allowed loudly proclaimed Egyptian announcements boasting it
had destroyed Israel's armed forces to go unchallenged. The Israelis
wanted to forestall a Soviet move toward a cease-fire if it thought its
client states were winning.

Dayan's ploy had one unexpected drawback: King Hussein also
heard Radio Cairo's bizarre and whimsical interpretation of the facts
and believed the reports. Israel had already contacted the king and
offered not to infringe on his territory if he would stay put. Perhaps

out of a desire for self-glory, Hussein ignored Israel's proposal and instructed his troops to begin shelling West Jerusalem. Hoping that was the limit of Hussein's military action, Dayan ordered the front commander in Jerusalem, Uzi Narkiss, to hold his fire. But just to be on the safe side, Israeli jets destroyed Amman's air force of twenty Hunter jets the same day.

At one o'clock that afternoon, the Jordanians made their move to overrun Government House on the south side of the city. It was the headquarters of General Odd Bull, the Norwegian chief of the United Nations Truce Supervision Organization. Surrounded by seven hundred acres, it would give Hussein easy access for his Patton tanks to invade Israeli Jerusalem.

An hour later Dayan gave the signal for Israeli troops to secure Government House. The Jerusalem Brigade drove the Jordanians from their objective and even farther south from "The Bell," a series of deep ditches used as protection from enemy gunfire. By midnight the brigade had accomplished its mission with the loss of but eight men.

About the time Dayan had ordered the Jerusalem Brigade to attack, Uzi Narkiss issued the command to Uri Ben-Ari, leader of the Harel Mechanized Brigade—tanks and motorized infantry—to take the ridges north of the corridor. He was then to intercept Jordanian tank columns advancing on Jerusalem south through Ramallah. Ben-Ari's men and tanks then moved into the Jerusalem corridor, and he began to send units into the ridges controlled by the Jordanians.

Ben-Ari chose four separate routes to ensure that at least one column would break through and reach the objective—Tel el-Ful. It was the place where the roads south from Ramallah and west from Jericho meet to form one road into Jerusalem. It was a strategic point. The principle obstacles to their advance were Jordanian troops and a minefield that stretched the entire length of the border in the area. The ground had been mined for so long no one knew where the mines were located. Sadly, Uri Ben-Ari and his troops would find many of them before the battle ended.

At five o'clock the command was given to commence firing. Israeli tanks—supported by jet fighter-bomber attacks—blasted the Jordanian bunkers blocking their way. The infantry moved forward while engineers, armed only with bayonets, cleaning rods, and other improvised equipment set out to find the mines. Many of the men lost legs that grisly night.

As dawn crept over the battlefield, Ben-Ari's units had managed to reach the outskirts of Tel el-Ful. They had only four Sherman tanks, some half-tracks, and a few vehicles from the reconnaissance unit. They soon spotted three Patton tanks moving toward them from Jericho and opened fire. If the three Jordanian tanks kept coming, there was little the Israelis could do to stop them, and lying just behind the advancing Patton tanks were twenty more awaiting orders of engagement.

Sitting in the turret of the tank with the disabled cannon was Sergeant Mordechai Eitan. He had been studying the tanks through his binoculars when he spotted metal containers mounted on the backs of the Jordanian tanks. Could they be auxiliary fuel tanks?

There was only one way to find out: He cocked the heavy machine gun on his tank's turret and opened fire on the containers. A direct hit on one of the containers caused the Patton to burst into flames. The terrified crew of the tank beside it bailed out and ran for their lives. One Jordanian tank kept coming toward the Israeli line. Just as its commander broke through, Israeli air support arrived and directed a well-aimed round. The remainder of the Jordanians turned and headed back to Jericho. Ben-Ari's troops had secured the road to Jerusalem and firmly blocked it.

In Tel Aviv, Colonel Mordechai Gur and his 55th Paratroop Brigade had been scheduled for deployment in the Sinai. Things were going so well there, however, that the high command offered its services to Narkiss. Colonel Gur and his staff arrived in Jerusalem a few hours ahead of their paratroopers. The battle for Jerusalem was bloody and costly. The Jordanians had withdrawn to entrenched positions on Ammunition Hill. There the Israelis encountered massive resistance. In the early morning hours, two prongs of the paratrooper attack crossed just north of the Mandelbaum Gate. One unit headed toward the Old City, the other toward several Arab strongholds. Both groups encountered fierce street-to-street combat. By noon, however, Jordanian resistance had ended.

Colonel Mordechai Gur arranged for detachments to enter the Old City through its gates. The main thrust would be through the Lion's Gate opposite the Mount of Olives. Resistance was minimal. The remainder of the day was relegated to rejoicing and the costly work of eliminating the last pockets of Jordanian opposition.

Years later in the office of my beloved friend, Mordechai Gur, who had risen to rank of general, he related:

> On Wednesday morning, June 7th, I and my paratroopers stormed into the Old City and advanced on the Temple Mount. I wept as I shouted over my communications system, "The Temple Mount is in our hands!"[153]

Gur continued:

> I had long looked forward to liberating Jerusalem as something sublime. For me it was the culmination

of my most personal goals as a youngster, as a Jew,
and as a soldier. To me, the Temple Mount was more
important than the Western Wall because the Temple
was the center of religion, the center of tradition. It
was also the center of the kingdom, of the state, of all
our hopes. The day we took it, I wrote in my diary,
"What will my family say when they hear we again
liberated Jerusalem just as the Maccabees once did?"
Jerusalem has only been a functioning capital when
the Jews have ruled it.[154]

By sundown on June 7, the Israelis had reached the Jordan
River. King Hussein had paid dearly for his gamble on the Egyptian
propaganda. His army suffered over fifteen thousand casualties—
dead, wounded, missing. His air force had been decimated and half
his tanks destroyed. He had lost his dynasty's claim to the Islamic
holy places. He had, however, lost even more than that. The West
Bank had been his richest agricultural land. Tourist income from
Jerusalem and Bethlehem had accounted for 40 percent of Jordan's
revenue. His only consolation was that the Jews had suffered more
casualties against his army (1,756) than they had in the much larger
Sinai campaign (1,075). One-fourth of Israel's losses had come in
Jerusalem.

Few Israelis found room for mourning. Chief Rabbi Shlomo
Goren related to me:

I managed to reach the Western Wall even before
the firing had died down. Like one of Joshua's priests,
I was running with the ram's horn, the shofar, in my
hand. When I placed it to my lips and blew, I felt like

thousands of shofars from the time of King David were blowing all at once.[155]

Jews from every nation were dancing and weeping as they touched the Western Wall. They sang, *"Yerushalayim Shel Zahav"* . . . Jerusalem of Gold. Prime Minister Yitzhak Rabin told me years later:

> This was the most holy day of my life. I heard rabbis crying that the Messiah was coming soon, and that ancient prophecy was fulfilled that day. You would have thought King David had returned with his harp and the Ark of the Covenant.[156]

Hardened veterans ran to touch the ancient wall, tears flowing down their faces in gratitude. "Next year, Jerusalem" was no longer a poignant cry; it was reality. To pray at the Western Wall was no longer a yearning; it was a certainty. The Temple Mount, on which stands the Dome of the Rock, remained closed to the Jewish people, but they could at least stretch out their fingertips and touch a portion of it.

Mayor Teddy Kollek wrote regarding the morning of June 7, 1967:

> At 10:15, a jeep bearing the Chief Chaplain to the Forces, Brigadier-General Rabbi Shlomo Goren, came flying through the Lions' Gate and across the Temple Mount, oblivious of sniper's bullets, and stopped near the southwest corner. The Rabbi jumped off and rushed down the lane which brought him to the Western Wall. There he offered a Hebrew prayer, and, drawing forth

a shofar, normally sounded only on the most solemn of Jewish Holy Days, he blew a long and powerful blast .... Battles were still raging elsewhere in the country, for this was only the third day of war. But every Jew, both in Israel and overseas, must have felt this to be a day of liberation. The city of Jerusalem was again united, and again, in its entirety, the Capital of Israel.[157]

Most importantly, Jerusalem was once again united and in Jewish hands. Today, the Western Wall, sometimes called the Wailing Wall, is all that remains of Herod's massive Temple Mount construction.

Gur expressed his feelings to a grateful nation:

For some two thousand years the Temple Mount was forbidden to the Jews. . . . The Western Wall, for which every heart beats, is ours once again. Many Jews have taken their lives into their hands through-out our long history, in order to reach Jerusalem and live here. Endless words of longing have expressed the deep yearning for Jerusalem that beats within the Jewish heart. You have been given the great privilege of completing the circle, of returning to the nation its capital and its holy center . . . Jerusalem is yours forever.[158]

33

THE TEMPLE AND THE
END *of the* AGE

T he question most often asked in regard to the end times is: Will the temple be rebuilt in Jerusalem, where, and at what cost? Many Jews, especially the ultra-Orthodox pray unceasingly for the temple to be rebuilt on Mount Moriah, the same location as the two previous structures. Those interested in prophecy are also aware of the reconstruction significance.

Members of the organization the Temple Institute in Jerusalem have made a concerted effort to gather all the significant items needed to prepare for a third temple—utensils, priestly robes, the altar on which the daily offerings are to be made, and the breeding of a red heifer needed for sacrifices. Members of the Levite tribe have been trained to assume the role of priests in the new temple.

Dr. Robert D. Luginbill, professor at the University of Louisville, said of the red heifer prophecy:

> I have no idea how common or uncommon an
> event the birth of a young red cow is. At some point,
> sacrifice of such a heifer to produce the ashes for the

> water of purification may take place. At some point,
> said water may be used to purify the temple mount or
> portions thereof. At some point (and scripture would
> indicate that this step, at least, is imminent), a third
> temple *will* be built.[159]

Where the temple edifice will be erected is of equal importance to Bible scholars, some of whom have proposed several sites for construction. The first and foremost location desired would be on the site of what is now the Dome of the Rock and Al-Aqsa Mosque, both highly acclaimed and, according to Muslim clerics, devoutly defended Muslim holy places. Jews claim it as the mount atop which Abraham was prepared to offer his son, Isaac, as a sacrifice to Yahweh. Muslims hold it sacred as the place from which Muhammad's winged horse ascended to heaven. For the Jews to demand possession of this land in Jerusalem would launch the greatest jihad ever fought in the holy city, and would draw the world's huge Muslim populace into the conflagration.

It was on Mount Moriah that both Solomon's and Herod's temples were erected, and stood north of the Dome of the Rock, according to Dr. Asher Kauffman, a Scottish-born physicist at Hebrew University. He suggests that a new edifice could be built without dismantling the Dome of the Rock.[160]

The second locale would have the temple sitting south of the Dome of the Rock according to Israeli architect Tuvia Sagiv, and the third site would be the traditional one occupying property now covered by the Muslim shrine.

A look at today's headlines and at recent history clearly echo events foretold in the Scriptures. As we look at all these things together, prophetic events and details of how they might come about begin to fit into a logical order, and we quickly realize there are only a handful of events that could represent the next domino to fall:

1. the attack of Gog's coalition on Israel,

2. the rapture of the church,

3. the rise of the Antichrist,

4. the rebuilding of the temple on the Temple Mount, or

5. the Antichrist's seven-year covenant of peace with the nation of Israel.

Whichever of these comes first, it seems very plausible that each of the others will follow in quick succession, very likely all within half a decade or less.

Of course, we must acknowledge that understanding and interpreting Bible prophecy is not an exact science. At best, God-given visions of the final stages of this Age have come in scattered sound bites and fragmentary visions spread between the interpretations of a dozen different writers. It has been left to prophecy scholars to interpret what was shown to Daniel, Ezekiel, Isaiah, Jeremiah, and Joel in visions, and what Jesus told us in the Gospels. Added to what John saw in the book of Revelation, the snippets provided in the Epistles, and the chorus of other prophets in the Old Testament it is possible to arrive at an overall pattern for prophetical events. This will inform us of approximately where we are in God's perfect plan.

The exact order in which these events will happen is still under debate by those who study end-time prophecy. Will the Gog coalition attack before or after the rapture? Will Gog's attack be after the rise of a one-world government that creates a covenant of peace with

Israel? Or will Gog's attack be the catalyst for the rise of the one-world government? Will it be the last attempt of desperate nations to hold on to self-rule in the face of a rising one-world superpower? Will it be the first step in another attempt by Islamic radicals to destroy the United States and Israel? As the exact details of when and how this attack will come about seem to perplex many, we can however see the gathering of the storm and the players coming into position. Even the motivations for such an attack on Israel are becoming clearer as the rhetoric of war and revolution in the Middle East rises toward a crescendo.

The Bible describes the battle of the end times in Ephesians 6:12: "For our struggle is not against flesh and blood, but against the rulers, against the authorities, against the powers of this dark world and against the spiritual forces of evil in the heavenly realms."

This kind of spiritual war is taking place in Israel today, and those evil principalities and powers are speaking into the ears of men. A new book from Iran's Supreme Leader Ayatollah Khamenei lays out in no uncertain terms what one Islamic country's leader thinks about the future of Israel. A review of the 416-page diatribe was offered by conservative Iranian author Amir Tahiri, who points out that the Ayatollah believes "Israel has no *right to exist* as a state."[161]

Tahiri further stated:

> Khamenei describes Israel as "a cancerous tumor" whose elimination would mean that "the West's hege-mony and threats will be discredited" in the Middle East. In its place, he boasts, "the hegemony of Iran will be promoted."[162]

In his book, Khamenei lays out a plan for a coordinated campaign of terror attacks, stopping just short of open warfare, to weaken and eventually destroy the Jewish state. He also called for a single state in the land of Israel to be called Palestine and for it to be a Muslim nation.

Today, great darkness surrounds the nation of Israel. Everywhere Iran's proxies are circling—Hezbollah in Lebanon and Hamas in Gaza, just waiting for an opportunity to strike. ISIL, another deadly threat, has made inroads into Syria and the Sinai. Sadly, in the midst of threatening times, her friends are too often walking away, leaving Israel isolated and alone just as she faces her most dangerous threats. With the recent addition of Soviet troops on the ground, its air force flying bombing sorties targeting, not ISIS so much as anti-Basher al Assad rebels, and a Russian warship offshore lobbing Cruise missiles at Syrian targets, the threat to Israel becomes even more menacing. The entire region is on the brink of war—a war that could very quickly become the most bloody and devastating in decades. The liberal media does its best to downplay the role of radical Islam in this crisis. President Obama has even gone so far as to say that the Islamic State terrorist group (ISIL) is not really Islamic[163] . . . but it is.

The world is trying to pretend that Iran is not working on nuclear weapons . . . but it is, and Israel is on the front line of this battle. It is a battle that would affect us in the United States eventually, of course; but the Jewish people are the first targets. War could break out again at any moment, and according to my sources in Jerusalem, there is a great concern, not just about the Iranian nuclear program but about the thousands of conventional rockets and missiles already in the hands of Hezbollah and Hamas. There are at least seventeen other active radical Islamic groups that may exhibit different ideologies and methods, but they all have one goal: to place the world under Islamic rule, regardless of how many people are killed in the process. These terrorists do not just hate the Jewish people—they hate all who oppose them, even other Muslims. Today, the tiny nation of Israel is truly standing at the forefront of a battle that would affect all of us. Whether it is Hamas or ISIS or Iran or Hezbollah or Al Qaeda, the motive is the same—to bring death and destruction to all who will not bow to their rule.

Perhaps it will be a Hezbollah or Hamas rocket that levels the Dome of the Rock in Jerusalem and makes it possible for a third temple to be erected on the site. Perhaps it will be a peace agreement that gives the Jews access to Mount Moriah. However access occurs, it has been predicted that with modern machinery and construction methods a new temple could be erected within months.

34

THE TEMPLE
in HEAVEN

W e have looked at the first "temple" where God walked with man—the garden of Eden. We watched as the tabernacle in the wilderness rose from the sands of the Sinai. The awesome buildings that were Solomon's temple and Herod's temple have vanished, but one temple remains.

The Scriptures are the only source of information about the temple in heaven. Glimpses can be caught through studying the tabernacle and the temples built in Jerusalem, which were but earthly reflections of the magnificence of heavenly grandeur, but ultimately, "Eye has not seen, nor ear heard, nor have entered into the heart of man the things which God has prepared for those who love Him" (1 Corinthians 2:9 NKJV).

The book of Revelation does provide insight that there is indeed a temple in heaven, a throne on which God sits, with the Lamb of God who is mentioned in several chapters. At the end of the millennium when the old earth is destroyed and the new heaven and earth descend, there will be no temple in New Jerusalem because God, the Father, and the Lamb will reside there. In Revelation 3:12 (NKJV) we read:

He who overcomes, I will make him a pillar in the
temple of My God, and he shall go out no more. I will
write on him the name of My God and the name of
the city of My God, the New Jerusalem, which comes
down out of heaven from My God. And *I will write on
him* My new name.

What a precious promise for the overcomer! After all the
struggle and strife, all the hardship and heartaches, God promises
eternal fellowship with Him! No more crying; no more dying. No
more pain; no more stain of sin . . . just love—full and unfathomable, and communion with God, the Father and the Son. This is the
promise that is woven through the pages of the Bible from Genesis
through Revelation.

Not only has God written His name on Jerusalem, He has
written His name on the hearts of His children—those who have
been bought with the most costly sum imaginable, the blood of His
Son. Revelation 22:4 (NKJV) reveals, "They shall see His face, and
His name *shall be* on their foreheads." Marked forever, not by the
mark of the Beast as recorded in Revelation 13, the saved, sanctified,
justified children of God will bear His name on their foreheads for
all eternity. And they shall "go out no more!" No longer will they be
"strangers and pilgrims on the earth" (see Hebrews 11:13); they will
have found Abraham's promised "city which has foundations, whose
builder and maker *is* God" (see Hebrews 11:10).

The Kings of Israel
(all were wicked)

1. Jeroboam I
2. Nadab
3. Baasha
4. Elah
5. Zimri
6. Omri
7. Ahab
8. Ahaziah
9. Jehoram (Joram)
10. Jehu
11. Jehoahaz
12. Jehoash (Joash)
13. Jeroboam II
14. Zechariah'
15. Shallum
16. Menahem
17. Pekahiah
18. Pekah
19. Hoshea

The Kings of Judah
(8 were good)

1. Rehoboam
2. Abijam
3. Asa (Good)
4. Jehoshaphat (Good)
5. Jehoram
6. Ahaziah
7. Athaliah
8. Joash (Good)
9. Amaziah (Good)
10. Azariah (Uzziah) (Good)
11. Jotham (Good)
12. Ahaz
13. Hezekiah (Good)
14. Manasseh
15. Amon
16. Josiah (Good)
17. Jehoahaz
18. Jehoiachim
19. Jehoiachin
20. Zedekiah[164]

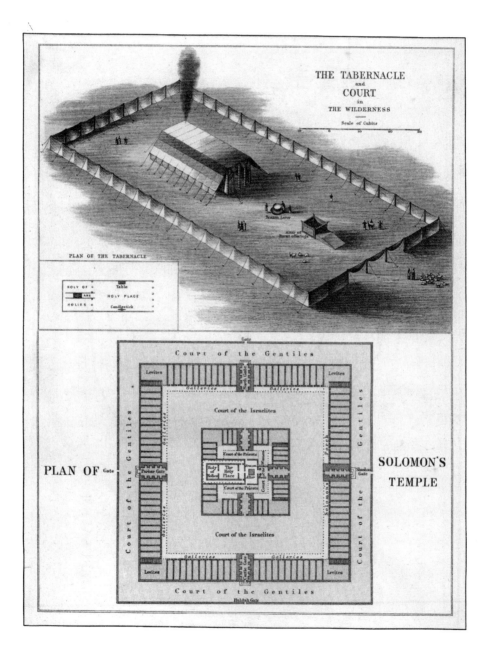

THE TABERNACLE
and
COURT
in
THE WILDERNESS

Scale of Cubits

PLAN OF THE TABERNACLE

PLAN OF

SOLOMON'S
TEMPLE

The Temple of Solomon.

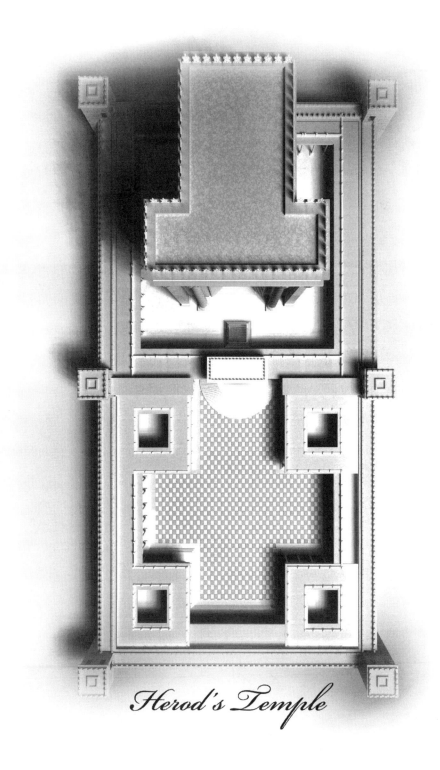

Herod's Temple

Herod's Temple

ENDNOTES

1. Dr. Henry M. Morris, *The Genesis Record: A Scientific and Devotional Commentary on the Book of Beginnings* (Grand Rapids, MI: Baker Book House, 1976), 116.

2. Doug Batchelor, "Fig Leaves and Pharisees," *Inside Report*, http://www.amazingfacts.org/news-and-features/inside-report/id/341/fig-leaves-and-pharisees.aspx; accessed February 2015.

3. *Strong's Concordance*, http://biblehub.com/hebrew/3801.htm; accessed February 2015.

4. *The United Methodist Hymnal* Number 365, words by Julia H. Johnston, music by Daniel B. Towner, http://www.hymnsite.com/lyrics/umh365.sht; accessed February 2015.

5. Wayne Stiles, "Eden and Gethsemane—Two Gardens and Two Choices," http://www.waynestiles.com/eden-and-gethsemane-two-gardens-and-two-choices/; accessed April 2015.

6. Morris, 122.

7. Charles Swindoll, "Jealousy," June 4, 2009, Insight for Living, http://daily.insight.org/site/News2?page=NewsArticle&id=14515; accessed February 2015.

8. *The MacArthur New Testament Commentary*, John MacArthur, Jr., (Moody Press 1983–2007.)

9. Morris, 190–191.

10. Dr. Boushra Mikhael, "Altars in the Life of Abraham," http://www.preciousseed.org/article_detail.cfm?articleID=81; accessed March 2015.

11. Morris, 375.

12. Dr. Henry M. Morris, *The Remarkable Record of Job: The Ancient Wisdom, Scientific Accuracy, and Life-Changing Message of an Amazing Book* (Grand Rapids, MI: Baker Book House, 1988), 12–13.

13. Ibid, 57–58.

14. Rev. Bob Deffinbaugh, "The Tabernacle, the Dwelling Place of God (Exodus 36:8-39:43)", https://bible.org/seriespage/32-tabernacle-dwelling-place-god-exodus-368-3943; accessed March 2015.

15. Price Randall, *Rose Guide to the Tabernacle* (Torrance, CA: Rose Publishing, Inc., 2008), 9.

16. Dr. Douglas K. Stuart, *The New American Commentary: An Exegetical and Theological Exposition of Holy Scripture, Exodus* (Nashville, TN: Broadman and Holman Publishers: 2006), 275.

17. Margaret Minnicks, "Number 10 and its meaning in the Bible," June 4, 2011, http://www.examiner.com/article/number-10-and-its-meaning-the-bible; accessed March 2015.

18. Dr. Martin Luther King Jr., "I've Been to the Mountaintop," April 3, 1968, Memphis, Tennessee, http://www.americanrhetoric.com/speeches/mlkivebeentothemountaintop.htm; accessed March 2015.

19. Pastor Robin Fish, "Mt. Sinai—God Gives Guidance," March 3, 2004, http://lcmssermons.com/index.php?sn=519; accessed March 2015.

20. Taken from "Ten Commandments and Jesus," http://www.allabouttruth.org/ten-commandments-and-jesus-faq.htm#sthash.A1RPFoB8.dpuf published by AllAboutGOD.com Ministries, C. Outlaw, M. Houdmann, P. Matthews-Rose, R. Niles, editors, 2002-2014. Used by permission; accessed March 2015.

21. David M. Levy, *The Tabernacle: Shadows of the Messiah* (Bellmawr, NJ: Friends of Israel Gospel Ministry, Inc., 1994), 18.

22. Dr. Charles Swindoll, *Moses: A Man of Selfless Dedication* (Nashville, TN: Word Publishing, 1999), 307.

23. Bible Q: Bible Questions Answered, http://bibleq.net/answer/4024/; accessed March 2015.

24. Dick Harfield, http://www.answers.com/Q/How_much_food_did_it_take_to_sustain_the_Israelites_in_the_desert; accessed March 2015.

25. The Tabernacle Place, http://the-tabernacle-place.com/articles/what_is_the_tabernacle/tabernacle_basic_layout; accessed March 2015.

26. http://www.bible-history.com/tabernacle/TAB4Preparing_for_the_Tabernacle.htm; accessed March 2015.

27. Henry Snyder Gehman, *New Westminster Dictionary of the Bible* (London, England: Westminster Press, 1970), 876.

28. *Jewish Encyclopedia*, Showbread, http://www.jewishencyclopedia.com/articles/13611-showbread; accessed March 2015.

29. Cwm Rhondda (Bread of Heaven), http://en.wikipedia.org/wiki/Cwm_Rhondda#cite_note-6; accessed March 2015.

30. http://library.timelesstruths.org/music/Come_and_Dine/

31. Dr. John MacArthur, "Jesus the Light of the World," http://www.gty.org/Resources/Sermons/1520; accessed April 2015.

32. Carolyn Adams Roth, "Galbanum, an Ingredient in Incense," http://godasagardener.com/2011/10/05/galbanum-in-the-tabernacle-incense/; accessed April 2015.

33. Dr. W. A. Criswell, "The Golden Altar of Prayer," http://www.wacriswell.com/sermons/1959/the-golden-altar-of-prayer; accessed April 2015.

34. Lt. Col. Robert Leroe, "Dwelling in Dagon's Tent," 2005, http://www.sermoncentral.com/sermons/dwelling-in-dagons-den-robert-leroe-sermon-on-gods-omnipotence-77777.asp?Page=1; accessed April 2015.

35. Dr. R. C. Sproul, *The Holiness of God* (Carol Stream, IL: Tyndale House Publishers, 1985), 108.

36. Hugh Stowell, in *The Winter's Wreath, a Collection of Original Contributions in Prose and Verse*, 1828. Stowell rewrote & republished the words in 1831, http://www.cyberhymnal.org/htm/f/r/fromevsw.htm; accessed April 2015.

37. "The Levitical Priests: Their Function and Role in the Holy Temple," http://www.templeinstitute.org/red_heifer/levitical_priests.htm; accessed April 2015.

38. *Barnes' Bible Charts*, http://www.biblecharts.org/oldtestament/oldtestamentpriestsandpriesthood.pdf; accessed April 2015.

39. Levy, *The Tabernacle: Shadows of the Messiah*, 163–164.

40. Dr. Douglas K. Stuart, *The New American Commentary, Volume 2, Exodus* (Nashville, TN: Broadman and Holman Publishers, 2006), 616.

41. *Pulpit Commentary*, Exodus 40:34–38, http://biblehub.com/exodus/40-34.htm; accessed April 2015.

42. S. Michael Houdmann, http://www.gotquestions.org/grain-offering.html#ixzz3YF7KPa9v; accessed April 2015.

43. "Awake, my Soul, and with the Sun," http://www.cyberhymnal.org/htm/p/r/praisegf.htm; accessed April 2015.

44. C. W. Slemming, *Thus Shalt Thou Serve: The Feasts and Offerings of Ancient Israel* (Fort Washington, PA: CLS Publications, 1974 and 2009), 42.

45. Dr. John MacArthur, "Why Did Jesus Cry, 'My God, My God, Why Have Your Forsaken Me?", http://www.gty.org/resources/print/bible-qna/BQ032913; accessed July 2015.

46. Ernie Brown, "The Peace Offering, A Figure of Fellowship", http://www.biblecentre.org/addresses/eb_the_peace_offering.htm; accessed April 2015.

47. Dr. Bob Deffinbaugh, "The Sin Offering," Bible.org, https://bible.org/seriespage/5-sin-offering-leviticus-41-513-624-30; accessed April 2015.

48. Robert Lowry, "Nothing But the Blood," http://www.cyberhymnal.org/htm/n/b/nbtblood.htm; accessed April 2015.

49. http://thinkexist.com/quotations/conscience/2.html

50. Paul Lee Tan, *Encyclopedia of 7700 Illustrations*, Item 819 (Rockville, MD: Assurance Publishers, 1979), 269.

51. http://www.plymouthbrethren.org/article/11848

52. Fausset, Andrew Robert M.A., D.D., "Definition for 'Hophni and phinehas' Fausset's Bible Dictionary", bible-history.com-Fausset's; 1878.

53. Rev. George Kirkpatrick, "From a Tent to a Temple," http://www.newfoundationspubl.org/tent.htm; accessed May 2015.

54. Eugene H. Peterson, *Leap Over A Wall: Earthly Spirituality for Everyday Christians* (New York, NY: Harper Collins, 1998), 160.

55. Ibid, 161.

56. Patricia Berlyn, "The Biblical View of Tyre," http://jbq.jewishbible.org/assets/Uploads/342/342_tyrefin.pdf; accessed May 2015.

57. http://jewishencyclopedia.com/articles/7720-hiram-huram; accessed May 2015.

58. http://www.brainyquote.com/quotes/keywords/pride.html#Io9VfBwDResoWYsk.99; accessed May 2015.

59. G. Campbell Morgan's Exposition of the Whole Bible, 2 Samuel 24, http://www.studylight.org/commentaries/gcm/view.cgi?bk=2sa&ch=24; accessed May 2015.

60. Dr. Charles Swindoll, *David: A Man of Passion and Destiny* (Nashville, TN: W Publishing Group, A Thomas Nelson Company, 2000), 470–471.

61. Teddy Kollek & Moshe Pearlman, *Jerusalem Sacred City of Mankind: A History of Forty Centuries* (New York, NY: Random House, 1972), 43.

62. http://www.brainyquote.com/quotes/quotes/j/jennifergr445033.html#b4spcUYuAAxkGy6P.99; accessed June 2015.

63. Rev. Charles Spurgeon, "One Worker Preparing for Another," June 19, 1892, Metropolitan Tabernacle, Newington, http://www.spurgeon.org/sermons/2261.htm; accessed June 2015.

64. Ibid.

65. President John F. Kennedy, Inaugural Address, January 20, 1961, http://www.bartleby.com/124/pres56.html; accessed June 2015.

66. Kollek and Pearlman, 43.

67. Randall Price, ThM, PhD, *Rose Guide to the Temple* (Torrance, CA: Rose Publishing, Inc., 2012), 24.

68. Simon Sebag Montefiore, *Jerusalem: The Biography* (London: Weidenfeld & Nicolson, 2011), 27.

69. Dr. Charles Swindoll, *Come Before Winter and Share My Hope* (Portland, OR: Multnomah Press, 1985), 52.

70. http://www.jerusalem-insiders-guide.com/temple-of-jerusalem.html#sthash.hXEIdAB7.dpuf; accessed June 2015.

71. Rabbi Dr. Raymond Apple, AO RFD, Emeritus Rabbi of the Great Synagogue, Sydney, Australia, http://www.oztorah.com/2014/11/pillars-of-the-temple-jbq/; accessed June 2015.

72. Price, 29.

73. Ibid.

74. Dr. Bob Deffinbaugh, "The Reign of Solomon," Bible.org, https://bible.org/seriespage/20-reign-solomon-1-kings-1-11; accessed June 2015.

75. Rev. Phil Christensen, "Dedication of Solomon's Temple, July 3, 2005, http://www.philchristensen.com/subpage37.html; accessed June 2015.

76. Orr, James, M.A., D.D. General Editor. "Definition for 'DOORKEEPER'". "International Standard Bible Encyclopedia". bible-history.com—ISBE; 1915

77. William Goodwin Aurelio Professor of the Appreciation of Scripture, Boston University, Frontline, PBS, "Passover", http://www.pbs.org/wgbh/pages/frontline/shows/religion/portrait/temple.html; accessed June 2015.

78. http://en.wikipedia.org/wiki/Puerperal_infections; accessed June 2015.

79. S.I. McMillen, *None of These Diseases* (Grand Rapids, MI: Fleming H. Revell, Revised edition 2000 by David E. Stern), 23.

80. David E. Lister, "Jesus our High Priest—The Day of Atonement," http://www.moriel.org/articles/sermons/jesus_our_high_priest.htm#; accessed June 2015.

81. Price, 42.

82. Words by Fanny Crosby, http://wordwisehymns.com/2013/09/30/redeemed-how-i-love-to-proclaim-it/; accessed June 2015.

83. Rev. Randy Moll, Good Shepherd Lutheran Church, Rogers, AR, "Lenten Devotions from Isaiah 53, http://www.goodshepherdrogers.org/tag/sacrifice/; accessed April 2015.

84. Dr. John MacArthur, Grace to You, "Celebrating the Passover," http://www.gty.org/blog/B130327; accessed April 2015.

85. The Seven-Feasts of Israel: the First and Second Coming of Messiah, 5. The Feast of Unleavened Bread, http://www.truthnet.org/Feasts-of-Israel/5-Unleavened-Feast/Index.htm; accessed May 2015.

86. Rev. Ken Overby, "Feast of First Fruits," February 7, 2014, http://www.jewishawareness.org/feast-of-first-fruits/; accessed May 2015.

87. "Rev. Mark Robinson, "Feast of Shavuot," February 7, 2014, http://www.jewishawareness.org/feast-of-shavuot/; accessed May 2015.

88. http://en.wikipedia.org/wiki/Shofar; accessed May 2015.

89. "Rosh Hashanah," http://www.aish.com/h/hh/rh/shofar/Shofar_Symbolism.html; accessed May 2015.

90. Slemming, 161.

91. Ibid, 162.

362

92. C. F. Keil, D.D., and F. Delitzsch, D.D., Professors of Theology, *Biblical Commentary on the Old Testament, The Books of the Kings* by C. F. Keil, translated from German by the Rev. James Martin, B.A., Second Edition (Edinburgh, Scotland: T. & T. Clark, 1866–1891), 38–39. (Online at: https://archive.org/details/thebooksofthekin00keiluoft)

93. "Who was the goddess Asherah/Ashtoreth?", http://www.compellingtruth.org/asherah.html; accessed June 2015.

94. http://amazingbibletimeline.com/blog/moloch-god-of-the-ammonites/#sthash.pFd9hkgl.dpuf; accessed June 2015.

95. Leon Wood, *A Survey of Israel's History* (Grand Rapids: Zondervan Publishing House, 1970), 340.

96. Herbert Lockyer, *All the Women of the Bible* (Grand Rapids, Michigan: Zondervan Publishing House), 33.

97. Kollek and Pearlman, 55.

98. Kollek and Pearlman, 61–65.

99. Jon W. Quinn, "The Man Who Killed Isaiah, "then Manasseh knew that the Lord was God." *The Bradley Banner*, December 16, 2007, http://www.bradleychurchofchrist.com/Bulletins%20of%20the%20Month/the_man_who_killed_isaiah.htm; accessed July 2015.

100. Jewish Encyclopedia—The Babylonian Captivity, http://www.bible-history.com/map_babylonian_captivity/map_of_the_deportation_of_judah_jewish_encyclopedia.html; accessed February 2013.

101. http://www.jewishhistory.org/jeremiah/; accessed July 2015.

102. Kollek and Pearlman, 74.

103. Alan Redpath, *Victorious Christian Service* (Westwood, New Jersey: Fleming H. Revell Co., 1963), 44–45.

104. Montefiore, 72.

105. Josephus, *Antiquities of the Jews*, book 14, chapter 4; translated. by William Whiston, available at Project Gutenberg.

106. *Dictionary of the Bible*, edited by James Hastings (New York, NY: Charles Scribner's Sons, 1927), 344.

107. Montefiore, 84–85.

108. Josephus, *Antiquities of the Jews—Book XV*, Chapter 11, http://www.sacred-texts.com/jud/josephus/ant-15.htm; accessed July 2015.

109. Price, 67.

110. Ibid.

111. Montefiore, 85.

112. Darrell G. Young, "The Eastern Gate in Prophecy," *Focus on Jerusalem*, Vol. 19, Issue 5, http://focusonjerusalem.com/easterngateinprophecy.html; accessed July 2015.

113. John MacArthur, "Testifying to Jesus: Joseph and Mary," September 26, 1999, http://www.gty.org/Resources/Sermons/42-28' accessed July 2015.

114. John Piper, "The Son of God at 12 Years Old," January 12, 1981, http://www.desiringgod.org/sermons/the-son-of-god-at-12-years-old; accessed November 2014.

115. Rev. G. Campbell Morgan, D.D., "Why Did Jesus Go to the Temple at 12 Years of Age?" *Adapted from The Crises of the Christ, Book II*,.http://www.jesus.org/life-of-jesus/youth-and-baptism/why-did-jesus-go-to-the-temple-at-12-years-of-age.html; accessed July 2015.

116. http://crossquotes.org/category/christmas/; accessed January 2015.

117. *The Pulpit Commentary*, Luke 3:23, Electronic Database. Copyright © 2001, 2003, 2005, 2006, 2010 by BibleSoft, Inc., Used by permission

118. Rev. G. Campbell Morgan, D.D., "What Was the Significance of the Temptation?" *Adapted from The Crises of the Christ, Book III, Chapter X*,. http://www.jesus.org/life-of-jesus/youth-and-baptism/what-was-the-significance-of-the-temptation.html; accessed July 2015

119. Paul Lee Tan, *Encyclopedia of 7700 Illustrations*, "Temptation: 6513, Our Weakest Moments" (Rockville, MD: Assurance Publishers, 1979), 1443.

120. C. H. Spurgeon, "Living on the Word," delivered by C. H. Spurgeon at the Metropolitan Tabernacle, Newington, March 15, 1883, http://www.spurgeongems.org/vols43-45/chs2577.pdf; accessed July 2015.

121. Ibid.

122. Ray Stedman, "The Temptation of Christ," http://www.raystedman.org/thematic-studies/the-life-of-christ/the-temptation-of-christ; accessed July 2015.

123. George Duffield, Jr., 1858, http://library.timelesstruths.org/music/Stand_Up_Stand_Up_for_Jesus/; accessed July 2015.

124. Alfred Edersheim, *The Life and Times of Jesus the Messiah*, eBook, *Book V, The Cross and the Crown*, Chapter 1, The First Day in Passion-Week, Palm-Sunday, http://philologos.org/__eb-lat/book501.htm; accessed July 2015,

125. Chuck Warnock, "Palm Sunday Sermon: On the Road to Calvary," March 27, 2010, https://chuckwarnockblog. wordpress.com/2010/03/27/palm-sunday-sermon-on-the-road-to-calvary/; accessed July 2015.

126. Kollek and Pearlman, 113.

127. Charles Swindoll, "The Gathering Storm," http://www.insight.org/resources/articles/pastors/gathering-storm.html?l=Jesus; accessed July 2015.

128. William Barclay, *The Gospel of Matthew, Volume 2* (Philadelphia, PA: The Westminster Press, 1958), 275.

129. Dr. John F. Walvoord, "23. Jesus Condemns the Scribes and Pharisees," https://bible.org/seriespage/23-jesus-condemns-scribes-and-pharisees; accessed July 2015.

130. http://www.forumancientcoins.com/catalog/roman-and-greek-coins.asp?vpar=812; accessed July 2015.

131. Barclay, 337.

132. Ibid.

133. George Eldon Ladd, *A Theology of the New Testament* (Grand Rapids, MI: William B. Eerdmans Publishing Co., 1974), 196.

134. https://en.wikipedia.org/wiki/There_Is_a_Fountain_Filled_with_Blood; accessed July 2015.

135. Rev. John MacArthur, "A Place Called Gethsemane," http://sermonnotebook.org/mark/Mark%2072%20-%20 Mark%2014_32-41.htm; accessed July 2015.

136. Rick Renner, "How Many Soldiers Does It Take To Arrest One Man?" http://www.cfaith.com/index.php/ article-display/31-articles/easter/15779-how-many-soldiers-does-it-take-to-arrest-one-man; accessed July 2015.

137. Ibid.

138. Ray Pritchard, "What Happened to Judas?" http://www.crosswalk.com/church/pastors-or-leadership/what-happened-to-judas-11532302.html?p=2; accessed July 2015.

139. John Greenleaf Whittier, "Maud Muller," http://www.poetry-archive.com/w/maud_muller.html; accessed July 2015.

140. Bible History Online, "The Roman Scourge," http://www.bible-history.com/past/flagrum.html; accessed February 2013.

141. Darlene Zschech, "Worthy Is the Lamb," http://www.lyricsmode.com/lyrics/d/darlene_zschech/worthy_is_ the_lamb.html; accessed February 2013.

142. "A Day in the Holy Temple," http://www.templeinstitute.org/day_in_life/chamber_of_lambs.htm; accessed August 2015.

143. Alfred Edersheim, "The Temple: Its Ministry and Services," http://philologos.org/__eb-ttms/temple08.htm.

144. Lonnie Branam, "The Three Hours' Darkness," http://sanfernandochurchofchrist.com/SermonView. aspx?ID=840; accessed August 2015.

145. Writer: David Phelps, Copyright: Winkin Music, Soulwriter Music Co. Inc., http://www.songlyrics.com/ david-phelps/end-of-the-beginning-lyrics/#3zwiBvW6dRwwQoXq.99; accessed August 2015.

146. Jewish Virtual Library, "Agrippa I," http://www.jewishvirtuallibrary.org/jsource/judaica/ ejud_0002_0001_0_00542.html; accessed August 2015.

147. Michael Farquhar, *A Treasure of Royal Scandals* (New York: Penguin Books, 2001), 209.

148. Flavius Josephus, *Antiquities*, 15, 403 ff. http://www.templemount.org/destruct2.html#anchor596423; accessed August 2015.

149. Ray C. Stedman, *What's This World Coming To?* (An expository study of Matthew 24–26, the Olivet Discourse), (Palo Alto, CA: Discovery Publications, 1970), http://www.templemount.org/destruct2. html#anchor615789; accessed August 2015.

150. "Julian and the Jews 361–363 CE" (New York: Fordham University, The Jesuit University of New York) and "Julian the Apostate and the Holy Temple," https://en.wikipedia.org/wiki/Third_Temple; accessed August 2015.

151. Walter Laqueur, *The History of Zionism* (London: L.P. Tauris & Co. Ltd, 2003), 557.

152. "History: The State of Israel," http://www.mfa.gov.il/MFA/AboutIsrael/History/Pages/HISTORY-%20 The%20State%20of%20Israel.aspx; accessed August 2015.

153. Personal Interview with Mordechai Gur, 1995.

154. Ibid.

155. Personal interview with Chief Rabbi Shlomo Goren, 1995.

156. Ibid.

157. Kollek and Pearlman, 269–270.

158. "The Six-Day War," *Committee for Accuracy in Middle East Reporting in America*; http://www.sixdaywar.org/content/ReunificationJerusalem.asp; accessed January 2015.

159. Dr. Robert Luginbill, "The Red Heifer and the Future Temple," http://www.ichthys.com/mail-red%20heifer.htm; accessed August 2015.

160. "On the Location of the First and Second Temples in Jerusalem," http://www.templemount.org/theories.html; accessed August 2015.

161. Amir Tahiri, "The Ayatollah's Plan for Israel and Palestine," http://www.gatestoneinstitute.org/6263/khamenei-israel-palestine; accessed August 2015.

162. Ibid.

163. CNN, September 11, 2014, http://www.cnn.com/2014/09/10/politics/obama-isil-not-islamic/index.html; accessed August 2015.

164. http://www.bible-history.com/resource/r_kings.htm; accessed June 2015.

ACKNOWLEDGMENTS

My sincere appreciation goes to Lanelle Shaw-Young whose assistance made this book possible. Thanks to Arlen Young for his excellent proofreading skills, to editor Janna Nysewander for her timely suggestions, and to Peter Gloege whose artistic talents turn my ideas into reality.

A book project of this magnitude demands a grueling schedule. For her patience, compassion, encouragement, and sacrifice, I am eternally indebted to my beloved wife, Carolyn.

MICHAEL DAVID EVANS, the #1 *New York Times* bestselling author, is an award-winning journalist/Middle East analyst. Dr. Evans has appeared on hundreds of network television and radio shows including *Good Morning America, Crossfire* and *Nightline*, and *The Rush Limbaugh Show*, and on Fox Network, *CNN World News*, NBC, ABC, and CBS. His articles have been published in the *Wall Street Journal, USA Today, Washington Times, Jerusalem Post* and newspapers worldwide. More than twenty-five million copies of his books are in print, and he is the award-winning producer of nine documentaries based on his books.

Dr. Evans is considered one of the world's leading experts on Israel and the Middle East, and is one of the most sought-after speakers on that subject. He is the chairman of the board of the Ten Boom Holocaust Museum in Haarlem, Holland, and is the founder of Israel's first Christian museum—Friends of Zion: Heroes and History—in Jerusalem.

Dr. Evans has authored a number of books including: *History of Christian Zionism, Showdown with Nuclear Iran, Atomic Iran, The Next Move Beyond Iraq, The Final Move Beyond Iraq,* and *Countdown*. His body of work also includes the novels *Seven Days, GameChanger, The Samson Option, The Four Horsemen, The Locket, Born Again: 1967,* and *The Columbus Code.*

✦ ✦ ✦

Michael David Evans is available to speak or for interviews.
Contact: EVENTS@drmichaeldevans.com.

BOOKS BY: MIKE EVANS

Israel: America's Key to Survival

Save Jerusalem

The Return

Jerusalem D.C.

Purity and Peace of Mind

Who Cries for the Hurting?

Living Fear Free

I Shall Not Want

Let My People Go

Jerusalem Betrayed

Seven Years of Shaking: A Vision

The Nuclear Bomb of Islam

Jerusalem Prophecies

Pray For Peace of Jerusalem

America's War: The Beginning
of the End

The Jerusalem Scroll

The Prayer of David

The Unanswered Prayers of Jesus

God Wrestling

The American Prophecies

Beyond Iraq: The Next Move

The Final Move beyond Iraq

Showdown with Nuclear Iran

Jimmy Carter: The Liberal Left
and World Chaos

Atomic Iran

Cursed

Betrayed

The Light

Corrie's Reflections & Meditations

The Revolution

The Final Generation

Seven Days

GAMECHANGER SERIES:
GameChanger
Samson Option
The Four Horsemen

THE PROTOCOLS SERIES:
The Protocols
The Candidate

The Locket

Persia: The Final Jihad

Jerusalem

The History of Christian Zionism

Countdown

Ten Boom: Betsie, Promise of God

Commanded Blessing

Born Again: 1948

Born Again: 1967

Presidents in Prophecy

Stand with Israel

Prayer, Power and Purpose

Turning Your Pain Into Gain

Christopher Columbus, Secret Jew

Living in the F.O.G.

Finding Favor with God

Finding Favor with Man

Unleashing God's Favor

The Jewish State: The Volunteers

See You in New York

Friends of Zion: Patterson & Wingate

The Columbus Code

The Temple

COMING SOON:
Netanyahu

Lights in the Darkness

TO PURCHASE, CONTACT: orders@timeworthybooks.com
P. O. BOX 30000, PHOENIX, AZ 85046